The Life and Death
of Aloysius Cardinal Stepinac

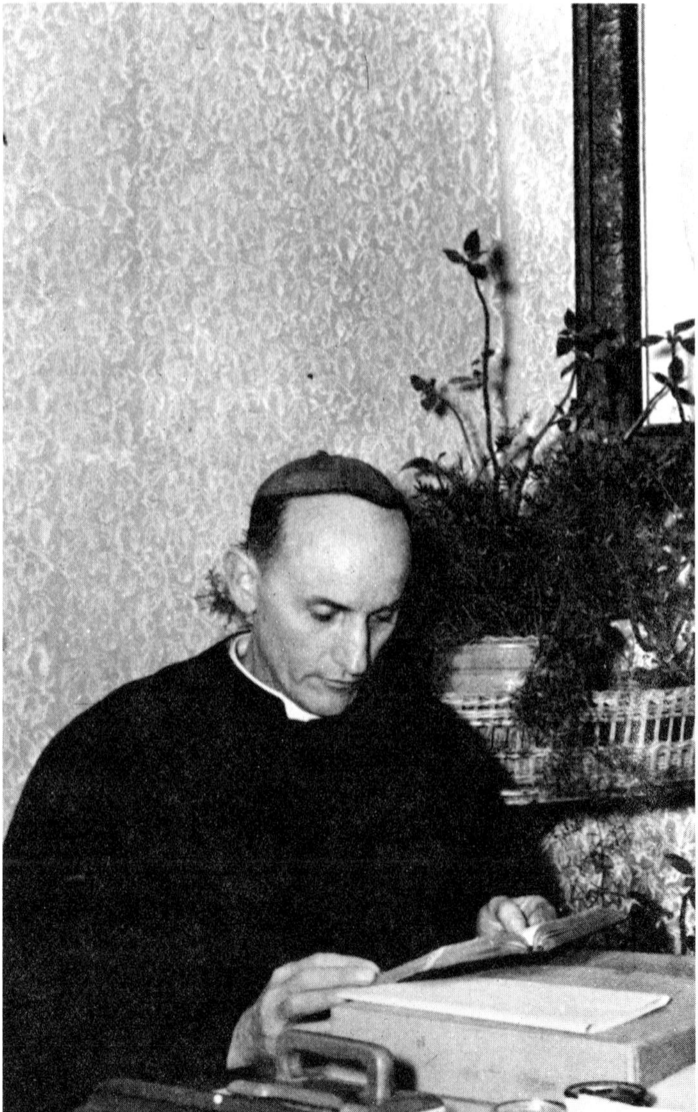

Religious News Service Photo

OTHER WORKS BY
FATHER M. RAYMOND, O.C.S.O.

The Man Who Got Even With God
Three Religious Rebels
The Family That Overtook Christ
Burnt Out Incense
Love Does Such Things
A New Way of the Cross
God, A Woman, and the Way
These Women Walked With God
The Less Travelled Road
You
The Trappists, the Reds, and You
This is Your Tomorrow . . . and Today
Now!
Your Hour
This Is Love
God Goes to Murderers' Row
The Mysteries in Your Life
The Silent Spire Speaks
Relax and Rejoice

alba house

A DIVISION OF THE SOCIETY OF ST. PAUL
STATEN ISLAND, NEW YORK 10314

Rev. M. Raymond, O.C.S.O.

THE MAN
FOR THIS
MOMENT

110896

Nihil Obstat:
Fr. M. Augustine Wulff, o.c.s.o.
Lector Ordinis

Imprimi Potest:
✝ Most Rev. M. Ignace Gillet, o.c.s.o.
Abbas Generalis Ordinis Cisterciensis
Strictioris Observantae

Nihil Obstat:
Rt. Rev. Msgr. Daniel V. Flynn
Censor Librorum

Imprimatur
Joseph P. O'Brien, S.T.D.
Vicar General
Archdiocese of New York
June 1, 1971

BX
4705
S823
R39

The nihil obstat and imprimatur are official declarations that a book or pamphlet is free of doctrinal or moral error. No implication is contained therein that those who have granted the nihil obstat and imprimatur agree with the contents, opinions or statements expressed.

ISBN: 0-8189-0220-5

Library of Congress Catalog Card Number: 77-169142

Designed, printed and bound in the U.S.A. by the Pauline Fathers and Brothers of the Society of St. Paul, 2187 Victory Blvd., Staten Island, N.Y. 10314 as part of their communications apostolate.

To
MAjKA BOZjA BISTRIcKA
the
Beloved Patroness of Croatia

and to

All Those who Sacrificed Their All
for God and Their Croatian Fatherland

✤✤

Foreword

"IN THE AGE OF THE COMPUTER, great men are
obsolete."

"What a statement! Damn it, man, why do we moderns
have to sound so ultra-sophisticated and thus manifest
not only our lack of wisdom but our actual abysmal ignorance?"

"Ignorance?"

"Yes, ignorance. Not agnosticism, note, but ignorance.
You and your like are not agnostic. You're ignorant in
the strict sense of that word; for you do not know what
you should know."

"You sound angry."

"Sound? I am angry. Who wouldn't be after hearing
a remark such as yours: 'In the age of the computer,

great men are obsolete.' Pff! That kind of talk reminds me of Mark Twain . . . ."

"Mark Twain? He didn't live in the age of the computer."

"No, but he anticipated many of the men of that age when he said: 'Man is a rational animal more often in definition than in deed.'"

"What in the world are you talking about?"

"About you—and thousands like you. 'No great men in the age of the computer.' Pff! I could name a dozen of them without the slightest effort . . . ."

"Name one."

"You wouldn't recognize him if I did. For you and your likes don't know what manhood is, let alone greatness . . . ."

"Well, name one, and let us see."

"Ten to one you don't recognize him . . . ."

"You're on."

"Aloysius Cardinal Stepinac."

"Who in the world is he?"

"There you go. Give me ten."

"Wait a second. Prove him a man first, then that he was great."

That heated—and it was very heated—conversation started this book. It is a *must*. For that there are thousands like the individual quoted above is unquestionable. Not agnostic, which is terrible enough, but actually ignorant, which is truly intolerable in this age of the computer. *This age needs to know what a man is.*

Further, when college students burn the flag of our country, when chronologically adult individuals tear up draft cards, when supposedly mature men support and commit "civil disobedience," when the streets of our cities are not safe in daylight let alone after dark, when assassins, seen in the very act of assassination, can hardly be prosecuted let alone penalized, when hippies, yippies and their ilk, when brought to court, show such contempt for court that they disrupt the very process of justice, when blackmail of the Churches is approved by churchmen themselves, what rational man would not grow angry?

Then look at man as a religious animal—and—every man is!—what a Babel. A few years back the Catholic Church looked like what she was named by her Founder: "The Light of the World." Against Communistic aggression and its militant atheism she was the focal point of resistance. Against the barbarism that was spreading over the entire globe the Church appeared as the one civilized and civilizing influence. She had a Creed, a Code, a Cult—and a genuine culture. Today . . . an anticlericalism that is growing with the speed of a mushroom but seemingly with the strength of an oak has the laity challenging the clergy at almost every turn, a "New Breed" of pseudo-theologians confusing the multitude with speculations that seem to question every doctrine and dogma, a number of moral theologians raising havoc with souls by their fallacious teachings of undigested existentialism, groups of priests boldly baiting their bishops, national hierarchies making puzzling public pronouncements, and even some Cardinals snidely sniping at the Pope. Indeed the Rock seems to be fragmenting, the Barque of Peter foundering, and the Bride of Christ, far from appearing "without blot or blemish" is made to look like some old hag. That "made to look" is no casual choice of words. For that is precisely how she does appear if we view her only from the reports of the press and her showings in some TV panels. Hence, this age of the computer, which is simultaneously the age of confusion, has an anguishing need to look upon, see, and even stare at *a Catholic of character.*

That last word is going to offend many. It is one of the "dirty" words of our day. For a man of character is one who builds his life on principles, and, thanks to the superficial silliness current among our pseudo-philosophers, principles are out. That is exact. "Philosophy," today, as taught even in some of our Catholic Universities, considers it naive to have principles, and horridly bad taste to discuss them. You can hear "philosophers" in the Academe actually congratulating one another in having found the "Queen of the Sciences" to have been an impostor. They give their students Nietzsche, Wittgenstein, Heidegger, Sartre, and Camus, but never Plato, Aristotle, Socrates, or that "dumb ox," Thomas Aquinas. And there you have a rather satisfying explanation of the radical students of today. Nourished on existentialism, how could they avoid relativism, subjectivism, moral, philosophical and theological nihilism? How could they fail to "mature" into individuals who are rootless in thought and enslaved to mere opinion, ready to follow every new fad and fashion and be open to mere suggestion? Hence the need to meet a man who realized that *Philosophia Perennis* merited her name, and far from being dead, is not even slightly ill; that she is as "relevant" today as she was in the ages past, and will be so tomorrow for the simple reason that principles are not only perennial but truly eternal.

I have met the man for this moment—and for every man living in this crisis filled moment. He is a man for our youth; for he is as modern as today's campus dissenter. He is a man who fought for the very ends these youngsters now espouse—and he won. Long before racism had led to any sit-ins, teach-ins, demonstrations or riots, decades before we had heard of Martin Luther King, Roy Wilkins, Eldrige Cleaver or Rap Brown, years before Watts, Detroit, Brooklyn, Boston, or New York were ravaged, this man was fighting against racism with intellect and will, and all according to law. Before our country ever heard of a Poverty Program, this man had one that worked. Years before our Senate ever thought of a law concerning "civil rights" this man was obtaining them. Although not an American citizen this man not only "held these truths . . ." but fought for the "inalienable rights" of every man to "life, liberty and the pursuit of happiness." He did all this because he was a man. Since he was a man he was, necessarily, a "man of God"; and because he was such, he was a man of love. All of which makes him *the man for the moment* . . . and this book a *must*.

Allow me a parallel . . .

Not too long ago the dramatic world, the literary world, and the entire thinking world sat up and took notice of a play by Robert Bolt titled *A Man For All Seasons*. The play was a world-wide success. It played to "standing room only" audiences in all English-speaking countries. But what is more astounding is the fact that it was translated into sixteen different languages—and the translations in print enjoyed almost the same success as the original in English enjoyed on the stage. Of course money-conscious Hollywood made it into a film, and Hollywood did not lose any money by that venture, though the play did lose some of its dramatic intimacy because of the adaptations made for the screen.

Now the astonishing part of all this lies in the fact that here was a play about a thoroughly English Englishman, and an outstanding Catholic amongst the Catholics, who was dead for more than four hundred years, and who had lost his life because of the stand he took on the question of divorce centuries before the divorce question became common, and on the matter of the Primacy of the Pope on such matters, centuries before Papal Primacy, or, at least, Infallibility, had been defined.

Surely no one will say that the "divorce" of Henry VIII is of piquant interest to modern man; and certainly the matter of Papal Supremacy is no great personal concern to Communists, Muslims, Buddhists, or Jews. Yet the play, translated into Hebrew, Japanese, Turkish and Russian, not only held the interest, but actually absorbed the readers of these languages, and the followers of those religions—for let no one fail to see that Atheistic Communism is a religion.

Why this absorption? Why this universal success?

No one dare say: "Dramatic suspense." For there is none. How could there be when the main action is determined by historical events, and most of the readers and playgoers already knew, at least vaguely, what the outcome of the clash between Henry VIII and Thomas More was?

Nor can one essay the surmise that it is the dramatist's technique. That Robert Bolt has technique is obvious. That he used it masterfully and with exquisite effectiveness is equally obvious. But it should be just as obvious that few indeed are the play-goers or readers who so appreciate technique that it would make a sell-out on the stage and a "best seller" in the book stores.

The appeal has been universal. Wherein does it lie?

Perhaps most will rest satisfied with the explanation that this universal appeal comes from Bolt's exquisite portrayal of More's character. Unquestionably there is much truth in this explanation; for Bolt portrays More as he was and has even managed to highlight those characteristics of the man and the saint that compel admiration and win warm affection if not genuine love: his charming affability, his warm affection for family and friends, his quick wit and deep wisdom, his urbanity and wonderful good humor, his abiding love for truth and justice, his consummate integrity. Anyone who knows of it might well suspect that Robert Bolt took not only his title but his every lead for the portrayal of More's character from a tribute written by one of More's contemporaries. Eight years before Thomas More became Lord Chancellor an acquaintance wrote of him: "More is a man of angel's wit and singular learning; I know not his fellow. For where is the man of that gentleness, lowliness and affability? And as time requireth, a man of marvelous mirth and pastimes; and sometimes of as sad a gravity; a man for all seasons."

Yet, Bolt himself gives the lie to that surmise when in the preface to the printed play he tells us: "What first attracted me was a person who could not be accused of any incapacity for life, who indeed seized life in great variety and almost greedy quantities, who nevertheless found something in himself without which life was valueless and when that was denied him was able to grasp his death."

There you have the whole truth, not only about the play and its protagonist, but also about its universal appeal. The play is not simply a portrait of a magnetically attractive character, but of a real man who knew that within him there was a tiny area he must rule and a time come when, with will stronger than any steel, in deference to the clear call of conscience, he must draw a thin, straight line which says: "Thus far I will go, but not one fraction of an inch further." Bolt shows us More ruling that area and drawing that line, and every human worthy of the name is fascinated by that show; for in Thomas More each recognizes the man each would be. Nor would Bolt have anyone miss the point. That is why he has More telling Dame Alice, who has been chiding her husband for not having said "Yes" to the King during his visit to More at Chelsea: "I neither could nor would rule my King," says More, "But there's a little ... little area ... where I must rule myself. It's very little—less to him than a tennis court." Then later Bolt has More explaining all by saying: "I can go no further, but put all in the hands of Him, for fear of whose displeasure, for the safeguard of my soul, stirred by mine own conscience (without reproach to any other man's) I suffer and endure this trouble."

Instinctively every man is "greedy" for life; and, had he the "capacity" and the opportunity, would grasp it, as did More, "in great variety." But, despite all the clamor of the present moment about "conscience," the "rights of the individual," "personal freedom" and "respect for the person," how many of our protesting contemporaries recognize that "little area" within him which he must rule? How many have the courage, or even the capability, of drawing that "thin, straight line" beyond which, "stirred by their own consciences (without reproach to any other's)," they will not go? How many are manly enough to "grasp death"? Failing the strength to rule that "area," the steel to draw that "line," the wit and the wisdom to "grasp" death rather than betray real manhood, how can any human call himself a man?

You may object and say that I am demanding saints and heroes. I reply by asking: Has life any other purpose? or manhood any other goal? The very objection proves the need for this book; for each of us needs to meet *"The Man for This Moment"*—Aloysius Cardinal Stepinac. He knew more about non-violence than Mahatma Ghandi or Martin Luther King. He can teach our protestors how to protest and our dissenters how to dissent. But what is more, he can teach every human all about that "little area within" that each "must rule," and how to rule it; show all of us where we must draw that "thin, straight line," and how to draw it. In short we can learn from him the man we ought to be; the man, the deepest anguish of our being longs to be.

Contents

Federation of Yugoslavia and its six republics. Shaded
area indicates the republic of Croatia.

✤✤

1 Some Necessary Knowledge

I BEGIN BY EXPOSING MY IGNORANCE—and maybe yours.

Have you ever heard of *Croatia?* Before meeting Aloysius Cardinal Stepinac, I had not; and I am the last to blame my education or my educators for that ignorance. From earliest youth I had been exposed to the geography of the Ancient, as well as of the Modern, World. I had poured over maps—even drawn them—of Europe, Asia, Africa, Australia, of North, South, and Central America, putting in the boundaries, mountains, rivers, lakes, and

1

plains, not to mention the names of cities, towns, and even of some villages. Yet never once had I printed the word *Croatia*. Can you say the same?

Now it is true that I was cloistered away from the world during those few years Croatia enjoyed sovereignty; that is, between the decline of Hitler and the rise of Tito. But the fact is that Croatia, as a people, a nation, a culture, a veritable civilization was there fifteen hundred years before Hitler was born or Josip Broz Tito came into being.

For my lack of knowledge concerning the country called Croatia I blame the cartographers. No map of ancient—or modern—Europe should ever be drawn without acquainting its readers with the fact that from as early as the fifth century there has been a geographical area in Europe inhabited by an indomitable people; a people who have always enjoyed some degree of sovereignty, and a people who has ever been—and it looks as if they will ever be—keenly conscious that they are a nation. Those people were, and are, the *Croats*.

That brings us into the realm of history—and again Stepinac will be a worthy guide. He opened my eyes not only to a geographical area I had never looked on before, and one that is worth while staring at, but led me into a realm of history I had completely missed—and one I am willing to wager millions of moderns, even many history majors, have missed. He opened my eyes to a people, a culture, and a civilization I had never viewed before. But what is more important, he made me stare and stare until I really saw what was before me. The operative word in that last sentence—as it will be in this book—

is "really." Stepinac made me look and look until I saw *reality*. He can do the same for you.

You are well acquainted with Yugoslavia. Our mass media will hardly let you forget it. Yet, what do you really know about it? Do not most moderns look upon it as one country, one political unity, and think of it as comprised of one people? It never was that. Is not now. And, with reason, one may doubt that it ever will be. Stepinac will show you why.

Officially, of course, it is described as a "People's Republic." That apostrophe is a lie. Its Constitution declares that it is "composed of the People's Republic of Serbia, the People's Republic of Croatia, the People's Republic of Slovenia, the People's Republic of Bosnia and Hercegovina, the People's Republic of Macedonia, and the People's Republic of Montenegro." But each apostrophe can be challenged, and in every case the word "Republic" questioned.

Only recently a journalist quite accurately described it as "a country of six nations, five basic nationalities, four languages, three religions, and two alphabets." With such a conglomeration can you imagine anything like true unity? Yet the enumeration of the ingredients gives you insight into the present political necessity for a dictatorship and the tyrannical rule of "the Party," even as it introduces you to the odd semantics necessary when they use such words as "democracy" and "liberty." And yet, Pan-Slavism has been a dream for decades, if not for centuries. But let no one ever think that, even in their

3

dreams, these nations and nationalities ever saw themselves as one. Stepinac will show you the real dream and the reality behind it, even as he produces incontrovertible evidence that anything beyond the semblance of a political unity will ever be possible among peoples of such clashing cultures.

The next revelation this man will make is in the realm of Ethnology; and what a revelation that is! First we learn that Yugoslavia is no new State. It was not brought into being by Josip Broz Tito and his then Communistic backers in Moscow. It would be much more nearly correct to say that it was created by America, and very specifically by Woodrow Wilson and his famous "fourteen points," especially that one about "self determination" for small nations as so strongly stressed during and after World War I. For on September 3rd, 1918, the United States of America acknowledged the justice of the Yugoslavs' aspirations for unity and freedom. Less than three months later, on November 23rd, the unity of the State was proclaimed, and on December 1st of the same year, accepted by Prince Alexander, a Serb. Thus it came about that the Kingdom of Yugoslavia or better, the Kingdom of Serbs, Croats and Slovenes was proclaimed to the world as being an independent State on December 4th, 1918. But it was a Kingdom made up, roughly speaking, of six and a half million Serbs, five and a half million Croats, and one million, one hundred thousand Slovenes; and while all derived originally from the Slavic People, they differed drastically in their loyalties — the deepest being that of Religion. And thereby hangs a tale that Stepinac will tell.

4

But before he begins let us grasp this one bit of very necessary knowledge so that we can understand his tale. Historically speaking it is possible that the Serbs and the Croats entered the Balkan Peninsula together, migrating from what, today, is Southwest Russia and Galicia, and that they headed toward ancient Illyricum and Dalmatia. But if they came together—and there is potent reason for that *if*—it was not long before they separated, the Croats moving toward the Adriatic and Italy, while the Serbs stayed further inland, and if attracted to the sea at all, it was toward the Aegean. That geographical split contributed in no slight degree to what was to become, and to remain for centuries, their religious alienation; for while the Croats became Roman Catholics, and, with that innate temper of their character, became, and yet remain, unswervingly loyal to the Holy See, the Serbs became, and still remain Oriental Orthodox Christians, and are just as determinedly attracted to Constantinople. That alienation, along with that deathless devotion, highlights the life and love of Aloysius Stepinac—and even contributed to his death.

This was the highlight that opened my eyes to the reality so many of us miss, and led me on to the realization that I had met the man for this moment. Stepinac opened my eyes to what is actually taking place in the world of today. He will open your eyes to that objective reality which we are all looking at, but which so few of us are seeing.

It was Gilbert Keith Chesterton who once gave us a directive which it is the height of wisdom to follow, yet one we very seldom use. This "tank of paradoxogen," as he was not unwittingly named, told us that we should "stare and stare at a thing we have looked at a hundred times and more," and then promised that we "would be seeing it for the first time." Stepinac forces us to do just that as he leads us into the realm of Theology.

In so-called "polite society" today one often hears it said that "Religion and Politics are two subjects that should never be discussed." You know the reason for that bit of unintellectuality. So do I. But I ask you: What other two subjects are of similar importance? What other two subjects involve the truly human being throughout his entire life as completely as these two should? What other two subjects are as worthy of intelligent discussion as these? You know the answer. So do I. None. Since the case of Aloysius Cardinal Stepinac revolves around these two subjects, there is no human being who can fail to profit personally from looking into that case; for the Cardinal and his case force us to stare and stare at Religion and Politics until we see them for what they are—and that sight gives *vision*. It is the vision of the reality which is our present moment. But how many moderns see that reality?

Most of our modern "seers" tell us that our world is falling apart, our civilization is being destroyed, our structures crumbling. When we look, but fail to stare, a case can be made for their contention. For on every continent we find not only unrest, but actual riot and rebellion. We "cry for peace, peace; but there is no peace." Shooting wars may be confined to Africa, the Middle East, and Southeast Asia, but when we stare, we see that the Third World War is on, and is being vigorously waged in both hemispheres. We work, and write, and speak for freedom; but how many in the world today enjoy true freedom? Emerging Nations declare themselves free, whole countries are said to have been "liberated" by those who call themselves "The National Liberation Front," or "The National Liberation Army"; but when we stare, we see on all sides of us "slave states." Youth, the world over, is clamoring for self-fulfillment—and yet, is finding such emptiness that among our own seven million college students the leading cause of death is not disease, but suicide. As for morals . . . who does not ask whether Rome, as it declined, was as immoral and as amoral as we? With the divorce rate climbing and the birth rate falling, with our stage, screen, literature and life itself becoming ever more sex-saturated, and crime ever more commonplace, you may be led on to agree with these "prophets of doom" and conclude that our world is very truly falling apart. But stop, don't look, but stare, and listen to a true prophet and a prophet of truth: Aloysius Stepinac. He will show you how to keep our civilization from becoming a shambles. All we need do is what he did: rule that "little area" within us . . . and draw that "thin, straight line." All we need do is what St. Thomas More did: become the men we are meant to be by being "stirred by mine own conscience (without reproach to any other man's)."

Yes, More and Stepinac take us into the realm of Religion. Now do not smile as you think of Bishop Robinson, Harvey Cox, Dietrich Bonhoeffer, Tillich, Bultmann, or Barth. Do not smile as you recall that "Religion is the opiate of the people," and that "God is dead." Learn from this Croatian Cardinal that far from being "dead," God

7

is the only ever-living One, the Lord of Life, and the one real reason for living, and, if need be, for dying. Learn that He it is for Whom you must rule your own "little area," and for Whom you must draw your own "thin, straight line"; for the real voice of your conscience is actually *the very Voice of God.*

That is the Voice which tells you how to become what you are: a real man. That Voice speaks not only to every man, but in every man. But it seldom shouts. That is why you must learn from Stepinac how to listen; for "above the din of these disordered years," that is the one Voice each of us needs to hear—and to heed.

Because, when one mentions Religion today, many can so readily name the above "elite," and recall so accurately the above clichés, we need to meet the man for this moment. He will show us that we not only must "live and learn" but more especially we must learn and live—*truth.* He may humble us, but it will be only to exalt; and we of this moment need both. For we are a highly sophisticated society and a toweringly conceited human race. We think we know, when we really do not. We claim to have open minds, open hearts, and wide open eyes; when the fact of the matter is that our conceit has actually closed all three. Stepinac will open each—if we but allow him to show us *Christ . . . and anti-Christ.*

If that last line shocks you, it is but proof that you have been looking without seeing, listening without hearing, touching without feeling. For that confrontation is the reality of this moment.

8

Now do not turn away in anger or irritation. For "there is no one so blind as he who will not see." Let us take this short, simple test: We have looked on pictures of the starving in Biafra. What did we see? Reality? Not if, in those shrunken bodies, pinched faces, and bloated bellies we have seen only starving Ibos. Not unless in those suffering faces we have clearly discerned the features of Jesus Christ. We look upon hands closer to home, begging hands of the unemployed, the undernourished, the poorly clad, and often more poorly housed in our ghettoes, but we are not actually seeing unless, in those hands, we find the stigmata of the Crucified. We listen to the sobbings of wives, mothers, sisters, brothers, sweethearts and friends of those killed in Vietnam and the other warring regions of the world, but we are not really hearing unless, in those sobs, we hear the crying of Him who wept over Jerusalem—and over all the world. Can you pass that test? Yet Blaise Pascal told us, more than three centuries ago, that "Jesus Christ will be in agony until the end of time . . ." He was telling us of reality. Then Francis Thompson has even more recently alerted us to actuality by saying:

"When men shall say to you: 'Lo, Christ is here';
When men shall say to you: 'Lo, Christ is there';

Believe them!—And know that thou art seer
When all your crying clear

Is but: 'Lo, here! Lo, there! Ah me, Lo everywhere!' "

Stepinac can loosen our tongues so that "all our crying

9

clear" will be the above; for he can open our eyes to reality, and open our ears to actuality. He can show us both Christ—and anti-Christ. We need that vision at this very moment.

In an especial way this book is addressed to Americans, first of all because this Croat has very special ties with America; he has a debt, as it were, to pay—and he can pay with interest. But more especially because he delivers a specifically American message to the world of our day.

I say that not only because it was an American President, with genuinely American principles, who led the Croatian people in this modern era to claim, and, in a way, achieve their independence, but also because it was due to an American woman that Aloysius Stepinac was enabled to become what he was. Here are the facts . . . .

In late 1923, a certain Mrs. Havlik, of Clyde, Missouri, summoned her thirteen children to her deathbed. Once they had all gathered about her she told them how, all through her life, she had ever held the priesthood as the highest and holiest calling any human being on earth and in time could receive. Consequently, since she herself could never aspire to the priesthood, she had saved all her life to finance the education of a priest. God had not called any of her sons to the priesthood, nevertheless, she would have her life-dream come true, and her life-ambition fulfilled. Hence, she asked her children to take her savings, send them to some trustworthy person, and have them used for the education of a priest. She died in 1923. Her children gave her money to the Benedictine

10

nuns of Clyde, Missouri, who, in turn, sent the sum to the German-Hungarian College in Rome.

Before her mother's first anniversary, Alice Havlik received a letter from Father Rauch, the Jesuit Vice-Rector of the College, telling her that her mother's money was being used for the benefit of an ex-officer of the Hungarian Army who had later joined and became an officer in the Yugoslavian Legion. Father Rauch gave Miss Havlik the ex-officer's name. It was Aloysius Stepinac. The Vice-Rector added: "He thanks you for your help; his case is certainly extraordinary. He promises to be an excellent priest, one who will do you and your mother honor" (Raoul Plus, *In Praise of God*, p. 167).

So, in a certain sense, we own Aloysius Stepinac, who most certainly became "an excellent priest" and did honor not only to the American ladies, Miss Alice Havlik and her mother, but to all America and the entire human race.

But that is not the only reason America should take Aloysius Stepinac to her heart. The deeper reason lies in his loyalty to Croatian tradition and the Croatian character; for therein lies his needed message for America and the world at this critical moment of time.

You have already read one account of the origin of the Croatian people. It is but one. There is another which tells that the Croatians stemmed from the Goths who had absorbed the Sarmatian and Slavic groups they had found on the steppes of southern Russia. The first evidence of the presence of this people was found in inscriptions carved in tombstones located near the Greek colony of Tanaïs, in southern Russia. These inscriptions date from the second and third centuries and bear the word CHRO-

11

ROATHOS. The etymology of the word, from which these people have been given their name of Croats, is difficult and somewhat doubtful. One account states that it comes from CHRO-BATOS, and means "A nation ever ready to defend its home and its rights." That such a translation, paraphrase, description—call it what you will—fits this people, and is true of this man, cannot be doubted by anyone who reads his story.

In his classic, *Decline and Fall of the Roman Empire,* Gibbon asserts the identical fact saying: "From the Euxine to the Adriatic, in the state of captives or subjects, or allies or enemies, of the Greek Empire, they overspread the land; and the national appellation of *The Slavs,* has been degraded by chance or malice from the signification of glory to that of servitude. Among these colonies, the *Chrobatians* or Croats, who now attend the motions of an Austrian army, are the descendants of a mighty people, the conquerors and sovereigns of Dalmatia" (p. 258, Book VI, 1890 edition).

That Americans need the spirit designated by *Chro-Batos* at this moment is evidenced by sit-ins, teach-ins, demonstrations, draft-card burnings, flag-desecrations, moratoria, and campus riots. When all the virtues that made our Nation great are ridiculed and scorned by so many; when what would have been recognized as treason in the days gone by, is now passed by Courts as "free speech"; when clichés, which cloak the real purpose of dangerous and destructive movements, are mouthed with seeming sincerity by intelligent men; when civil disobedience, defiance of authority, confrontations, contestations, and even open avowal of intention to destroy our structures and abolish the "Establishment" go, not only unpunished, but often even unchallenged, it is obvious that the temper, character, and spirit of Aloysius Stepinac make him the man for this moment, which writhes in such great anguish for a "prophet"—a man who will show us the light, lead us on the way, and give us the truth.

This anguish is not limited to America; it is world-wide. But such a longing has always created "vocations." That is why we are hearing so much about "charisms" these days of confusion. The wise among us will recall that when the lone prophet of God challenged the "charismatic" of his day, Mount Carmel was covered with "prophets"; yet there was only one Elisha. We could cover many a mountain today with the so-called "charismatic"; but there is only One Christ. And Stepinac shows us Him clearly!

Since Tertullian was not wrong when, centuries ago, he said: "The human soul is naturally Christian," Aloysius Stepinac is the man for every man, be he baptized Christian or not; for every human will have an "hour" similar to Christ's in Gethsemani. In that "hour" there will come the critical moment when the "thin, straight line" must be drawn, or life, no matter how measured by years, will have been a failure.

It costs to draw that line. It is the costliest cost of all; for it is the price we have to pay for what the Apocalypse calls a "pebble," but which is "the pearl of great price." You have the price. So have we all. But how many of us are willing to pay it? Stepinac will show us how as he shows us the *costliness of love*—which, after all, is what life is all about.

2 He Is Caught In A Multipronged Vice

IT WAS THE EVENING of November 30, 1938. Monsignor Shimrac, editor of *Hrvatska Strazha,* the leading Catholic daily in Zagreb, was talking to Count Anthony H. O'Brien of Thomond, who had arrived that very morning from Austria, with a tale of escape that, in any days before this momentous year, would have been dubbed "unbelievable." With a title such as "Count" and a name such as O'Brien, you would have thought him safe in Vienna in the year 1938. But no. Hitler was on his way to dominating Europe. Hence, noblemen, no matter what their race or nation, who had had anything to do with the "free and independent Austria" were far from safe with the Feuhrer. Ten hours after Dr. Kurt von Schuschnigg had broadcast his last speech as Chancellor of Austria, Hitler's SS men were searching the Count's home; for what he did not know, but, after their search, they took him off to Police Headquarters where he underwent forty-eight hours of incessant questioning, after which he was taken off to the Central Police Prison. There, for three seemingly interminable weeks, he lived with fifteen other people in a single cell, thirteen feet by seven. But that was only the beginning. Next came three and a half months in the County Court Prison. Even as he still wondered, and strove to find out, what it was all about, he was as suddenly told he could go home as he had been taken from that home. Of course he headed for home with puzzlement still present, but also with great relief. That relief, however, turned to consternation when he entered his former home only to find that it, and everything in it, had been requisitioned for, and was being used by, the Hitler Youth.

Nor was that the end. As he looked about for a place to stay and was considering the advisability of getting out of the country, he received a confidential warning that Herr Hitler had issued orders to confine him in Thuringia. That set the Count fleeing. But flight was no easy matter. In the dead of night some friends rowed him across the river March, which formed the border between Austria and Czechoslovakia. He got across safely, and felt he could breathe more freely in Prague. The air was not only clean and fresh, but filled with a determination to resist Hitler, despite his threats and fulminations.

But the Count had not been in Prague three months when he was told by an official in the Ministry of Foreign

Affairs that the Germans were demanding his extradition because of his connection with the Austrian Auxiliary Army in 1934 after the assassination of Chancellor Dollfuss. Being a journalist of standing, the Count had numerous connections in the various Foreign Offices in central Europe. Thanks to these, he had been forewarned in Austria and now in Czechoslovakia. Owing to his profession he had much more knowledge and far keener and deeper insights into what was actually transpiring than many in the individual Offices themselves. Hence he knew that the German grip on the Czechoslovak government was much firmer than was generally realized. Therefore, he concluded that he must again be on the move—and hastily; for the Czechs could not afford getting into trouble with Hitler over a single foreign correspondent. His friends in the Foreign Office supplied him with a genuine passport, but under an assumed name, and urged him to get out of the country and into Yugoslavia as soon as he could. An Hungarian transit visa and a Yugoslav entrance visa were readily obtained, but the use of them was another matter. For, since the Munich Conference, which brought the Agreement into being in September, the train service between Czechoslovakia and Hungary had been discontinued. Of course it was "to be opened any day"—but when the Count arrived at Bratislava, he found out that the reopening was not to take place that day!

He could walk twenty miles to the next Hungarian railroad station, or he could cross Austria. Danger of being detected at the passport control centers in each country was high. What should he do? Some sixth sense told him that, though Austria was more hostile to him personally, the chances of passing through undetected were a little higher there than in Hungary. For eight long hours, as the train crossed the country, Anthony O'Brien, Count of Thomond and Foreign Editor of *The Standard,* of Dublin, sweated. Would Hitler discover him under his alias? Night's blackness was hesitantly yielding to November 30th's daybreak when the train whistled and belled its way into the station at Zagreb and a tense and tired journalist all but slumped out of the carriage onto the station platform and sighed with relief.

He needed rest, but he took very little. There was one man in this city he must see. But how to arrange a meeting? No Foreign Office this day. They had not been gentle with him these past few months, even though they had been more than kind. So he sought out a fellow journalist, the Editor of the leading Catholic daily, and told him his desire.

"Archbishop Stepinac?" Monsignor Shimrac had queried. "I believe a meeting can be arranged. He is easily accessible. I'll see what I can do. I'll wager he'll see you shortly."

"Not too shortly," said the weary Count.

The Monsignor glanced at the clock in his office and smiled as he said, "Well, it won't be tonight." The clock struck ten and, weary as he was, the Count himself had to smile. But less than five minutes later that weary face was lighted, not with smile, but with surprise and delight mixed with something close to disbelief.

"At ten o'clock tomorrow morning? Are you sure?"

"Positive," replied the Monsignor. "I told you he was accessible. And I could tell you much more, but wait and see for yourself." Then stepping closer to O'Brien the

Monsignor went on, "You've known me for twenty years, Count. And you must admit that I am not a man given to exaggeration or sentimentality. Our profession kills the one and curbs the other. But wait until you meet our Prelate. Once you get to know him you will see why I say with real sobriety that he will become one of our great Croat Bishops, perhaps even the greatest. He's young, but he is already a sage, and I claim, a saint."

At quarter to ten the next morning Count O'Brien was standing in the office of the Archbishop's secretary, presenting his card. The young cleric arose immediately, assured the Count that he was expected, and escorted him down the long, high-ceilinged corridors of the *Kaptol*, the centuries old residence of the Archbishop of Belgrade and Primate of Yugoslavia.

The secretary knocked. A firm yet gentle voice answered. When the young cleric swung the door open, the Count saw a tall, slim figure rising from a desk covered with papers and books. A few swift strides carried the prelate to O'Brien's side. Out went both hands, and, before the Count could speak, he heard: "Praise be to God that you are here. Cardinal Caspar sent me word through Switzerland of your departure from Prague. I have been praying—and anxious—ever since." The Count could only marvel at the delicacy, the diplomacy, and the dispatch with which these prelates, without any request from him, had concerned themselves with his danger.

They sat then and O'Brien had the rare experience for a correspondent: to be the interrogated, rather than the interrogator. The Archbishop was alive with questions.

At lunch that same day Count O'Brien was sitting with the Editor of the *Hrvatska Strazha* and saying, "You win.

I agree one hundred per cent." Then he went on with quiet exclamations: "What a man! What a patriot! What a priest! What a Prelate!"

The Monsignor smiled and added, "And what a mind and heart!"

Then O'Brien recounted the substance of the conversation. They had talked of Hitler and before the Count could opine that Chamberlain of England had made a mistake by adopting a Policy of Appeasement, the Archbishop had knifed to the heart of the matter by saying: "The Sudetenland is not the end of Hitler's demands; it is but the beginning. England and France have not been wise. Munich was sunset; not sunrise." The Count pointed to the receptions given the returning diplomats: London, Paris, even Rome and Berlin had welcomed their representatives at Munich: Chamberlain, Daladier, Hitler and Ribbentrop, Mussolini and Ciano, with jubilation. The Archbishop agreed that the peoples of these lands actually wanted peace, and thought the Agreement would bring them the same; but he insisted that the Berlin-Rome axis had been formed, and the leaders in those two cities were greedy for power and land. They would not let the world enjoy peace. "Before a year has passed," said the intent young prelate, "Czechoslovakia will have ceased to exist, Germany will dominate central Europe, and there will be war."

When O'Brien exclaimed: "What a journalist he would make! His knowledge of world events, the politics and diplomacy of the various countries, his insight into the motives for their various moves . . ." the Monsignor interrupted with: "I hope he is not a prophet. I hope there will be no war."

"I'm no prophet," countered the Irish journalist, "but I've watched these same European powers for years—and at close range. The Archbishop is right. My only question is: Is he premature? He thinks that it will come within ten or twelve months. The man does know what is going on. He told me things even I did not know. But the most revealing thing of all was his knowledge of Croatian history and his love for Croatia. The man—and he is a real man—is a true patriot."

"He proved that long before he was a priest, let alone Primate of Croatia. Did you know he fought on both sides in the First World War, yet was fighting all the time for Croatia?"

"What do you mean? He did not mention that...."

Then followed the story of how Aloysius Stepinac, as soon as he had reached his eighteenth year, had been inducted into the Hungarian Army; for Croatia was then part of the Austro-Hungarian Empire. He had been assigned, after his basic training, to the 58th Division, which was then fighting on the Italian Front. The Empire showed wisdom by filling this Division with Croats, whom, they knew, had no great love for the Empire itself, but who were aflame with love for their homeland. It was wisdom, too, that had the Empire assign this Division to the Italian Front; for, fighting there, they would be fighting for their homeland more than for Austria, Hungary, or Germany. The Italians learned this when, on thirteen separate occasions, they, under General Luigi Cadorna as Commander-in-Chief, tried to force a passage along the Isonzo. Thirteen separate times the Italians were repulsed.

"Stepinac was promoted rapidly," the Monsignor

inserted here, "and fought as Cadet Warrant Officer along the Isonzo for over a year; fought in such a way that the Hungarian government twice decorated him."

"But you said he fought on both sides . . . ."

"He did; for in 1917 he was taken prisoner by the Italians, along with some other Croats. While in prison he heard of the 'Yugoslav Legion' and finally joined it. The 'Legion,' as you may not know, was composed exclusively of Croats, Serbs, and Slovenes from the Monarchy. It had been conceived by the 'Yugoslav Committee,' whose thought it was that, by contributing to a military victory, they would obtain a sympathetic hearing for the Yugoslav cause when peace came . . . ."

"Oh, the Archbishop talked long about the 'union of the Southern Slavs.' He said he had heard about it from his father and his uncles. What a closely knit family his must have been, and what a love for their country they had." Then with a wry smile he added: "You know, Monsignor, as I listened to the Archbishop talk about Croatia, I could not keep from thinking, what a wonderful Irishman he would have made. . . ."

"Irishman?"

"Haven't you ever realized how parallel the history of the two peoples has been: Two Catholic nations—the proportions of Catholics is about the same in both countries. You know, roughly speaking, about a hundred per cent."

"A hundred per cent?"

"Roughly speaking," laughed the Count. "Then, for that Catholicity we have suffered three hundred years and never had full freedom as a nation. You have suffered longer—and for the same reason. . . ."

22

"Almost from the beginning," said the Monsignor softly.

"Yes, the Archbishop told me about that. How proud he is of the titles you Croats cherish . . . ."

"And have earned . . . ."

"Yes," said O'Brien, "the Archbishop brought that out, too. I've been associated with Yugoslavia for twenty years now, and I thought I knew something of her history. But I learned more in twenty minutes this morning than I had learned in twenty years. He is proud of his people. He took me back twelve hundred years to the first treaty ever entered into by the Croats. That was in 679, and you could see his eyes light up as he told that it was a treaty between the Croats and the Holy See. Agatho was Pope, and your people promised never to enter an 'aggressive war.' Do you think they kept that promise?"

The Monsignor's eyes now lighted up as he said, "Absolutely! We have been in many a war, but every one was in defense of our homeland. That's what our very name means: 'A Nation ever ready to defend its homeland and its rights.' Why do you think we fought the way we did along the Isonzo in the First World War? It was not for Austria. It was for Croatia. The 58th Division, to which the Archbishop belonged at that time, was one of the best fighting units in the Austrian Army. They were reminiscent of the *Hrvatsko-Domobranstvo* of the mid-nineteenth century . . . ."

O'Brien's eyes twinkled as he said, "Not so fast, Monsignor, nor so furious. I don't speak your language well. What does *Hrvatsko-Domobranstvo* mean?"

"Just what it says: Croatian Home-defenders. That's what the Archbishop was doing along the Isonzo in

1917, and what he was doing in the Yugoslav Division at Salonika. He became an officer in that Division, too. And I have heard that he was decorated for the way he served. I have never verified it, but I have heard that he received the *Karogeorge Star*—the highest honor possible in Yugoslavia. Of course you heard nothing about that from him, did you?"

"No. He never mentioned his days in the Army."

"He wouldn't. He's not that type. I have never looked into the matter. But I do know that the Yugoslav Division, as it was then called, played a mighty part in the breakthrough of the Bulgarian and German lines at Salonika in 1918. I have often wondered just how much fighting the Archbishop actually did; for, as I have told you, he came from an Italian Prison camp to the 'Legion' as it was first called. Most of the others came from Russian prison camps and there lies a sorry tale . . . ."

"This gets ever more interesting. I thought the Archbishop was my teacher in Croatian history, but now I see I can learn much from you. What's this sorry tale you have to tell?"

"One I'd rather not recall. But it seems that the Serbian government, with the agreement of the Allies, obtained permission from the Russian authorities, just how I don't know, to have a voluntary draft among the prisoners in the Russian camps for the 'Legion.' The response was not much. You see, our Croats on the Russian Front in that War did not have the same spirit as those on the Italian Front; for they were not fighting near or for their 'homeland.' Most prisoners taken by the Russians were Croats. But Serbia let it be known that their idea of Pan-Slavism was anything but a union of peoples with equal rights; they wanted to rule the others. Neither

Croats nor Slovenes could accept that. So there were few volunteers for the 'Legion' amongst the prisoners in Russian camps. The next mistake the Serbs made was to change that draft from voluntary to compulsory. You can imagine what happened. The Croats rebelled. Disturbances broke out in the camps. They were put down with utmost cruelty. At Odessa there was a mass murdering of prisoners and their corpses were thrown into the Black Sea. No one knows the exact number of the murdered, but it has been estimated at between ten and thirty thousand."

The Count whistled softly, and then remarked, "Small wonder there is so little love lost between the Serbs and the Croats. Yet the Archbishop, a Croat amongst the Croatians, fought in that 'Legion'?"

"As I said," the Monsignor continued, "it was in the 'Division' he fought. Further, never forget he came from an Italian Prison camp, and had fought on the Italian Front. That made all the difference in the world. He felt himself to be an *Hrvatsko-Domobranstvo* along the Isonzo, and an *Hrvatsko-Domobranstvo* at Salonika."

The Count smiled at the way the Monsignor used his native tongue when aroused and could not refrain from using the same tongue as he now said, "And I think he feels himself an *Hrvatsko-Domobranstvo* right now. He used the word 'homeland' and 'Croatian People' with a vigor, and yet with a lilt in his voice at the same time, that made me think of a strong-willed father and a love-filled mother together."

The Monsignor looked long at the Count before he rather quietly said, "You have looked into the heart of our Primate. He is both father and mother to his people, and he is both strong-willed and love-filled. As I said last night, he may yet be one of our greatest Croatian prelates, a sage and a saint . . . ."

"I use neither word loosely, Monsignor. In fact, I seldom use either; for I've met too many men called one or the other who never measured up to my concept of sage or saint. But I must say that your young Archbishop proved that he is filled with knowledge, especially about Croatia, and there was a light in his eyes, a light in his face, a veritable aura about his whole person this morning that touched some memory in me that I am only now identifying. I have seen pictures of his namesake, the young Jesuit saint, Aloysius Gonzaga. There is a resemblance between him and your Archbishop. He is a handsome man . . . ."

"He is a holy man . . . ."

"Maybe I saw what is called 'holy indignation' this very morning," the Count broke in. "The Archbishop was talking about the present condition of the State and he was particularly outspoken about many of the moves by the government in Belgrade. He openly named it 'a Serb regime.' But it was when he told me of the policy of the school authorities of sending young Catholic school teachers into remote villages where they had to work with young Orthodox teachers. He saw it as a deliberate effort on the part of the authorities to promote mixed marriages. He was indignant indeed—highly indignant. But now I see I can call it 'holy' indignation. Yes, I'd say he is a holy man, but, believe me, I would hate to rub this holy man the wrong way. I'd hate to have to fight him physically, mentally, and certainly not morally. But I almost challenged him once this morning. He called

26

Croatia *Regnum Catholicissimum* and seemed to be saying it was, not '*a most Catholic nation*' but '*the* most Catholic nation'—and you know I'm Irish."

The Monsignor chuckled and said, "Well, it was a Pope who named us '*Scutum solidissimum et Antemurale Christianitatis*'—'The Impregnable Shield and the Outmost Rampart or Bulwark of Christianity. . . .'"

"I know. The Archbishop told me about that. It was Leo X who conferred that title on you. And the way the Archbishop told it, he did so with reason. His Excellency took me back to the thirteenth century, then on to the fifteenth, and finally wound up in the nineteenth, telling how you Croats fought the Tartars and the Turks, and actually saved the Church and Western Culture. He was eloquent as he talked of Nicholas Zrinski, naming him the 'Croatian Leonidas,' and likening Siget to Thermopolae."

"Is not the similarity obvious?" queried the Monsignor, and then went on with ardor, "Think of it: Zrinski, Ban of Croatia, with a mere seven hundred men, facing Solyman the Magnificent, with his hordes of mighty Turks. Did His Excellency tell you the battle cry?" Without waiting for reply, the aroused Monsignor all but shouted, "*Reliquiae reliquiarum Regni Croatiae*—yes, 'the remnant of the remnants of the Kingdom of Croatia' was the cry with which they plunged into battle. Only seven hundred of them. The seven hundred died that day, but not until they had strewn that field at Siget with the corpses of twenty thousand Turks. Did Leonidas do better at Thermopolae?"

"You Croats are fiery," said O'Brien with a smile. "I

27

wasn't challenging you, nor was I questioning the accuracy of the Archbishop's comparison. I was just admiring his eloquence . . . ."

"Eloquence? You should hear him preach. The Cathedral is packed every time it is known His Excellency will be in the pulpit. I tell you he is one of our greatest . . . ."

"But so young for an Archbishop."

"When consecrated in 1934 he had just turned 36 years of age, and was then the youngest Archbishop in all the world. What is more, he had been a priest for only four years when he was made Coadjutor 'cum jure successionis' to His Excellency, Ante Bauer, an old man, a capable man, and a man of very sound judgment. He made an excellent choice in Father Aloysius Stepinac." When Monsignor Shimrac saw O'Brien's eyebrows lift in surprise and with question, he quickly added, "Oh, I know, such selections come from Rome, but only after they have been made by those most concerned. Pius XI nominated Stepinac Titular Archbishop of Nicopsis, and appointed him Coadjutor 'cum jure successionis' to Archbishop Bauer, but I can assure you it was Bauer who told Pius whom to nominate. It was something of a surprise to many of us here in Zagreb, especially amongst the clergy. But as for the people, they were delighted."

"I've heard about that. You know Dr. Mazhuranic?"

"I should. He was President of the Yugoslav Senate, and at one time Minister of Justice. He is from one of the oldest and most famous of Croat Patrician families. But he was never very friendly to us in the clergy and not outstanding as a practicing Catholic. Why do you ask?"

"He spoke to me just this morning. I told him I was to see the Archbishop and he waxed enthusiastic, told me about His Excellency's work amongst the poor of the city. I actually detected a note of envy in his voice when he said something very like what you just said. He claimed that while the people rejoiced over Stepinac's elevation, it was the poorest of the poor who actually exulted. He said he wished he could elicit such a response from them; for it was evidence not of mere admiration, but of actual love."

"We all love him. And don't forget he has been Archbishop for almost five years now, though actual Primate for less than a year. Ante Bauer died December 7th of last year. I happen to know Stepinac was functioning as Primate, though without the name, for some time before Bauer died. The point I make is 'the honeymoon,' which we all enjoy after any elevation, should have ended long ago were it only a 'honeymoon.' I know mine as Editor did not last anywhere near as long. But in the case of Stepinac it *is* love, especially among the poor."

"Why is that? Was he from a poor family?"

"Not exactly. In fact he is from what you could call 'well-to-do.' Certainly the Stepinacs belong to the highly successful middle class. Not truly wealthy. Yet anything but poor. We had to run a biographical sketch of him when he was consecrated. That is how I came to know all about him and his family. He was born in Krasic, not too far from here. He was the seventh in a family of eleven. Actually, his oldest brother, Max, and his two eldest sisters, Teresa and Barbara, are only half-brother and half-sisters to him. For his father, Joseph Stepinac took Maria Matko as his first wife. She died shortly after Barbara was born. Realizing he needed a woman's hand to help raise his tiny tots, he wisely married Barbara Penic not too long after his first wife's death. And did he get a blessing in that woman! She gave him nine children,

29

but one died soon after birth. That is why I say Aloysius was seventh in a family of eleven, when actually his father brought twelve children into the world. You can see the Archbishop's old home if you wish. Some of the family are still there. Krasic is not a large town—maybe 3000 population. But the Stepinac place is worth seeing for its beauty if nothing else. I'd say it was about 150 acres, which is a fairly good sized estate for people in Krasic. It has some delightful woods on it, excellent meadows for pasture, and a magnificent vineyard. Our Archbishop was a farmer's son, and you can be sure, in his early years, he was a farmer's boy. The family is well-known as diligent workers. But I was telling you about his mother . . . ."

"Barbara Penic . . . ."

"Yes, and if ever I met a saint she was one. It was she who named our Archbishop Aloysius. His middle name, Victor, was given him by Father Stephen Huzek, who was Pastor of Holy Trinity church, wherein Stepinac was baptized. He gave the name to the child because it was the Feast of St. Victor, May 9th, 1898 when he baptized the boy. He had been born just the day before."

"You don't waste any time in Croatia . . . ."

"Barbara Penic didn't. But what very few know is that on that very day, if not the day before, that woman took a vow to fast on bread and water three days a week. She offered that fast in petition for a priestly vocation for her newly born son, Aloysius. You know something about the way European women work not only in their homes but also on their farms when married to farmers. So you can imagine what it cost this woman with that size family, living on that size farm. But she got her request didn't she?"

"But tell me, did her son, Aloysius, always show signs that he would be a priest?"

The Monsignor laughed before he answered. "What would you think of our Primate if I told you he was not only engaged to be married, but that all, even the final arrangements, had been made for the wedding?"

"Who backed out: he, or the bride-to-be?"

"Oh, it was he. But can you imagine the state of mind of Barbara Penic Stepinac as she saw her Aloysius courting, then engaging, and then all but getting married? You can be sure that wonderful woman never said a word to dissuade him. But I can be sure, she prayed and fasted even more. She was a saintly mother."

"But what happened? Why did Stepinac back out?"

"First love, I'd say," was the Monsignor's reply. Then he told how Aloysius Stepinac, after finishing his elementary schooling at Krasic, took six years of gymnasium at Karlovac, then moved on to Zagreb where he entered the Archbishop's lyceum, with every intention of going on for the priesthood. In 1916, just as he was completing his seventh year, he was called to the colors. The students who were drafted were allowed to take their final examinations early and thus obtain their degree, *Grade Matura.* Young Stepinac had always been a good student. He had no difficulty obtaining his degree. After the war, most people expected him to resume his ecclesiastical studies. But Aloysius chose the College of Economics where he majored in Agriculture. Once again his abilities were manifest and his assiduity soon had him at the head of his class. He was almost twenty-five years old when about to graduate and he must have given serious consideration to his future. It was at this time that he became engaged. But suddenly, there came a resurgence of his boyhood ideal: the priesthood. He went through anguish and even agony for some time, but was finally convinced, through prayer and consultation, that God was calling him to the life of a priest. He told his fiancee, not without some human sorrow. But in the fall of 1924 he was enrolled as a student in the Pontifical German-Hungarian College at Rome. With characteristic thoroughness he plunged into his seminary life and his studies. Six years later he was in possession of two doctorates: one in Philosophy and one in Theology. But these were nothing compared to what was given October 26th, 1930. That day was the Feast of Christ the King that year, and on it Aloysius Stepinac was made priest of the Great High God and a vicegerent on earth for Christ the King of Kings. No one was happier than his aging mother, Barbara Penic Stepinac. Her years of fasting were rewarded when she knelt for his first priestly blessing.

The lunch was over. As Monsignor Shimrac drew back his chair he was saying, "His first assignment was to Tresnjevka, the poorest section of Zagreb. But he was not there long before he was transforming the place. He founded an organization that was more than a St. Vincent de Paul Society, more than International Red Cross. He called it *Caritas*—and it has lived up to its name. It is an organization that ministers to the poor, in every and any sense of being poor, whether it be economically, socially, spiritually, or any other way. Even as Archbishop he retains the Directorship of the organization. It is the work of his heart and of his life. He is even called 'The Father of the Poor.'"

O'Brien was smiling as he left the table and joined

the Monsignor. The Editor noticed the smile and asked quizzically, "See something amusing?"

"Myself," replied the Count. "I see I was taken in. Would you believe me, His Excellency told me he needed me to help him with *Caritas*. The way he spoke you'd think he was desperate for leadership—and he still the Director. What a man. But, tell me, how did he manage to grasp all the details of his office so quickly? He is still only in his fortieth year, and from what you tell me he is a priest of only eight years. . . ."

Then followed the account of how in early 1934, the aged Ante Bauer called young Father Stepinac, whom he had removed from Tresnjevka after little more than a year and had made him his Secretary and Master of Ceremonies, and said: "I am an old man. The day of my death cannot be too far off. But before I die I'd like to settle what could easily be the most important work of my life—the matter of my successor. You know already these are difficult times. But I can tell you the years just ahead will be more difficult. My successor must be a strong man, a man of robust health, a holy man, an energetic one. I think you are the man."

Stepinac's own mother tells that her son fell on his knees and with tears in his eyes said: "Excellency, have pity on me!" The aged Archbishop laid his hands on Stepinac's shoulder, looked deep into his eyes, and said, "You will be my successor." When the young priest made no reply, the Archbishop more quietly said, "I will not ask you to decide right now. Pray over it. I'll see you in two days." Stepinac spent most of those two days before the Blessed Sacrament. When he entered the Archbishop's presence two days later he was much more composed and felt he had unassailable arguments against his appointment. He put them before His Excellency as strongly as he could: he was too young, too inexperienced; he had not really learned how to run a parish, far less an Archdiocese; he was not a competent Secretary to an Archbishop, let alone competent to be an Archbishop; there were more experienced priests, Monsignors, and pastors right here in Zagreb; finally, he was a Croat and any appointment of Primate of Yugoslavia would have to be approved by King Alexander, a Serb. He ended with: "too young, and too inexperienced, Your Excellency."

Very quietly the aged Archbishop Bauer said, "I see you have thought this out thoroughly. I am sure you have prayed it through, also. Your youth does not make me apprehensive. It is an asset in my sight. Your inexperience, however, is another matter. Let us both pray God to spare me long enough to give you the fruits of my experience. All will not be pleasant to the taste, I assure you. You will be my successor."

"But, Excellency . . . ."

"Enough, Father. My mind is made up. But you are to tell no one. We must keep it from the press for the very reason you mentioned: the King's approval."

Ante Bauer then worked rapidly. He told the Apostolic Nuncius in Belgrade of his choice and asked him to get the *Placet* from the Holy See as quickly and as quietly as possible. There was no need to explain the reasons. The Nuncius knew the agreement between Rome and the government about Royal Approval of the one selected. As soon as word came to him that the Holy See had said *"placet"* the aged Archbishop sought a meeting with King Alexander. He was not with His Majesty long before he had outlined his need for an Auxiliary "with the right of succession." Then, smiling, he asked: "Would Your Majesty have any weighty objections to have as my successor a very good young priest who was once your reserve officer and a volunteer to the Yugoslav Legion during the first World War?"

Even His Majesty smiled at the way the query had been put. "No very weighty objections," he replied. "Who is this ex-officer of mine?" When the Archbishop gave the name and added a few remarks about Stepinac's character and abilities, His Majesty nodded his agreement as he said: "No objections." Bauer immediately released the news to the Press. That same day Yugoslavians learned of the nomination by Pius XI of young Father Aloysius Stepinac to be Titular Archbishop of Nicopsis and his appointment as Coadjutor to Archbishop Bauer *"cum jure successionis."*

The very next morning the Archbishop was summoned by the King, and told by His Majesty that he had reconsidered his approval of the Archbishop's selection of Stepinac. Some one had gained the King's ear the day before. Who it was, the King alone knows. But His Majesty did not get far with his excuses, and nowhere with his retraction; for Ante Bauer fixed King Alexander with stern gaze and almost indignantly said: "Your Majesty, We, your subjects, are well acquainted with, and have always believed, the saying: 'A King's word is never revoked.' Your subjects already know you have given your word." The King hesitated, but then said: "Be it done. I approve your choice."

"Most of us expected the consecration to take place in May that year; for we Croats have a special devotion to our Lady. But Stepinac himself selected June 24th as the day, the Feast of John the Baptist. Do you think it was indicative?"

O'Brien was putting on his coat by this time and obviously intrigued by the whole account. As he took his hat from the Monsignor's hand, he said: "I don't know whom to admire the more: Bauer or Stepinac. That press release was clever."

As the Count hurried back to his hotel for his next meeting, he was asking himself what the connection could be between the young, courtly Aloysius Gonzaga and the rugged man from the wilderness, John the Baptist. Stepinac looked like his namesake, Aloysius; yet he spoke like the Baptist. It was a fascinating combination and yet something of a puzzle to the Count. Still, what puzzled him more, now that the Baptist had been brought to his consciousness, was the statue he had noticed on the Archbishop's desk during the recent interview. Most prelates had a crucifix on their desks he had noted. Stepinac did not. But there was a small statue standing where most had the crucifix. He had not been able to identify it while with the Archbishop, but now as he headed more briskly toward his hotel, he told himself: "It certainly was not that of the Baptist."

But then he began to recall the Archbishop's tone, the fire in his eyes, and his expressive gestures as he had talked about the position of Yugoslavia at the moment. There was something of the Baptist about the man. He was direct, fiery, pierced to the heart of every topic, and had a note of intransigency about him. He had told the Count that his people—and how often he had used that term instead of "the country"—were between the prongs of three powerful, dangerous, and utterly untrustworthy movements. He had spoken rapidly, but had drawn a vividly clear picture. There was Mussolini and his Black Shirts to the south. Just above them, to the north, was Hitler with his Brown Shirts, to the east was Stalin and his Reds. Each, in his own way, was courting the favor of "his people." Ciano had been to Belgrade only recently. Prince Paul, reigning for the boy, King Peter, had just been invited to Berlin. While Moscow had been infiltrating for years. "No one of these men or their Movements is favorable to the Church. My people face difficult days."

As O'Brien crossed the foyer and before he entered the lift he was recalling what the Archbishop had had to say about "internal conflict." This, for the moment, disturbed the Count more than the picture of the triple prongs without the country. Stepinac had told him about the Croat Peasant Party and its leader, Machec; about Stoyadinovic and his dictatorial ways in Belgrade as head of the Cabinet; about the *Frankovitzi*, as the people called them, or the *Ustashi*, as they called themselves, and their leader, Ante Pavelic; then he had much to say about a certain Communist who called himself Tito.

It had been an informative morning and noon for the Count. He knew Monsignor Shimrac's source of information: every editor is fed continuously by his news gatherers, and pick up much from others in the profession. But what, he wondered, was the source of the Archbishop's information?

It was not long before he gained some insight to at least one source; for, when he went to help out in *Caritas,* his eyes were opened to Europe—or at least one part

37

of the continent, as they had never been opened before. The Count thought, from the descriptions he had been given of this organization, that he would be working among the poor of Zagreb, and most of these, he expected would be Croatians. But he had not been there an hour before he was interviewing Austrians, Germans, Poles, and Czechs—men and women of Jewish origin who were fleeing Hitler and his anti-Semitic purges. As the days moved on he saw that thousands on thousands of these persecuted people were pouring into Croatia. The Archbishop had broadened the base of his *Caritas* and had set up a Relief Committee for Refugees.

Now he was looking more deeply into the heart and mind of Archbishop Stepinac as the Count saw that the Committee's function was to find habitation and employment for these frightened people, and to do everything possible to enable them to live honest and decent lives on Croatian soil, or to aid those who so desired to leave Europe for England, United States, or South America. O'Brien's eyes opened wide when he found the Archbishop using the reserve funds of the Archdiocese to pay the travelling expenses of these refugees, since neither *Caritas* nor the Relief Committee had anything like adequate means at their disposal.

He was not within *Caritas* a fortnight when he heard Stepinac talking about the Protestants of Jewish origin now in Croatia. His Excellency pierced to the heart of the situation immediately. One day he told the Count that the Relief Committee must seek these people out; for many of their co-religionists could not, or would not, help them. Some were secretly sympathetic to the Nazi regime, while others feared it. The Protestant Bishop of Zagreb had been approached. He was a good man, said

Stepinac, but, obviously, a frightened one. He sincerely desired to help his flock, but dared not. So the Primate of Yugoslavia would take over. When O'Brien mentioned funds, His Excellency smiled a wry smile and said he would manage somehow.

It was not long after that the Count learned how His Excellency had contacted the head of the Protestant Relief Fund in England and had arranged for them to shoulder half the weekly cost for the subsistence of these frightened people, while he and his *Caritas* took care of the other half. As O'Brien saw this assistance to Protestants swell and the original stream of those of Jewish origin become a rushing river, he began to think of Archbishop Stepinac as some sort of a Midas; for money was never wanting.

The Count spent over two years in Zagreb and in that time gave himself generously to the work of *Caritas* —and learned what true Catholic Christian charity actually is. For, after the Nazi occupation of Czechoslovakia and Poland, thousands on thousands of Jews fled to Yugoslavia as the first step on their flight toward the Near East and their compatriots. Archbishop Stepinac and his organizations in *Caritas* immediately went into action, and aided these almost panic-filled people across the country to their place of safety. It mattered not what their religious convictions or their political ties were. No questions were asked. And the Archbishop himself had laid down the rule, which was law: They are human beings—that is all that matters. Help them!

O'Brien himself has told one of the most striking cases. A young German Communist came to them in Zagreb, asking assistance to get to the Soviet Union through Bulgaria and Rumania. It was not only a different case, it was a difficult case. It was labor to get the passports and visas through other countries, but at this point in history, to get what was needed to take this German Communist through Bulgaria and Rumania on to Russia seemed impossible. But Archbishop Stepinac said only one sentence: "He is a human person; he merits our help." They got him through.

Another facet of the Archbishop's life that fascinated Count O'Brien was his seeming contradiction of never meddling in politics, forbidding his priests to ever meddle in them, and yet being caught up, because of his love for "his people" and his country, in the middle of all movements. It was the Archbishop himself who filled O'Brien in on the historical movements and moments of Croatia—and Yugoslavia.

At the time King Alexander, a Serb, had accepted to rule the new State which had practically been brought into being by the Pact of Corfu in 1917, and had been formally proclaimed as "The Kingdom of the Serbs, Croats, and Slovenes" in 1918, friction was already felt between the Croats and the Serbs. A Constitution had been drawn up and, by 1921, recognized as the Constitution for the Kingdom. But the Croats, who had an imperishable dream and even a demand for independence—and to some extent had always enjoyed it to some degree, even when they were part of the Austro-Hungarian Empire—did not find in the Constitution anything like a realization of their dream, or a satisfactory answer to their demand. For Alexander was a Serb, and the Croats were always conscious of the fact. In their country was organized a powerful and patriotic party called The Croat's Peasant's Party.

At its head was a brave and intransigent man: Stepan Radic.

In 1928, Radic was assassinated in parliament. Vladimer Machec took over the leadership of the Croats, set up a separatist Parliament in Zagreb, and refused to have anything more to do with the Government in Belgrade. King Alexander did all in his power to effect some sort of a compromise. But by 1929 he realized that his efforts were in vain. He did what he thought best for the State. He set aside the Constitution of 1921, declared a dictatorship, and, in an effort to wipe out the old historic divisions between Croats, Serbs, and Slovenes, named the country "The Kingdom of Yugoslavia." It was in this year that Ante Pavelic, a member of the Croat bloc in the Belgrade Parliament, founded a revolutionary organization known as the *Ustashi,* whose aim was the creation of a Croat State within the territories traditionally belonging to the Croatians.

In 1931 the King announced the end of the dictatorship and introduced a new Constitution which called for a two-chamber Parliament. The electoral law left no place for purely local parties. On November 9 of that year, elections were held. But, since the Government named most of the candidates, it won an overwhelming victory. But it was truly a Pyrrhic victory; for most of the opposition groups had abstained from participation. Alexander found himself forced to arrest Croat and Slovene leaders on the charge of "treasonable activity." Vladimer Machec was sentenced to three years imprisonment, whereupon his Party denounced the regime and again demanded autonomy.

In 1934, while on a visit to Marseilles, King Alexander was assassinated by a Macedonian revolutionary who was

41

working with some Croat revolutionists who had their headquarters in Hungary. War between Hungary and Yugoslavia, on account of this, was barely averted, thanks to the good offices of the League of Nations. Peter II, the lawful heir to the throne, was then only a boy of eleven. Prince Paul, cousin of Alexander, took over the Regency. Now the Croats, hoping for concessions from the conciliatory Regent, promised to cooperate with the Government. The only concession Prince Paul made was to pardon Machec. The Croats soon resumed their boycott of the Belgrade Parliament. It was in this year that Stoyadinovic became head of the Parliament. He was not in office a month when he blasted all hopes for a "federalist" union of the Serbs, Croats, and Slovenes—each nation enjoying some definite autonomy.

It was shortly after his arrival in Zagreb that O'Brien saw the people of Croatia, in a Parliamentary Election, give almost a hundred per cent vote to Machec. This forced the resignation of Stoyadinovic. Within a year it looked as if Machec would win what most Croats would accept: a federation of the three peoples with separate autonomy for each. In late August of 1939 a Democratic Government was reestablished and new elections, by secret ballot, arranged for. The State was to be reorganized on a federal basis, the Croats receiving complete autonomy in all cultural and economic matters. Machec became Vice-Premier, and five other Croats joined the Cabinet. Things were looking better—but then came September and the *Blitzkrieg* into Poland.

It was history's irony. Just five days before World War II broke out, a *Sporazum*—that is, an "Agreement"—had been entered into by Croats, Serbs, and Slovenes, which might very well have ended years and years, yes, even centuries on centuries of conflict between these peoples. It was provided for that Croatia, Bosnia, parts of Slovenia and Dalmatia be set up as an autonomous *Banovina*. It allowed for provincial control of economy and cultural affairs, while communications and foreign affairs, along with defense, would remain within the jurisdiction of the central government in Belgrade. It was an advance. But resentment was soon manifested; for while Croatia was given a certain amount of local autonomy, other parts of Yugoslavia were not. The Serbs, as usual, could never accept this state of affairs. But, had the war not come, there was a possibility that the *Sporazum* might have worked, and, in time, the federation of autonomous states might have become a reality. But Hitler saw the importance of Yugoslavia for his plans.

O'Brien had seen some fast moves and mighty upheavals in Europe during his twenty and more years as foreign correspondent, but never had he witnessed anything like what now took place in the year 1941. He realized, and the Archbishop made it even more evident, that Prince Paul and all Yugoslavia was caught in a vise. No help would come to them from Russia; for the Nazi-Soviet Pact was still in force. Great Britain was in no position to give assistance. If the Government yielded to Hitler's pressures, it meant German occupation and possible subsequent dismemberment of the country. If it did not. . . .

It is true that when Prince Paul had visited Berlin in 1939, a few months before the rape of Poland, Hitler, in a toast, had assured him of the "inviolability of the Yugoslav frontier." But who could trust Hitler now?

By 1941 Germany had practically occupied both Bulgaria and Rumania, and was demanding the use of Yugo-

43

slavia for transportation of troops and war material. If Prince Paul refused, occupation of the land seemed a certainty. On March 25, 1941 he signed the Pact.

Two days later, March 27, the Prince learned how unpopular his act had been with his people. A *coup d'etat*, organized by officers in the Army and a few politicians, eliminated Prince Paul. General Simovic, a Serb, a centralist, a strong, stern Serbian nationalist, took over the Government. This was anything but pleasing to Herr Hitler. The Yugoslavs learned just how displeasing it was on Palm Sunday, April 6, when their country was blitzed. Belgrade was brutally bombed by the Führer's famous —or infamous—*Luftwaffe*. German troops poured into Yugoslavia from many frontiers. By April 10, Belgrade was occupied by the Nazis. On that very day Croatian nationalists severed all ties with Yugoslavia and proclaimed the existence of "The Independent State of Croatia." One week later the Yugoslav forces capitulated. Five days after that, Italy and Germany partitioned Yugoslavia in eight directions—and made Croatia, Bosnia, Hercegovina, and a part of Dalmatia into the Independent State of Croatia, with Ante Pavelic, head of the *Ustashi, Poglavnik* —or President.

The Count sought out the Archbishop to ask what he thought of these lightning-like events. He received another lesson in history, and was given deeper insight into the man, the patriot, the priest, and the prelate who was Aloysius Stepinac. As Croatian patriot he exulted in the creation of the Independent State. It was the age-old dream of his people realized. He said it was only just. But, as Catholic priest, he had his reservations about the way it had been brought into being. The ties between the *Ustashi* and the Nazis were too evident, and too strong.

44

The presence of the Fascists in the proclamation of the State's existence pleased him no more than the appointment of Pavelic as *Poglavnik*. He respected the conscience of every man, but he never hesitated to tell any man when his conscience was an erroneous one. No one could love Croatia more than Stepinac did. But, at the same time, no one had clearer concepts of the difference between a nationalist and a patriot. He admired many of the men in the *Ustashi* movement, but he had no admiration for the movement itself. It was too nationalistic, despite its claim to be patriotic.

With customary clarity, as well as brevity, he drew the true picture of the country: Five Armies—two being Occupational Armies of Foreign Powers, Germany and Italy; three being those of Yugoslavians—*Chetniks* under Draza Mihailovic, the Serbian nationalist; the *Ustashi,* under Pavelic as *Poglavnik*; and the *Partisans,* under Josip Broz Tito. Further it was a country in which five different ideologies were being held out to the people: Nazism from Germany, Fascism from Italy, Communism from Russia, Serbianism from Belgrade, and Croatianism from Zagreb. Finally, it was a country in which there already were at least two wars in progress: that of the Nazi-Fascists against the Allies, and the civil war: that between the Croats and the Serbs and Communists. He ended his vivid description by promising a third war: "The *Partisans* seem negligible just now, but they are backed by Moscow. They will turn on the Serbs; Tito and Mihailovic will never be partners. My poor country! My poor people! God alone can help us."

When asked what he knew of Mihailovic, the Archbishop told the Court that he was, undoubtedly, a well-meaning man, but too narrow in his outlook. He, like many other military men, was devoted to his country and would discharge his duty under the most trying circumstances, but appeared better versed in military history than in political, and seemingly was unaware of the depth of antagonisms between the different peoples. He was a Colonel when the Yugoslav Army surrendered and Simovic capitulated. Mihailovic repudiated that capitulation, and proclaimed the continuation of the struggle against the Nazis. He had but a small group of army men with him, yet proudly named his followers the "Yugoslav Army in the Homeland." That last word, the Archbishop claimed, told the whole story—and promised little comfort to his Croatian people; for Mihailovic held that Serbia should dominate any future Yugoslavia, and had let it be known that he was convinced that the collapse of the Yugoslav Army under the blitz was due in no small measure to the betrayal of Yugoslavia by Croats.

About Tito he was briefer, but, obviously, considered him a much greater threat. He told O'Brien that Josip Broz was a Croat who had been born, like himself, in a small village. He, too, served in the Army during World War I, but, unlike Stepinac, had been sent to the Russian front where the morale of the Croats was low. Like the Archbishop he had been taken prisoner; but unlike him, he had never joined the Yugoslav Legion. Instead he had stayed in Russia and studied Communism. He had been sent back to Yugoslavia to infiltrate the Unions. He had been imprisoned for years; then seemed to drop out of sight. He had adopted the name "Tito" while working as a Communist long before the War broke out. He kept it now and used it more than his real name, Broz.

Then the Archbishop urged the Count to leave the country. When O'Brien argued that His Excellency

46

needed him now more than ever, for the case-load at *Caritas* had increased by leaps and bounds, Stepinac simply shook his head. "No, you must go. We will manage with God's help. The Gestapo will get you if you do not leave."

The Count was almost stunned by the Archbishop's mention of the Gestapo; for though both were well aware of the fact that there were agents of that dread arm of Germany's secret police in every congregation to which the Archbishop spoke, His Excellency had actually thundered against a law promulgated by the Pavelic Government on May 1, 1941, less than a month after the creation of the Independent State. It distinguished between Croat *citizens* and Jewish *nationals,* then confiscated the radio sets of Jews and Serbs, and shortly afterwards dismissed from public office all Jews and Serbs. Finally, the Government stipulated that all Jews should wear a special insignia—the Star of David. "Promulgated from Zagreb, but written in Nuremberg" was Stepinac's summation. But what he had not said about the injustice of the law was not worth saying—and all in front of agents of the detested and feared Gestapo. Yet, here he was now warning the Count about them.

"How about your good self?" the Count asked.

"I'm different. I'm a Croat; you're not. I'm a priest; you're not. I'm a prelate; you're a man of the press. The Gestapo, at the moment, has more fear of me, than I of them. My place is with my people; but your place is any place but here."

O'Brien had tried to argue that as a newsman, he could be at no better place than Zagreb; for that was where things were happening. He soon saw he made no impression on the Archbishop with that line of argumentation, so he mentioned *Caritas*.

"That's why you must go. . . ." Then he told the Count how both *Caritas* and the Relief Committee had been under the careful surveillance of the German Consul-General almost since its inception, but now the watch had intensified. Before the blitz on his country Archbishop Stepinac had been reported again and again to the Yugo-slav Minister of Foreign Affairs by the German Minister in Belgrade. But now the Gestapo was upon them. "You know what they did to you in Austria, and what they would have done to you in Czechoslovakia. I know what they will do to you in Croatia if. . . . No, Count, you must go."

Again O'Brien put the question, "And what of your-self?" He saw the Archbishop's eyes flash toward the statue—the statue the Count had not yet identified, and about which he had not, as yet, asked a question which had haunted him since that first meeting over two and a half years ago. He might have posed it there and then had not His Excellency, with a speed that almost dazzled O'Brien, presented his position with a clarity that kindled to brighter blaze the admiration which had grown and grown in the mind of the Count from the first day, even as it struck with sharper poignancy into his heart.

"A priest is not his own. A prelate belongs to his people. As a Croat and as a Catholic I praise God for allowing my people to realize their dream. For ten centuries, despite occupations, usurpations, seeming defeats and actual dominations, my people have been conscious of their right to nationhood. The Law of God, and the Law of Nations, Woodrow Wilson's Fourteen Points, the principles enunciated by the League of Nations, the innate sense of right on the heart of every man of good will attest to the right of small nations and national minorities to freedom. Justice and Truth are on the side of my people and my country. But both my country and my people are now in danger. The Pavelic Government is the *de facto* government at the moment. We must not only accept it, we must work with it when it is right, and oppose it whenever it is wrong—and tied in as it is with the Axis Powers, it will often be wrong. The Croat People need a Croat Prelate even more than the Croat State needs a Croat *Poglavnik*. My place, as a man, as a priest, as a prelate, and especially as Primate is with my people. Pavelic and the *Ustashi* would have been difficult and dangerous at any time, but now, dominated by Nazis and Fascists. . . . Don't you see, Count? Just look at the law against the Jews. That would never have been dreamed of by any Croat. But you've seen how the Croats under the Nazis are prosecuting it. I see that I shall have to fight on four or five fronts simultaneously; oppose those from without my country and even some from within."

"Then, let me stay and help. You know the Irish: we are always spoiling for a fight." The slightest semblance of a smile touched the Archbishop's lips. He rose from his desk, walked to the Count, and gently said, "Because you are Irish you must go. Believe me when I say it is harder for me to press you to go than it is for you to go. No man likes to be alone, and I—But no, *He* is always with me."

They parted shortly after that, but with no promise on O'Brien's part that he would leave; he simply asserted that he would "think it over." But he gave Stepinac insight into his mind and heart when he asked the Prelate for a copy of his first Circular Letter published shortly after the creation of the State of Croatia. The Archbishop added two other letters to the first.

Before the sun had set the Count had read all three, and referred to them as he was bidding Monsignor Shimrac goodbye. "I've met many Churchmen in my day," the Count was saying, "Most of them I have esteemed. Many, I have admired. But two have made an impact on me that is imperishable. In 1923 I met Eugenio Pacelli in Berlin. We call him Pius XII today. I've met his equal, if not his greater, in Zagreb in the person of Aloysius Stepinac. I've just read three of his Letters. He could teach diplomacy to diplomats, philosophy to philosophers, theology to theologians—and, if they only knew it: Statecraft to statesmen."

The Monsignor smiled. "Do you recall what I said to you on your arrival: Sage and saint?"

"You are more expert on that last category than I. But I do know I met a man—every inch of him. I met a priest and a prelate—*par excellence*. And what a patriot! He is a fearless man. I hope he'll never become foolhardy...."

"Never fear...."

"I don't know. I heard von Galen in Germany. You have your own von Galen here in Croatia. I have been thinking of comparisons all afternoon. What would you say if I called him the Mercier of our day?"

"Not bad. But I'm a Croat. I think him better."

The Count's smile was tribute. Then he asked his question: "Whose representation is that on the Archbishop's desk? It has always been there whenever I visited. That desk could be piled high with papers and books obscuring everything, but that statue—not so very big—stood out...."

"So, you didn't recognize it? It is of 'one of the twelve'...."

"Never. I believe I can recognize the representation of any and all the Apostles...."

"Count, I was quoting. It is a statue of 'one of the twelve'...."

O'Brien hesitated. He frowned. Then he shook his head. "I still don't get it."

"Whenever the Evangelists refer to Judas they always add 'one of the twelve'...."

"Judas Iscariot?"

"Judas Iscariot—'one of the twelve'...."

"But, why?"

"That is the question we all have asked ourselves and one another, but no one has yet asked His Excellency. So your surmise, Count, is as good as mine."

As O'Brien left the country that night, provided with all he needed in the way of passports and visas, he was thinking of the vise he saw closing in on Croatia. The prongs were powerful: two of them, Nazism and Fascism had already closed in, but had not crushed. The third prong, which the Count considered the most dangerous had, as yet, not moved with all its force. But he felt that Communism would yet effect what Nazism and Fascism might fail to crush. But then he thought of the man no force could ever crush—and he saw that he stood alone, and open to pressure from all sides.

"That's what it takes to be a man," he told himself. "It's a price no man has within himself. If he is to be what he has been made to be, his grasp must exceed his reach; and he must do what Stepinac has already done: he must grasp God."

✣✣✣

3 The Thunder of A Voice... Like God's

MONSIGNOR SHIMRAC AWOKE next morning with a feeling of loss and a gnawing curiosity. His stimulating friend, Count O'Brien, had left the country. But he had not gone without leaving the Editor of the Catholic paper a puzzle. What was it, the Monsignor wondered, that O'Brien had seen in the Archbishop's Letters that he himself had missed? As Editor of *Hrvatska Strazha* he had received the earliest release of the first Circular Letter after the creation of the Independent State. He

He had even read it from the pulpit to a large congre-
had read it before ever handing it over to his type-
setters. He had proofed it as it came off the press.
gation. Yet he felt that O'Brien had seen more in it than
he himself had seen. His first task that morning would be
to get that Letter out of his files and reread it.

His first impulse was to go into the "morgue" and dig
up the issue in which the Letter had been printed, but
then he decided to look in his private files where he felt
certain he had placed the original release from the
Chancery. As he remembered it now, it had seemed to him
to be little more than the usual call for a *Te Deum* that
any Ordinary would put out after such an event as the
creation of the Independent State. But O'Brien had said
something about diplomacy, philosophy, theology, and
statecraft. Shimrac hoped he himself was not slipping.
He admired O'Brien's quickness of mind, the journalist's
keen nose for news, but, even more, his ability to see
more in an event than what met the eye.

"Ah!" he exclaimed. "Here it is. Good." And he took
the Letter to his desk. He noted the date: April 28, 1941,
and began to read:

Venerable Brethren:

There is no one among you who has not been
a recent witness to the momentous events in the life
of the Croat nation, in which we are all laboring as
messengers of Christ's Gospel.

Strange, thought the Monsignor, how that opening
sentence struck him now. He had not noted before that
the Archbishop was doing in this opening sentence what
he seemed to be always doing: reminding his priests
both of their dignity and their duty. He never tired of

54

telling them they were Christ's vicegerents who were to preach His Gospel. The Monsignor had read this Letter at first as the enthusiastic reaction of a patriot. He now saw it was a priest's letter to fellow priests. He read on more attentively:

These events are the culmination of an ideal long cherished and desired by our people. This is a time when the tongue speaks no more, but only the sense of heritage and community in the country in which we first saw God's light and with the people from whom we descend. It must be stated that in our veins, too, the blood coursed more strongly and the heart in our bosom beat faster. No reasonable person can condemn, and no honest one can cast blame, because the love towards one's own people is inscribed in the human heart by God, and is His commandment.

And who can blame us, when we, as spiritual pastors, contribute to the national joy and enthusiasm, when we turn our hearts full of deep emotion and warm gratitude to the Majesty of God? For, however complicated is the web of contemporary events; however heterogeneous the factors which influence the course of affairs, it is easy to see the hand of God at work. "A Domino factum est istud, et est mirabile in oculis nostris" (Ps. 117:23).

Today, from this ancient castle in the shadow of this old Cathedral, this silent witness to our Croat history, I speak to you not only as a son of the Croat people, but even more as the representative of Holy Church. I speak to you as the representative of that divine institution which has sprung from eternity, and the end of which is in eternity in the full sense of the word. As a representative of that Church which is *"firmamentum et columna veritatis"* (1 Tim 3:15) and which was not afraid to speak the truth through my mouth when it was necessary, although, unfortunately, her voice remained frequently "a voice crying in the wilderness" (Jn. 1:23).

"Whew!" the Monsignor whistled as he hitched his chair closer to his desk. "How did I miss so much on earlier readings? O'Brien is right. There is philosophy here. That first appeal is to the Natural Law. But how soon he rose to the theological aspect. And what a facility in quoting apt texts from Scripture. This is quite a Letter." He read on:

As the representative of the Church and as pastor of souls, I pray and exhort you to work with all your might that our Croatia may be the country of God, because only in that way will she be able to fulfill the essential tasks for the benefit of her members. Faithful to God and to Christ's Holy Church, our Croatia will achieve that noble mission which is the function of our earthly Fatherland of promoting the supernatural interests of its members. Faithful to God and to the Church, she will show her belief that the final aim of all human strife is Eternity—where our true home is. In respect for religious and moral values she will prove her belief that the earthly home is a true mother only when she teaches us to pray, and to "give to God what is God's," and that she is a solicitous mother in our life only when she directs our steps on the roads which lead to God, and when she casts aside tribulations from the souls which God created for Himself.

Faithful to God and to the Church, our Croatia will not only perform its duty in the promotion of the supernatural destiny of the Croat people, but will erect a solid foundation of sound progress in the natural order. The Church, which has already seen two thousand years of changes in the world's history, is the historical witness of how "*regnum de gente in gentem transfertur propter injustitias et injurias et contumelias et diversos dolos*" (Ecclus 10:8). We must, therefore, regard as our supreme duty in these crucial times in the history of our nation to spiritualize our whole national being with deep insight into eternity. We must warn and teach that the holy enthusiasm and noble zeal in building the foundations of the new Croat State must be inspired by the fear of God and by love of God's law and His commandments; for, only through God's law, and not on false natural principles, can the Croat State be solidly established. Answer, therefore, promptly this appeal of mine in the noble task of conserving and advancing the Independent Croat State.

The Editor of Zagreb's leading Catholic daily stopped there and sat back a moment. His mind was racing. It was condemning himself for having missed so much, and admiring Count O'Brien for having missed nothing. In the paragraphs he had just read, he saw the diplomacy and the Statecraft the Irishman had mentioned. The Archbishop was addressing his own priests and people directly, but, quite assuredly, he was addressing those in power indirectly. He was telling his people that if they would be Croats they must be Catholic, and if they are Catholic they must be Croats; but he was also telling Pavelic and all in the Government that they, if they would be statesmen and not mere politicians, will look through time to Eternity, and have as their ultimate goal the ultimate good of their people. In other words, Religion must be the very basis of the State. That reference to "give to God what is God's" was pointed. But the omission of the balanced phrase "and to Caesar what is Caesar's" was even more pointed. To follow that with the long quote from Ecclesiasticus telling how "a kingdom is translated from one people to another because of injustices and wrongs, injuries and diverse deceits" was the most powerful and piercing of all. If those in power read this Letter they must have seen that while they had an ally who would exhort his people to cooperate, they also had a potential adversary—and a powerful one.

The Monsignor consoled himself inasmuch as he felt that even the Count had missed something: he had not mentioned the holy mind and holy heart evidenced in this Letter. He had said nothing about the manifest God-consciousness of the Archbishop. That was really the substance of this appeal to the people and the indirect address to the rulers. All must be God-conscious if they would make Croatia what the Primate saw it called to be: "the country of God." Consoling as that thought was to the Monsignor, he was still chagrined at having had to have an outsider alert him to the wealth contained in the first Circular Letter the Archbishop had penned

58

after the birth of the Independent State. He lifted the last page of the Letter closer to him as he completed his reading:

Knowing the men who are today at the helm of the Croat nation, we are deeply convinced that our efforts will find understanding and assistance. We believe and expect that the Church in the newly erected Croat State will be able, in complete freedom, to preach the principles of eternal Truth and Justice. She will, therefore, fulfill the words of Holy Scripture: *"Verbum Dei non est alligatum"* (2 Tim 2:9). And she will regard as her holy duty *"opportune, importune, arguere, increpare, obsecrare in omni patientia et doctrina— et cum omni apostolica libertate"* (cf. 2 Tim 4:2).

May God grant that this shall come to pass. And that it may be so, I appeal to you, venerable brother priests, that you do not cease exhorting to prayer the faithful entrusted to you, and that you yourselves at God's altar raise up your hands the more to the "Father of Lights" from whom descends every good gift and every perfect endowment (Jas 1:17), that the Chief of the Croat State may have the spirit of wisdom in order to fulfill this noble and responsible office for the Glory of God and for the salvation of the people in justice and truth; so that the Croat people may be people of God, attached to Christ and to His Church, founded on the rock of Peter!

It may be that prayer seems to the world a superfluous thing; We regard it as the most vital thing in life—for "when the Lord does not keep the city, in vain he watches who keeps it" (Ps. 126:1).

The Church of God has never wasted herself on empty slogans, and has never failed in the patient work on which are laid the foundations for the happy future of individuals, of nations, and of states. Prove yourselves, venerable brethren, now, and fulfill your duty toward the young Croat State.

I have decided that on Sunday, May 4 of this year, a solemn *Te Deum* will be held in all parish churches, on which occasion the parochial officers should invite the local authorities....

The Monsignor did not finish the last few lines. He knew what they said. But again he sat back and marvelled at all the Archbishop had managed to put into this Letter which had to have been composed quite hurriedly. It was dated April 28—the Croat State had not been recognized (or set up) by Hitler and Mussolini until April 23. Five days—and he knew how crowded every day was for the Archbishop—to crowd so much truth into a few paragraphs!

At this point in his reflections he was interrupted by an assistant editor who held out a sheaf of papers containing the news of the late night and early morning. Before he so much as glanced at them Monsignor Shimrac asked: "Have you ever reread the Archbishop's first Circular?"

"The one about the *Te Deum?*"

"It's about much more than that," said the Editor. "Count O'Brien alerted me before he left." Then gesturing toward the copy before him, the Monsignor asked, "Have you ever been conscious of the Archbishop's careful choice of words?"

"Not particularly."

"It would be worth your while to notice it. I have just realized that in this very first Letter he distinguishes throughout between the Croat people and the Croat State. . . ."

"Between the governed and the governing?"

"If you want to put it that way. I see now that His Excellency was not being subtle so much as being consistent. The distinction is legitimate. But from his pen it means that he is more priest than patriot, or, better, patriot because priest. He loves his country. No one can doubt that. But it is "his people" as he calls them, who make up that country, who are his first—and I'd say, his final—concern. The man is all priest. He rejoices in our independence—and yet he fears. He wants God's people in Croatia to be the Croatian people of God. I'd dare say that, running through his mind, as he hastily penned this Letter, was that title we all should cherish: *Regnum Catholicissmum*. He wants Croatia a "most Catholic country." Did you notice his insistence on loyalty to the Holy See?"

"In that Letter?" It was an exclamation of incredulity that came from the assistant editor.

Monsignor Shimrac laughed good-naturedly. "God bless the Irish. I see you can reread with profit the Letter I have just reread. Yes, His Excellency stresses unity to, and loyalty to, the Pope."

"But why? Haven't we always been?"

"Father," Shimrac now said with calm seriousness, "there is fear in this Letter."

"But our Archbishop is fearless. . . ."

"In one sense, yes. But read that Letter again, and you'll see that he has deep fears about the government. I just discovered that there is both a threat and a plea in his lines. Yes, he pleads for freedom for Religion. . . ."

"In Croatia?"

"In Croatia . . . but at the same time he warns those in power that they will not only fail, but fall, if they do not grant it. And that warning is on theological, not political grounds: 'When the Lord does not keep the city, in vain he watches who keeps it.' That is the Psalm he quoted, and while the Letter is addressed to the people, that line is directed to the *Poglavnik*. This Letter is loaded, Father. It's a bomb. It is brave, bold, demanding, and fearful. It comes from a fearless Primate, a patriotic priest, and a man who not only knows what has gone on in the world, what is going on, but foresees what may yet go on in this newly erected State of ours. He fears Pavelic because of his connections with the Nazis. I guess, actually, it is the Nazis he fears."

"Fears the Nazis?" It was almost a snort of derision that came from the assistant editor. "Read what I just brought you and you'll see how much he fears the Nazis. He is practically dictating to them. And look how he not only disregarded, but actually showed disdain for them whenever they tried to interfere with his *Caritas*. You and I know who was behind all that harassment. Why he defies the very Gestapo. There were plenty of them in the Cathedral last Sunday when he tore into the *Poglavnik* and all in the government for the way they are enforcing those laws against the Jews. Fear the Nazis— he almost disdainfully despises them. Though I can't use that last word about the Archbishop, can I?"

"No. He actually does despise Nazism. But he'll never

despise any man no matter what his '-ism.' But I guess I was not careful of my own choice of words when I used 'fear.' What I meant was that this Letter shows His Excellency is aware of possibilities that can harm the State and the people. But what have you this morning?"

"A bomb. . . . You know how he has been working for the Serbs. As soon as he heard of those two hundred and fifty the *Ustashi* were holding as hostages he went to work. You remember that, don't you? It was just after the State came into existence. He told Pavelic plenty about the inalienable rights of every individual human be he Muslim, Orthodox, Jew, Protestant or fallen away Catholic. Pavelic must have been a trifle shocked. You know I think the *Poglavnik* is a Catholic fanatic, or should I say fanatical Catholic?"

"Same difference," laughed the Monsignor. "I remember that case well. Stepinac certainly laid down the law to the *Poglavnik*. I remember his passages on justice. Superb. Unanswerable."

"Pavelic would make the country Catholic overnight. He is actually forcing conversions. I've heard the *Ustashi*, at least many of them, are real 'hold-up men.' But instead of 'Money or your life' it is 'Convert to Roman Catholicism or you die' with them. The Archbishop will never stand for that. You saw his first directive to the clergy. His Excellency knows Canon Law and human nature. Who wouldn't convert with a gun at his head or a bayonet at his belly? But what kind of converts will such people be? But read that bomb you have in your hand. It is to the *Poglavnik* directly, but to Mussolini and Hitler almost as directly. That letter calls for asbestos. Every sentence burns. But wait until you get to the end. . . ."

The Monsignor sat in to his desk as the assistant went out the door. He arranged the papers more firmly in his hands and began to read:

Poglavnik:

Allow me to address you on the following matter:

At Zagreb, as well as in the provinces, panic exists because of the measures against non-Aryans which have been announced, and we await the consequences with great fear. Many people are afraid that their legitimate spouses will be separated from them despite the fact that they were validly married in the Catholic Church.

Poglavnik, if it is a question of marriages which have been validly contracted in the Catholic Church, I raise my voice as representative of the Catholic Church, and I energetically reject the interference of the State in the question of such marriages, which are indissoluble regardless of the race of those involved. More than that, no State has the right to invalidate these marriages, or effect divorce by force, and if it uses physical power, then that State commits nothing other than an ordinary crime—from which no good can come.

Meanwhile, I know that there are similar marriages among the chief ministers of the National Government, but these marriages are protected. It is against logic, and it is against justice that these marriages are protected while others are abandoned to the favor or the disfavor of a different law which has no basis in common sense, and which, moreover, does not accord with the true interests of the people or the State.

If even dumb animals protect their young, and will

not let themselves be separated by force, who among the judicious will believe that thousands of people of mixed marriages will be able to watch passively while their families are destroyed by force, and their children are abandoned to an uncertain fate? Is it not exactly in this way that the *Partisans*—so much decried —were created? Is it not by exactly such measures, full of injustices, that the people are driven by force into the ranks of the same *Partisans,* as is the case with many Croatians who can no longer tolerate the injustices of the occupation forces?

In the same way I ask you again, as representative of the Catholic Church, to protect the most elementary right—the right to life—of those among the subjects of the Independent State of Croatia who have become members of the Catholic Church during the time of the State's existence, whether they were "rebaptized" or whether they came into the Catholic Church from the Orthodox; and against whom no one can prove any personal crime against the interests of the Croatian people or the State.

Next, I ask in the name of the humanity that our people have always respected, not to permit any longer, *Poglavnik,* that the people of our State suffer unjustly. There are many in the concentration camps who are innocent or who have not deserved so severe a punishment.

Poglavnik, I am sure that such unjust measures do not come from you, but rather from irresponsible persons who have been guided by passion and personal greed. But if there is here an interference of a foreign power in the internal and political life, I am not afraid if my voice and my protest carry even to the leaders

65

of that power; because the Catholic Church knows no fear of any earthly power, whatever it may be, when it is a question of defending the most basic rights of man.

There is no one in our country who desires more the happiness and prosperity of our people and our new State than the Catholic Church. But this happiness and prosperity depend on our respect for the natural and positive law of God, by the respect of this law by the Government of the State, as well as by the people; and it is the Catholic Church which must exert vigilance. Since it does not possess physical force, but only moral, it will in the future intrepidly use this moral power, the power of protecting the rights of man, and, by means of this, of contributing to the happiness and prosperity of our people.

Poglavnik, in Italy there are some tens of thousands of innocent people, mostly of women and children, from Gorski, Kotar, Primorje, and Dalmatia, exiled in concentration camps. Hunger, sickness, and suffering of all kinds have caused a very high death rate among these wretched people. It is seriously to be feared that by some means the extermination of the population of these parts of the country is sought. When my delegate recently attended, with delegates from the Croatian State and humanitarian institutions, a meeting of the Italian Ministry of Foreign Affairs in Rome for the purpose of freeing and helping these poor people, the Italians said: "Why do you interfere in our treatment of these people, after the way you act in Croatia?"

Poglavnik! Do not let these irresponsible and unwelcome elements violate the true welfare of our people. The violation of the law of nature in the name of the people and the State will bring vengeance to the people and even to the State. The bitterness which will spread the spirit of vengeance is being born within the country, while from outside the enemy attacks our moral values.

Please accept, *Poglavnik,* the sincere expression of my deep respect for you.

Dr. A. Stepinac — Archbishop of Zagreb

Monsignor Shimrac pressed a button. The assistant editor who had given him the sheaf of papers just a few minutes before, entered. "Where did you get this letter? Is it official, or is it a leak?"

"It's authentic. . . ."

"I know that. No one else could, or would write like this. Stepinac is written all over it. But is it for release officially?"

The assistant editor smiled a bit self-consciously before he said, "I'd call it an official leak. I did not get it officially from any of the Archbishop's secretaries, but a friend of a friend of mine. . . . You know what I mean."

The Editor frowned in thought. "If it's not official I don't think I'll break this story. You summed it up. This letter is a bomb. That reference to Hitler is too obvious—and it is defiant. . . ."

"Why not call the Archbishop?"

"I've called him too often of late. He's not getting testy, but he is tired." Then after a few seconds more of reflection the Editor took his pencil and wrote across the top of the Letter: *Kill*—"If His Excellency wants the public to read that, he'll release it to *Katolicki List.* That's his official organ."

At that same moment, in his office in the *Kaptol,* the Archbishop was pondering the same question: should he release this personal letter to the *Poglavnik* to the press? A trace of a frown of displeasure appeared on his forehead as he looked at the word *Poglavnik.* He did not like it. It was the equivalent in Croatia to Hitler's *Führer* and Mussolini's *Duce.* It was proper enough as a title in ordinary times, but with Italian and German occupational soldiers seen all over Zagreb, the title smacked too much of Nazism-Fascism and dictatorship for His Excellency to use it with ease. Before he had decided about the release of the Letter he buzzed for a secretary and asked him to give him the file on protests against anti-Semitism. Soon he was flashing through four letters, each of which had been addressed to Dr. Andriji Artukovic, Minister of the Interior, for the Independent State of Croatia, Zagreb.*

The first was dated April 23, 1941. It drew Artukovic's attention to the fact that the anti-Semitic Law made no distinction whatsoever between Jews who had been converted to the Catholic Church and those who had not. As the Archbishop read his own sentence: "There are good Catholics of the Jewish race who have been converted by conviction from the Jewish religion; there are among them those who have been converted for dozens of years, and there are among them those who have excelled as good Croatian patriots," he muttered to him-

---

* The Archbishop was vigorously antagonistic to the Nuremburg Laws in themselves, as he had clearly shown by his generous care of all those Jews who had escaped from Nazidom into Croatia. But in these early letters he thought it proper to plead for those Jews who had converted to Catholicism and who were, consequently, his very own "children." Later he would openly protest unconditionally against the laws in themselves.

self: "The *Ustashi* were called *Frankovitzi* after a converted Jew, Pavelic is married to a Jewess, so is his Minister, Zanic. What can they be thinking about?" He was glad to note he had added to his above sentence: "I think it necessary to take account of such converts in the promulgation and application of the law."

Perhaps I was too gentle, he thought. The fact is obvious. Anyone with common sense, a logical mind, and the barest sense of justice would see the point. But where did it get me? He looked at the next letter, dated May 22, 1941. He saw immediately that he had been more pointed. The opening paragraph ran:

Mr. Minister:

I had the honor on April 23 of this year to address you a memorandum, No. 103/BK (Episcopal Conference), in which I asked you in the promulgation of the anti-Semitic laws you respect those members of the Jewish race who had been converted to Christianity. The laws promulgated on April 30, however, took no notice at all of religious affiliation. We were told then that the laws had to be promulgated in that form for reasons independent of us, but that their practical application would not be so harsh. In spite of all that, we note daily the appearance of more and more severe provisions which hit equally the guilty and the innocent. Today's newspapers carried the order that all Jews, without regard of age or sex or religious affiliation, must wear the Jewish insignia. Already there are so many measures that those who know the situation well say that "not even in Germany were the racial laws applied with such rigor or speed."

His lips pressed closer. That thrust, telling the Minister

69

whence the laws came, and the cowardly toadying to the Nazis by the Pavelic government, was well deserved, he was telling himself. His eyes raced through the next few paragraphs in which, after admitting the justice of having a national State ruled by sons of that nation, he had immediately pointed to the injustice of "taking away all possibility of existence (in that national State) from those who were members of other nations and races." His eyes lighted as he read his statement: "to mark them with the stamp of infamy is a question of humanity and morals. And moral laws have application not only for the lives of private individuals, but also for those who govern states."

How could he have been clearer or more pointed, he wondered? He knew what he had feared at the time he penned this particular letter, and he now knew his fears had been well grounded. What had happened in Germany after Jews were compelled to wear a yellow "Star of David" on their persons, had happened also in his Croatia. Easily recognized as Jews, rabid anti-Semites had brutally assaulted these persecuted people on the streets; senseless mobs had vandalized their homes; and bullying gangs of thoughtless youths had beaten a few innocent, helpless Semites into insensibility.

"Good!" he quietly exclaimed as he scanned the next passage: "The social organization of our day, and the general moral conceptions which are dominant, do not brand as infamous or criminal those who have been released from prison to which they had been sentenced as murderers—because it is desirable that even these persons become again useful members of the human community. Neither notorious adulterers nor common prostitutes are marked with visible signs. And, since it is not the practice of human society to hold in aversion those persons who have deserved such treatment because of their personal crimes, why treat in this way those who are members of another race through no fault of their own?"

He was interrupted here by an urgent buzzing beneath his desk. He pressed another buzzer and one of his Suffragan bishops entered his office. The two prelates conferred for only a very short while, then Stepinac seized his biretta, ordered his car, and had himself driven to the residence of the *Poglavnik*. He was well known througout the building and marched directly to the office of Pavelic. He was hardly announced when he strode in, faced the *Poglavnik*, who was slowly rising from his chair, and before Pavelic was standing, the Archbishop all but shouted: "It is God's command that *'Thou shalt not kill!'* " Without another word His Excellency turned on his heel and strode out of the office.

It was an aroused Archbishop who hurried back to his own desk in the *Kaptol*. He sat in to his desk with a jerk, took up the papers he had laid down when his Suffragan had entered and rapidly read the rest of the letter he had been scanning. He had already decided that he would not release his most recent letter to the *Poglavnik* to the press. He had resolved to bring this whole matter to a head by preaching to his people on the Feast of Christ the King—the anniversary of his ordination. But he would review what he had written to assure himself that he would be consistent and to note whether he had omitted any phases of the subject that should be stressed.

He saw that he insisted on "personalism"—a matter that was not yet receiving enough attention in Philosophical circles, though it had always been part of his Scholastic Philosophy. He had told Artukovic that "it is necessary

71

to take into account the fact that, as a result of all this, the instinct to revenge and the so-called 'Minderwertikeits-Komplex' (inferiority complex) will become well developed, especially among the youth who are now growing up and will be affected by these measures, and that this will exert an overwhelming influence on their spiritual development. Have we the right to commit such an outrage on the human personality?"

He was still smouldering from his meeting with Pavelic as he came upon the passage he particularly wanted to reread: "In regard to what I have said, I ask you, Mr. Minister, to give appropriate orders so that the Jewish laws and others similar to them (the measures against the Serbs) be executed in such a way that the human dignity and personality of every man is respected. The provision that the Jewish insignia must be worn ought to be generally suppressed. To reimburse the State for the expenses it has incurred in procuring these insignia, it could be ordered that those in question buy them, but that they may cease wearing them. Let the guilty, and the exploiters be submitted to the punishment they deserve. No intelligent person is opposed to that. But let not the irresponsible mob be judge and executioner of their punishment."

That is as far as he got when the same secretary, Father John Salic, who had first interrupted him by bringing Aloysius Misic, Bishop of Mostar, in to his office earlier in the morning, now entered with the announcement that Bishop Goric, of Banja Luka, another Suffragan to His Excellency, had been there while the Archbishop was out on his visit to the *Poglavnik*, and said he would be back before noon. Stepinac simply nodded. Then Father Salic told him that there was a Serb, accompanied by a German soldier awaiting him. "He says he is from Archbishop Ujcic of Belgrade."

"Oh, I know. That's about Sava Trlajic, Orthodox Bishop of Gornji Karlovic. They think he is prisoner at Lepoglava. I went to the *Poglavnik* with the Apostolic Delegate, Marcone. Pavelic investigated. Said the Bishop was not in Lepoglava."

"From what I gather, Excellency, this Serbian messenger has some other business...."

"Show him in."

"What shall I note about Bishop Misic's visit? Anything?"

"Three words: *Murder—Saw Poglavnik.*"

Father Salic went back to his small office thinking that His Excellency was becoming more and more succinct in his speech. Never stingingly short. The Archbishop was always a perfect gentleman. Brief, thought Salic, not abrupt. He ushered the Serb and the German soldier back to the Archbishop's office. Then, just as he was entering the note about: *Murder—Saw Poglavnik*, into his record, Father Stepan Lackovic, another of the Archbishop's secretaries entered.

"Well, John, how's His Excellency this morning?"

"Busy as ever. Busier. He all but stormed out of here for the *Poglavnik's* office. The only note he gave me is: 'Murder.' Now he is in there with a German soldier and a Serb."

"Never a dull moment in His Excellency's service— and what a variety."

Father Lackovic had hardly completed his sentence when His Excellency appeared at the door of the secretaries office. He had his biretta on. "Good morning, Father Stepan. Hope you are well—and ready for work. Plenty of it here." Then to both secretaries: "I'm running down to see the Minister of the Interior. I'll be back shortly. If Bishop Goric comes, hold him here." With that he swept out of the office and the *Kaptol* accompanied by the soldier and the Serb.

"Things are apoppin' this morning," said Lackovic merrily. "What's this about murder?"

"Haven't the slightest. . . . His Excellency of Mostar was in. The two talked together for a very short while. Misic left. Stepinac blew out of here with his face set. It was still set when he came back after what must have been the shortest visit on record to Pavelic."

"Mostar . . . Mostar . . . Murder. . . . Just a second," said Father Lackovic as he strode to his desk, fished in a drawer, and came out with a letter he quickly unfolded. "Have you met Teddy Benkovic?"

"The American priest who stubbornly stays in our country despite everything? Yeah."

"He's writing a book. Here is the last bit he sent me to criticize. This will tell you all you need to know about that cryptic entry after Bishop Misic's name: Murder. Read it. I'll be right back."

Father Salic sat down and read:
The match that touched off this smouldering confla-gration of hate and revenge was the *Chetnik* bestiality perpetrated at Illici and Cim, villages two kilometers from Mostar.

Croatia had been declared free April 10, 1941, and on the 13th, 14th, and 15th of the same month the terrorist *Chetnik* bands of Draza Mihailovic began their bestial work. In villages close to Mostar, the

74

Chetniks murdered 25 Croat peasants; at the village of Struge by Capljina, the *Chetniks* poured four dum-dum bullets into Francisca Vego, who was holding her six-months-old child in her arms and was surrounded by four of her younger children.

At Illici and Cim, the *Chetniks* burned down to the ground 85 houses, and many of the inhabitants were either killed or seriously wounded.

The atavism displayed by the *Chetniks* surpasses many a violent chapter in Balkan history. In Central Bosnia, the *Chetniks*, in the pay of the Italian Army, wiped out the village and surroundings of Prozer, razing to the ground 2400 houses, and butchering 1062 Croatian women, children, and old men. In some Croatian villages in Bosnia, all over twelve years of age were put to the knife. Not even the *Partisans* committed such crimes as the *Chetniks*. To the Croats in the village of Nunich, Dalmatia, the *Chetniks* sent the barbecued body of their assistant Pastor to them as a present—Fr. John Kranjac. . . .

Rev. Kresimer Barisisch, Pastor of Krnjeusa, Bosnia, was captured by the *Chetniks*, who then proceeded to cut off his ears, amputate his arms and legs, and finally hurl the remains of the still living priest into his burning church.

Five Sisters of the Society of Daughters of Divine Love watched their Orphanage at Pale, by Sarajevo, pillaged and destroyed by the *Chetniks* who killed Sister Berhmana Leidnix, age 80, on the spot. The four remaining Sisters were taken by the *Chetniks* to their hideout at Gorazda, where they were subjected to all kinds of bestial indignities, finally mur-

75

dered, then thrown into the Drina river. This happened in 1941.

When Father Lackovic returned he found his fellow secretary white. "Nasty, isn't it?" Father Salic seemed incapable of speech. Father Lackovic took the letter from him, folded it and put it back in his drawer. Father Salic was still in a state of shock. Finally, in a very subdued voice he said, "Suppose those nuns were your own sisters; those priests, your brothers...."

Before more was said the buzzer sounded. The two secretaries looked at one another. "Back already? I'll go," said Lackovic.

"Please take this note for me, John," said His Excellency even before Lackovic was half way across the room: "This Serbian, sent by Ujcic from Belgrade, came to me accompanied by a German soldier so that no harm should befall him. He thanked me for what I had done for the Serbs, then asked me to intervene. I told him I was against mass conversions to the Catholic Church, to which he replied: 'Excellency, let all be converted so that they may save their lives.' I promised to intervene. Went directly to the Minister of the Interior. What result came of it I don't know. But we did what we could.—Thank you, John. Send in that Muslim I saw waiting."

So the morning went. So went the afternoon and evening. Late that night His Excellency still had the file of his letters to Artukovic before him. He sat in to read what he had said to him about the anti-Semitic laws. He found his place in the letter of May 22. He read:

I especially ask you, Mr. Minister, that you respect the baptized members of the Jewish race. Some of

76

them were baptized a long time before the persecution of the Jews began, hence at a time when Baptism meant a hardship to them, especially in a material way. Many of them are already completely assimilated, and no one knows they are Jews. There are also those who have stood out in the national revolution, and in that of the *Ustashi*. I, personally, know several of them who are good and enthusiastic Catholics. How will these persons now perform their religious duties? Are they to go to Holy Mass and receive Holy Communion with a yellow ribbon around their arms? In such a case, I would be forced to tell the Jewish Catholics not to wear these insignia in order to avoid trouble and difficulties in church.

Is it opportune to create an atmosphere of distrust and discord at a time when the Holy Father has just so graciously received our *Poglavnik* and our delegation, and when steps have been taken to get the Holy See to recognize our State?

He turned to the last letter before him, dated May 30, 1941. He remembered this one quite clearly. He had specifically referred to marriages between converted Jews and Croats, to the education of the children of such marriages, and to rightful employment for such individuals. He had reminded the Minister that "it is precisely Catholicism which has been the cohesive and assimilating agent which has tied the different parts of our Croatian people into a whole, and which has nationalized numerous foreign elements. Consequently, conversion has created, even among Jews, a strong tie with the people among whom they live and work." That was teaching the Minister of the Interior his work.

77

Toward the end of this letter he had stated that "it is the duty of their ecclesiastical superiors to take care of them and to be responsible for them before God, but the State would also sin against its duty to the Church and Religion by hindering Christian non-Aryans in the fulfillment of their religious duties."

The weary Archbishop placed his head in his hands at this juncture and recalled how Pavelic, for propaganda purposes at least, had announced, shortly after this last letter, a mitigation in the application of the laws. He stated that he and his colleagues realized that a person not Aryan by birth, if one regards only blood, could prove by his actions that he had Aryan qualities. Such actions as "active fight for ideals, a life of sacrifice, and the like." It was a concession, even something of a mitigation. But it did not satisfy the Archbishop. The words could be interpreted in a Catholic sense; for who had ideals as high as Catholics, or ideals as worth fighting for? As for a life of sacrifice, that is what the Catholic life is all about. But Stepinac knew that to the minds of those in power "active fight for ideals" meant the ideals of the *Ustashi*. "Aryran qualities" came down to "collaboration with the pro-Fascist State." He had fought on for all Jews. His first insistence had been for those Jews who had been converted to Christianity. But he never closed his mind or his heart to those Jews who had not been converted. They were human beings. They had the same rights as any other human being. He told Pavelic so. As man, as priest, and especially as prelate, he would fight for the rights of every human being. Since he had heard that very afternoon of some arrests of Jews who had not been converted, he now seized his pen and, weary as he was, he wrote Artukovic another letter. It was short. It was pointed.

"Recently," he wrote, "there has again been talk about the arrest of Jews, and about their having been taken to concentration camps. Insofar as there is really something to this talk, I take the liberty, Mr. Minister, of asking you to prevent, through your power, all unjust proceedings against citizens who, individually, can be accused of no wrong.

I do not think that it can bring us any glory if it is said of us that we have solved the Jewish problem in the most radical way; that is to say, the cruelest.

Hoping, Mr. Minister, that you will prevent the violation not only of the Christian law of love of one's neighbor, but of the most basic natural law of humanity."

It was not weariness that led him to such brevity. The news from his two Suffragans in the morning had convinced him that things were getting out of hand, and that it was high time for him to speak out to the people in place of addressing letters to those who were supposed to be governing the people for the welfare of all. He would do so the next time he preached.

He looked calm as he ascended the pulpit. He sounded calm as he spoke his text with reverence: "Christ, You are the King of the Centuries, You are the Prince of all peoples. You are the Sole Judge of all minds and of all hearts." He told his congregation, which had packed the

Cathedral, whence his text had come: "Words taken from the Hymn of First Vespers for this Feast of Christ the King." Then he began quietly enough:

"Catholic men and women, Catholic Faithful!

When we look about us in this world, and when we consider what goes on around us, we conclude that all that is created on this earth is subject to change. There are the mineral and vegetable kingdoms which are subject to change. There are the seasons which are subject to change. There is the firmament and the depths of the sea which are subject to change.... And there is man who is also subject to change. On leaving his crib, where his mother's hands had put him, he learns to walk; from the age of a little boy he grows to adolescence; from the age of adolescence he grows to manhood, only to find himself in a short time a weak old man at the edge of the tomb, to become again the dust from which he was made. And human power is also changing on earth. Today millions tremble before individuals whose names will evoke no memory tomorrow.

He paused. The people knew the purpose of his pause. That last sentence was meant to sink in. Its truth was to be grasped. Here today; gone tomorrow. Today seemingly all-powerful; tomorrow, dust. Today peoples shudder at your very name; tomorrow, who recalls you? But then His Excellency lifted his voice:

"There exists one power which knows no end, which knows no change.... That is the Royal Power of Jesus Christ, Son of God, of whom the Apostle said:

'Jesus Christ, yesterday, and today, and the same forever!' (Heb 13:8) It is to this immortal King that the Church sings today from the Canticles: 'Christ, You are the King of centuries, You are the Prince of all peoples, You are the Sole Judge of all minds and hearts.' It is to this 'King of kings, and Lord of lords' (Apoc 19:16) that we have come today, to adore Him, full of lively faith, of profound humility, and with hearts full of repentance.

Let us reflect on His royal power and on our relations to Him both as individuals and as nations. If individuals and people were conscious of what they really are before God, and of what their functions were, there would be less misery on earth and more happiness.

The Archbishop was warming to his theme. The people sensed it and many straightened in their pews.

"What are we as individuals?—As individuals we resemble Lazarus in his tomb. He would have stayed for all eternity in this darkness, if the Light of the World, Jesus Christ, had not bent over his tomb and if He had not said: 'Lazarus, come forth!' (Jn 11:43). Each of us is nothingness and would have remained so eternally if the love of God and the power of God had not called him to life and if He had not maintained him in life. All men of good will join with St. Paul the Apostle and say: 'By the grace of God, I am what I am' (1 Cor 15:10).

"How, then, must we judge those individuals who raise their heads proudly as if God no longer existed on the earth and as if the law of the Gospels were superfluous? We ought to say to them that which Christ said to the unfaithful city of Capharnaum: 'And you, Capharnaum, will you raise yourself to the sky? You will descend into hell!' (Mt 21:23). A very short pause preceded: "And what, before God, are the peoples and races of this world? It is worth while to suggest this subject at a time when the theories of class, race, and nationality have become the main topics of discussion among men.   ·

The first thing we affirm is that all nations, without exception, are as nothing before God. 'All nations are before Him as if they had no being at all,' says the prophet, 'and are counted to Him as nothing, and vanity' (Is 40:17). These words of the prophet have already found their affirmation many times in the history of the world, when the Divine Hand, for various reasons, has swept individual nations from the face of the earth. It is, moreover, in the act of doing that today to every nation, if as nations they do not conform to the laws given by God, because 'The Lord made the little and the great' (Wis 6:8).

At whom was that directed, many in the congregation were wondering? Was he referring to Yugoslavia, which Hitler had declared non-existent? Was it to France, Belgium, Holland, which had already been overrun by Germany's seemingly indomitable forces? Or was it to Croatia itself? Or was he reminding the Axis Powers that God is God? It was not like their Archbishop to leave them wondering this way. He was usually most specific. . . . But then it came:

"The second thing we affirm is that all nations and

all races have their origin in God. *Only one race* really exists—and that is *the divine race*. Its birth certificate is found in the Book of Genesis, when the Divine Hand formed the first man from earthly clay and breathed into him the spirit of life (Gn 2:7). He made him as well a woman, blessed them saying: 'Increase and multiply and fill the earth' (Gn 1:28). Among all who belong to *that* race, entrance into the world, and their departure from it, is the same—and will remain the same until the end of time; for it is written by the Divine Hand for all: 'For dust thou art, and unto dust thou shalt return' (Gn 3:19). Those who belong to the race may have a greater or lesser culture, may be white or black, separated by oceans, live at the North or the South Pole, but they remain essentially the race which comes from God and which must serve God according to the norms of the divine natural and positive law, written in the hearts and in the souls of men and revealed by the Son of God, Jesus Christ, Prince of all peoples.

His hearers could infer much from what His Excellency had so far said. He had spoken of change—and assuredly they were living in a decade of swift changes. He had spoken of nations—and talked about their destruction. He had told about the pride of man. He could be talking about individuals, but he had not specified. Now, even on race— and their day was filled to the overflowing with talk about Aryan race—Jewish race—he was still quite generic. Was he hesitant to specify? It was not like their Archbishop. Of course they were sure the Cathedral held members of the Gestapo, members, too, of the *Ustashi*. But their Primate had never shown fear of any of these. Now he was going on talking about variety. He showed it in the mineral, vegetable, animal kingdoms. He was following, very much, the categories he had mentioned in the very beginning. Where was he heading? Was this it: nationalities, their multiplicity as evidence of God's infinity? But what was this: his voice had changed. His whole appearance had changed. He sounded not only severe, but even angry as he vehemently said:

"But this diversity must not become a source of mutual destruction. For the third thing we affirm is that all nations and all races, as reflected in the world today, have the right to lead a life worthy of men, and to be treated with the dignity with which one treats a man. All of them without exception, whether they belong to the race of Gypsies or another, whether they be Negroes or civilized Europeans, whether they are detested Jews or proud Aryans, have the same right to say: 'Our Father, who art in Heaven' (Mt 6:9). And if *God* has given this right to all, where is the *human* power that can deny it? All nations, no matter what their names, have the same duty: to beat their breasts and say, 'And forgive us our trespasses as we forgive those who trespass against us' (Mt 6:12).

His voice rose in power as he went on:

"That is why the Catholic Church has always condemned, and condemns today as well, every injustice and every violence committed in the name of the theories of class, race, or nationality. One cannot exterminate intellectuals from the face of the earth because it may be agreeable to the working class, as Bolshevism has taught and done. One cannot extinguish from the face of the earth Gypsies or Jews because one considers them inferior races. If the racist theories, *which have no foundation,* are to be applied without scruples, is there any security for any nation at all? The Catholic Church had the courage in the very recent past, as it always has when it is necessary, to lift its voice against the secret work of international Freemasonry, against the moral deprivation of our youth by the unscrupulous press, against crimes of abortion practiced by those who, without conscience, are eager only for material gains. It had the courage to defend our Croatian national *rights,* and to hurl that word of defense before crowned heads. It would be unfaithful to its duty if it did not raise its voice today, with the same energy, in defense of all those who suffer from injustices, without consideration of the race to which they belong. *No one has the right* to kill or harm in any way those who belong to another race or another nation. That can be done only by the legitimate authorities, if they have proved the crime of an individual and if the crime merits such punishment.

"These things, moreover, are those which look to the interests, *justly understood,* and the love, *well comprehended,* of one's own country, which are, and remain, for a Catholic, not empty words, but the moral duty for which he is responsible to God."

Was that a thrust at the *Poglavnik?* Before they could

answer, they found themselves the object of the Archbishop's direct address:

"Catholic men and women! Faithful Catholics! Today is the Feast of Christ the King. Not a King whose power lasts for today and tomorrow, but the feast of the Prince of princes! and of this Prince it is written: 'For the nation and the kingdom that will not serve Thee, shall perish, such nations will be totally laid waste' (Is 60:12). That is what history has shown many times. It will show it again if the present-day nations reject the law of the Gospels and if they should repel Christ. Your duty is to work in such a way that the spirit of the true Gospel may be introduced into our public and private life. For in the Gospels man is closest to God, and, that human personality, which our modern age has degraded to the rank of slave to creatures, must again become the center around which revolves, according to the plan laid down by the Creator of the world, all creation. Because the least human being, whatever his name, to whatever race or nation he belongs, carries upon himself the imprint of the living God: an immortal soul.

One of the reasons that impelled Christopher Columbus, convinced that he would find land beyond the sea, was the desire to lead new nations to Christ. After his return, when he was questioned about the new countries, he described the wealth and the marvels of the new world with enthusiasm. But he concluded his description with the words: 'India,'—for he thought that America was India—'India is beautiful and rich, but the most beautiful jewel of India is the souls of the Indians.' Yes! That is the most beautiful jewel of every man, for which, when it was lost and in order to restore it, the Son of God, Jesus Christ Himself, descended from heaven, to give up not only all that He had, but even to give His own life on the Cross to redeem this jewel—the soul of man—from the mire of sin, to pick it up, and save it.

"Catholic men and women! Catholic faithful! It often happens, as a man walks across fields and climbs mountains, that he treads upon jewels or upon gold which is hidden under foot, and of which he has no inkling. But in this ignorance there is no tragedy. It is much more tragic that men pass over that which is most beautiful in man, that which renders him like unto God, over his own immortal soul—and that of others! Away with that ignorance! Let everyone be conscious of his dignity as man! Let him be conscious of his royal vocation as a child of God, above all today, when we celebrate the Feast of Christ the King, the King of centuries, the King of peoples, but especially the King of the immortal souls of men, to Whom be glory and honor throughout the centuries. Amen."

The next morning Monsignor Shimrak had the text of that stirring sermon before him when his assistant editor came to bring the usual sheaf of reports of the news of the night and early morning.

"Were you there last night? Did you hear the Archbishop?"

"Couldn't make it. Had to work on today's Editorial."

"You missed something. His Excellency was in magnificent voice—and did he use it!"

"From reports coming in, I'd say he used it for the whole world. He must have released a copy to some journalists. . . ."

"He did. I got this," said the Monsignor, "some days ago. But I failed to read it. In one way I'm glad. It is superbly composed. But you should have heard it delivered. All I could think of was the old definition of the 'Queen of the Arts' as our old Professor used to call Rhetoric. His Excellency was 'Logic on fire.' He also recalled for me Cicero's old dictum about '*Si vis me flere, flendum est tibi primum*,' only the Archbishop was not weeping, he was aflame with indignation, and he would have fired asbestos, to use one of your favorite metaphors."

"He certainly fired up many foreign correspondents and news commentators. I suppose they got their leads from Rome. London cites the Vatican Radio as its source. New York picked up either London or the Vatican. Read these reports."

The Editor took the cabled reports from his assistant. He was a bit surprised that reactions came so rapidly. But his eye had not gone down two lines when his mind told him what had happened: Vatican Radio had gone on the air as soon as Stepinac had stepped out of the pulpit. The London news commentator had said:

"In the moral sphere the Axis have been dealt a heavy blow by the highest moral and spiritual power by the medium of the Vatican Radio. This blow was directed against Nazism and against its satellites, of whom Pavelic is one, who must do as they are told. Last night the Vatican station transmitted certain portions of a sermon by the Archbishop of Zagreb, Dr. Aloysius Stepinac, in protest against the

88

persecution of the Jews. The Archbishop delivered this sermon after the *Ustashi* Government had ordered that the Nuremburg laws be applied to all the Jews in the Independent State of Croatia. Previously the Archbishop had declared himself against the exaggerations of the racist theory, following which the *Ustashi* Government ordered the confiscation of property and the wearing of special insignia. The Vatican station described the Archbishop as a resolute champion of moral rights and of freedom. The Archbishop said in his sermon:

'Last Sunday I had the occasion to see the tears and listen to the groans of stalwart men, and the wailing of helpless women who were threatened with the destruction of their family life, for the sole reason that their origin was not in accord with the theory of Nazism.' And Archbishop Stepinac added: 'The Church cannot remain tranquil before events of this kind, because the fundamental rights of man are violated by these measures.' Following this he said: 'Every man, to whatever race he belongs, bears the stamp of God, whether he has studied in a European University, or whether he hunts in the jungles of Africa. Every man has the right to physical and spiritual life, to marriage, to a religious education, and to the use of material goods. The laws of society cannot prevent this, because all destruction of the rights of men can have only grievous consequences.' Previously the Archbishop had said: 'God has given to man certain rights, and there is no power here below which can take them away. That is why the Church rises against all acts of violence committed against these rights.'

The most important prelate in Croatia has spoken out against the *Ustashi* authorities who imitate Nazi crimes. This expression needs no commentary."

Neat, thought the Editor. But some sentences from the Archbishop's text did not read the same as he had heard last night. He picked up the cable from New York and read:

"We are reproducing the statement of Archbishop Dr. Aloysius Stepinac against the persecution of the Jews. At the end of a sermon the Archbishop of Zagreb said: 'No one has a right to destroy the intellectual class in order to aid the working classes. Thus, neither Jews nor Gypsies may be persecuted for the sole reason that they are considered inferior races. If the so-called racist theories are imprudently applied, all security will disappear from the earth. Yes, We ask the *Ustashi* if they have any reply that would refute the Vatican and that would destroy the truth, preached by Christ, of the brotherhood of men and peoples.'"

The Editor ran those cables and spoke of "the Voice heard round the world." A week later he was more than surprised, and highly pleased, when he learned that even the Soviet sponsored radio station in Tiflis, U.S.S.R., repeated the Archbishop's message, and that this broadcast was caught up and carried over secret wireless transmitters to Tito's *Partisans*.

Yet he had an even more interesting and arousing story to run a few days later, for the Government seemed to be about the only ones in the world who had not caught the Archbishop's message. They ordered two priests and six nuns in the Zagreb Archdiocese, who were of Jewish origin, to wear the insignia. The outbursts of indignation which followed, and the fiercely frank condemnations of the Government which immediately broke out, moved the officials to order police action. This was brutal in certain places, but utterly useless; for the protests continued with even greater fierceness. Pavelic thought it prudent to publicly exempt these eight people.

He may have thought this would appease the Archbishop. But, on the very next day he learned how wrong he was when His Excellency told the thousands who had come to the Cathedral to hear him speak: "I have ordered these priests and nuns to continue wearing the insignia that by doing so they may proclaim to all that they belong to the very people from whom our Savior was born. I have ordered them to do this so long as any others in this land have to wear the yellow band with its Star of David."

That did it. Pavelic knew when he was beaten. A few days later that part of the Nuremberg laws was rescinded.

"I hope Count O'Brien has been listening to his radio and has read this latest bit of news," said Monsignor Shimrak to one of his proof-readers who had just returned the copy on this latest development. "He will appreciate our Archbishop the more."

Had Count O'Brien been able to visit Croatia's Primate about this time he would not have found His Excellency exulting in his triumph over Pavelic with the Nuremburg laws. Instead he would have found him deeply concerned, and not a whit happy about the condition of his people and his country. His Excellency might well have described that condition with the one word: *Schizoid*.

With characteristic honesty he would have told O'Brien

that it could be said with a good deal of truth that the Croatian people greeted the fall of Yugoslavia with a great degree of joy, and were, in a sense, grateful to the Germans for contributing to the destruction of what had often been named "the jail of the Croation nation." But he would have been quick to add that the greater part of the people, and he himself without any reserve, not only distrusted Hitler and his policies, but denied the validity and detested the implementation of his basic ideology. Further, right now, they were fearful of the possibility of his future success with arms. Then he would have told the Count that it was because of their antipathy to Nazism that they, for the most part, did not have complete trust in Pavelic and the *Ustashi* Government—they were too closely allied to the Nazis and the Fascists. Political expediency, perhaps; but, nonetheless, a fact.

Had O'Brien asked the Archbishop to account for German-Italian acceptance, and, in a way, the construction of the present State, he would have learned more about the Primate's realism and insight into European Statecraft of the moment. For Stepinac knew well that neither Germany nor Italy was enthusiastic about the Independent State of Croatia, but neither would suppress it; for each saw in it a certain amount of "propaganda value." Since both Hitler and Mussolini had more than once mouthed their support of the ideal of freedom and liberation of "oppressed and enslaved peoples," they could point to Croatia as having been "liberated" after centuries of "oppression" and now standing "free." But the Archbishop would then have gone on to say that, while they did not suppress it, they both occupied it, and were using it and its people for their own ends.

Then would have come the proof. The Italians had

sabotaged almost every effort of the Croatians in the political, economic, and military fields. Since this last was, at the moment, the most important field, he would have told how the Italians were hindering the operations and movements of Croatian troops, and openly aiding those who rebelled against the *Ustashi*, especially giving tremendous support to Mihailovic's *Chetniks*.

As for the Germans—they were using Croatian troops chiefly to protect their own communications with the Balkans, at the moment, and in certain other areas they considered vital to the Nazi economy. Thus they kept these magnificent fighting units far from regions that were vital, truly vital, to the Croatian national interests. It was clever. It was cruel. And, while it helped the Axis cause, it was destroying the morale of the Croats.

But then would have come the sad lament: "And yet the worst of all enemies are those of one's own household. These are the ones who are producing the real schizophrenia. Our Army is really split. Almost from the beginning they divided into two very separate factions: the Regular Army or Croatian *Domobans,* and the *Ustashi* Militia. Of course the Government favored the Militia. They were their own, as it were. But such favoritism has shaken the morale of the *Domobans* who have been bearing the brunt of whatever fighting there has been for our men, and who may well be the better soldiers."

This, as was inevitable, had its effect on the ordinary citizens. It looked as if schizophrenia were contagious. For to the Nazis, the Fascists, and the *Ustashi,* were added the *Chetniks* and the *Partisans*. O'Brien would have recognized the summation as the filling in of the outline His Excellency had given him the night he told him he had to leave the country. But he would have listened intently as the Archbishop told how the poor people did not know exactly where to turn; for they hardly knew whom to call "friend" and whom, "enemy."

The *Chetniks* with their strong Serbian bias which in many cases amounted to a veritable hatred for the Croats, and the *Partisans* with their Communistic "religion," were almost equally repulsive to the ordinary Croatian. To whom should they turn?

The Germans appeared as "allies" to the people, since the Nazis opposed both the *Chetniks* and the *Partisans;* and to the loyal Croat, this was their real war—not that between the Allies and the Axis. For no Croat wanted anything like what Mihailovic had put forth as his ideal: a united Yugoslavia under Serbian domination. As for Communism, no Catholic Croat could countenance that— and they recognized Tito and his *Partisans* as Communists. But these same Germans were also their present day oppressors inasmuch as they were occupying their country, using the armed forces of Croatia for their own personal objectives—and were Nazis: an ideology as repulsive to Catholic Croats as Communism.

As for the Italians—they would never be their friends.

So the poor people saw themselves facing four enemies: Germans, Italians, *Chetniks* and *Partisans.*

When they looked at their own Army they felt just as bewildered. For the *Domobans,* who were democratic in outlook, were becoming more and more distrustful of their fellow-soldiers: the *Ustashi* Militia, and of the Government itself. For they considered both too pro-Fascist. Hence, many of the *Domobans* were beginning to hope for, and when they could, work for an Allied Victory; for they saw this as their only hope for freedom from the Nazi-Fascists and from the Communists.

As for the *Ustashi*—they were fanatically nationalistic and were showing it by attacking the Orthodox Serbs of the country. This was an especially sore point with the Archbishop. "As one writer has put it," he could have told O'Brien, "the task of the *Ustashi* is not only to crush, with Axis aid, those loyal to the Yugoslav Government, but to eliminate the Serb minority, nearly all of them belonging to the Orthodox Church, who dwelt within the newly drawn frontiers of Croatia."

The Archbishop, with his customary clarity of vision and love for truth would have added that the writer was a bit extreme in his statement, but not altogether wrong; for some of the *Ustashi* were offering these Orthodox Serbs as options: conversion to the Roman Catholic Church—or death.

That violation of men's consciences could never be allowed to pass. When Stepinac heard of what some were calling "mass conversions" he went into action. He summoned an Episcopal Conference. His Suffragans gathered in Zagreb to listen to their Primate and to give him firsthand information on what was going on in their respective dioceses. Before the Conference was very old the Primate was shaking his head in sorrow and saying: "Indeed those within one's own household are the worst enemies one can have." But soon that sorrow and the shaking of that head changed to a stern set face within which eyes were blazing and a strong determination was born. "This must not go on!" were his words to his Suffragans . . . and later to his priests and his *Poglavnik*.

4   Enemies In One's Household

"ARE THESE CONVERSIONS SINCERE? Are they based on conviction or is it coercion? How stable will they be?"

Those rapid fire queries came from the Primate as he faced the Croatian hierarchy assembled in Zagreb. He had heard how not only entire parishes, but whole villages of Orthodox Serbs had converted to Roman Catholicism.

His Excellency, Jazo Garic, Bishop of Banja Luka arose. "Excellency," he began, "I do not know what I can say on this subject. . . . Generally speaking, I am not an optimist. In many cases, not only of individuals but of entire villages, I think that there will be defections at the first opportunity. From now on the *Chetniks* and the *Partisans* will take revenge on those who have become converted to the Catholic religion. They will burn their houses, steal their cattle and other properties. And on the part of the Mohammedans, crimes of indescribable savagery have been committed on the poor Orthodox population. Called to account for this, they said in their defense that they did but what they had been ordered to do. Many of those who had already been converted to our religion have died in the districts of Bihac and Cazin after having been forced to convert to Islam. The only consoling thing among all this tragedy is that our priests conducted themselves very nobly in taking what care they could of these poor people. They took no notice of the threats made to them by the others. Banja Luka has suffered, but Banja Luka has known moderation in comparison with the bestial cruelties committed in other places. . . ."

"In my place, for instance," put in Aloysius Misic, Bishop of Mostar. When Bishop Garic nodded to him, Bishop Misic took the floor. "Excellency, you have just heard something about 'orders from those higher up.' Now it is true that on several occasions already the high State Officials in Zagreb have given to subordinate officials instructions regarding conversions from another religion. But, according to general indications, these instructions are not of a kind to serve the general welfare of the Church, or even of that of the State."

"A bit more specific, Excellency."

"Gladly. By the grace of God we have been given a chance today, as never before, to help the Croatian cause, to save the souls of innumerable men of good will;

that is, of the peaceful peasants living in the midst of Catholics. They know the Catholics, and the Catholics know them. Conversion is acceptable and easy. But, unhappily, the authorities, by their extreme views, are, without perhaps intending to, placing obstacles in the way of the Croatian and the Catholic cause. The leaders are not guilty. But all kinds of people are interfering in this matter, youths without learning or experience. In place of intelligence and reason, there is force and violence. . . ."

"More specific, if you will, Excellency."

"In many parishes of the Diocese of Mostar, for example, Duvno Polj, Stolac, Klepeci, Goranci, Gradac and others, a number of honest peasants announced their intention of being converted to Catholicism. They went to Holy Mass, they learned the Catholic Catechism, had their children baptized, but then the intruders came and gave their orders. While the neo-converts were at Church, assisting at Holy Mass, they seized them, the young and the old, the men and the women, and drove them before them like cattle . . . and soon sent them to eternity *en masse*. That can serve neither the holy Catholic cause, nor the Croatian cause. Everyone condemns such unreasonable acts and we have lost an excellent opportunity which could have furthered the Croatian Catholic cause. We might have emerged into a majority in Bosnia and Hercegovina, and instead of coveting favors from others we could have dispensed them ourselves. . . ."

"But I do not understand," said the Primate. "You say it is the under-officials."

"Those who have been *Stozernik*, designated *Logornik—Ustashi* under-officials—have abused their positions, exploited the worst instincts of the masses, and the weakest side of human nature, with the result that a reign of terror has come to pass. Men are captured like animals. They are slaughtered, murdered; living men are thrown off cliffs. . . ."

"Excellency, please! Names and places. . . ."

Two things were evident to the assembly: first the Bishop of Mostar was aroused, he had suffered, his people had suffered, in near desperation he was crying for direction; but at the same time the Primate was looking for specifics so that he could give that direction. While Bishop Misic was almost passionate in his denunciation and descriptions, Archbishop Stepinac was cool, but insistent.

"Mr. Bajic," came back the Bishop of Mostar, "a Mohammedan, under-prefect of Mostar, has stated with the authoritative voice of his position—he should have kept silent—that at Ljubinje, in a single day seven hundred schismatics were thrown into their graves. From Mostar and from Capljina a train took six carloads of mothers, young girls, and children of ten years of age to the station at Surmmaci. They were made to get off the train, were led up into the mountains, and the mothers together with their children were thrown alive off steep precipices. In the parish of Klepci seven hundred schismatics from the surrounding villages were murdered. In the town of Mostar itself they have been bound by the hundreds, taken in wagons outside the town, and there shot down like animals. Must I continue this enumeration?"

"No. But tell me do these conditions and acts continue?"

"Excellency, there has been a change. But I wonder if it is for the better. You see, these same under-officials began to deport the Serbs back to Serbia. In tears, lamentations, and misery, they gradually disappeared. A delegation went to wait on Mussolini in Rome and we can readily imagine what they asked for. The result was a renewed Italian occupation of Hercegovina with civil as well as military authority in their hands. The schismatic churches came to life all of a sudden. The pastors of the Greek churches, coming out of hiding, showed themselves freely, because the Italians were friendly and favorable to the Serbs. Good. For the Catholic Church does not countenance the commission of acts of violence. She condemns violence, and She condemned it on these very occasions. But the transition from one extreme to another is significant. The new occupation authorities have suddenly become friendly toward the Serbs, severe toward the Catholics. There have been imprisonments, even executions. The poor have paid the bill for this tyranny. It is not astonishing that, in the light of these events, the conversion of Orthodox to Catholicism has been a complete failure. The ferocity and the savagery of certain individuals, the lack of understanding of the highest authorities, have seriously damaged the welfare of the State as well as of religion. If the Lord had given the authorities more understanding on how to handle the conversions to Catholicism with skill, with intelligence, with fewer clashes, and at a more appropriate time, the number of Catholics would have grown to five or six hundred thousand."

The Bishop of Mostar sat down. There was pain evident in his every feature. His fellow bishops sympathized fully. His address had left them all somewhat shaken. If both the *Ustashi* and the Italians, who were Catholic, could so antagonize whole masses of the people, whom were they to trust?

The Archbishop of Vrhbosna next arose, Stepinac bowed to him with his head. He began much more quietly than had Bishop Misic. "For my part I note there is a tendency among civil authorities to seek the conversion of more Orthodox in my region. But, unhappily, they do not do what must be done. From many places where the highest positions are occupied by Moslems, I have received complaints that these officials are not carrying out the requests of the Orthodox who wish to be converted to the Catholic religion. In other places overly high taxes are imposed on religious conversions, taxes which these poor people cannot afford to pay."

"Can we have a specific?" asked the Primate quietly.

"At Sarajevo the authorities demanded by way of a tax, five hundred kunas." A gasp was heard from many in the assembly. "We felt obliged to petition the government in Zagreb to have this order revoked. As is understandable, such acts on the part of local authorities make great difficulty in the matter of conversions."

"Has Zagreb given you any satisfaction? Has the tax been revoked?"

"It is a bit early, Excellency, for me to have had an answer."

Then up spoke Bishop Butorac of Kotor, Apostolic Administrator of the Diocese of Dubrovnik. "The recent order from the Minister of the Interior indicates that a more precise understanding of the subject of conversions to the Catholic religion has been grasped by those in the highest authority. But we must insist that any use of force, any whatsoever, can have the most catastrophic effect on the reputation of the Catholic Church. It is necessary to consider all eventualities, even the possibility that the Serbs, through caprice, might decide to be converted *en masse* to Islam. Precisely for this reason I think it is necessary to choose with special care the missionaries

102

who are to be sent among the Serbs and not to entrust this charge to priests or religious who are not prudent and in whose hands a revolver might better be placed than a crucifix."

"Strong words, Excellency. Care to mention names and places?"

"Will the Primate excuse me from naming priests? I am endeavoring to handle the situation prudently, mercifully, but with insistence on proper procedure. . . ."

"But did I not make it abundantly clear in my Circular Letters just what was required before converts could be accepted?"

"Abundantly clear, Excellency, and I believe your directives are being followed quite generally. But I am sure more than one in this assembly will agree with me when I say there are some priests who are more than favorable to the *Ustashi*—and even to the *Nastashi*—those young rebels who are rightly named 'Upstarts.' We can charitably call it 'excessive zeal.' It is zeal. But it is also tremendously excessive—and, therefore, quite wrong."

There was a shadow of a smile at the corners of his mouth as the Primate said, "Isn't it strange how different things look from different points of view? Let me read you two recent communications from the Government. The first is from the District Authority of Pozega. He writes from Nova Gradiska. He says:

'By reason of absolutely accurate information, and personal observation, it appears that several of the priests here do not show sufficient interest in the movement for the conversion of the people from the Orthodox to the Roman Catholic religion. Without doubt all the pastors here, as well as their assistants, are very busy with their regular duties as priests, but that ought not to be a hindrance—in the opinion of the undersigned—to sacrificing a little time in the interests of the converts or to instructing them. It is my opinion that each priest, as soon as he has received the decision of the authorities that they will permit the conversion of certain persons, or of whole villages, ought immediately, on his own initiative, to establish contact with the people, without waiting for special petitions or delegations, in order to associate himself personally, as soon as possible, with those who are preparing themselves for conversion; and that he ought to encourage them and strengthen them in their decision and at the same time refute the propaganda of the opponents of conversion who in such cases ordinarily become most powerful and dangerous, because at that moment—as we have been shown by our experience up to the present—intimidation and threats reach their peak.' "

The Archbishop looked up, smiled and said: "That is one sentence. Loose. Somewhat involved. But we cannot miss his meaning, can we? Isn't it kind of the Government to permit conversions—especially of whole villages? But let me go on:

'Too long a time passes from the moment a decision is made to allow conversions to the initiating of religious instructions, and the opponents of conversion are the only ones to profit by it while our spiritual leaders have remained waiting, arms folded, "for the Orthodox to agree with them and send their carriages for them." When the Primate saw a few of the bishops stir in irritation if not anger, he paused and smiled.

"Brothers, you haven't heard anything yet. This gentleman is deeply concerned. He hesitates not to lay down the law for us. Listen:

'This conduct can no longer be excused because of overwork. It shows that they are not taking their obligation seriously, which is scandalous, because the conversions are a patriotic duty for every priest.'"

The Archbishop stopped there, looked at his fellow prelates and said, "There is the difficulty. These men are sincere. They mean well. But, first of all, they don't know the difference between patriotism and nationalism. The first is a virtue, part of the very virtue of Religion, and part of Justice. The second is not even Catholic. But the second mistake is worse than the first: They consider it their duty to make converts. They forget the First Cause—God—and they take it upon themselves to force people into the Catholic Church, forgetting that while they may be helpers, it is the priest's function, especially pastors, to care for the flock. I can accept the term 'patriotic duty' only when that refers to our true Fatherland: Heaven; only when it is the Kingdom of God we are seeking to build, and as Christ said: 'My Kingdom is not of this world.' But listen further to this man. He may have something to tell us after all. He says: 'What is even worse'—than neglecting their 'patriotic duty'—'is when a priest at his first meeting with the 'Converts' declares frankly that the Church is not at all happy about their conversion!'"

"That, of course, is true if the conversions were forced in any way. We must ever respect every person as a person, and have the highest, holiest respect for their consciences. History has much to tell us about 'forced conversions.' They have been, and are today, wrong from every aspect. Yet I like the next paragraph in this letter. It reads:

'For this reason it would be useful to advise the clergy, by some adequate means, to undertake this work with devotion and tact so that progress may be made in this district as soon as possible and with greater success.'"

"We can't fault him on that bit of sagacity, can we: Devotion, tact? Two indispensables in this kind of work. I believe most of our priests have both. But he goes on to caution me about a few. He says: 'I emphasize especially that the priests in this district, on account of their national Hungarian feelings, as the pastor at Rusevo and the chaplain at Kutjevo, are not suitable persons for work of this kind, because they are lacking in the spirit of nationalism.'"

The Bishop of the Pozega district half rose from his chair. The Primate held up his hand and read on: "The apathy with which they work leaves a very disagreeable impression on Catholics as well as on those preparing for conversion. For this reason it is indispensable that others come to take their place and that they be sent elsewhere where they will not be required to fulfill this sort of mission.'"

Again the Bishop of the Pozega district half arose. "I know, Excellency," said the Primate kindly. "I have investigated. The second letter I was about to read you came from Zagreb. It carried all I have just read plus a demand, practically speaking, that I remove both priests mentioned in this letter. I didn't. For, on investigation, I learned that these are exemplary priests. Further, that they had displayed real tact in not doing as the District officer wanted them to do; for that would have been in violation of laws the District officer seems to forget; namely, that such people report to the parish office after they have manifested their intentions to the State offices. I had my Vicar-General, Dr. Salis, write a letter that minced no words. I had him inform both Zagreb and

Nova Gradiska that the pastor of Rusevo had shown such zeal for converts that he had begged me to send two helpers to his parish. I sent them. I also had my Vicar-General remind both Zagreb and Nova Gradiska of their own laws along with the laws of the Church. Never fear, Brothers, about our priests. No priest of this Archdiocese will ever be misrepresented to me by any of the *Ustashi,* or by anyone else. They are, thank God, for the most part, what they are called: 'Salt of the earth.' I am proud of them, and will ever be what God wants me to be for them: a father. But I wanted all of you to hear this man using the word 'nationalism' and speaking of 'patriotic duty.' We as Pastors of the People of God cannot be other than patriotic. But as Pastors and especially of these people of God, we can never be, nor can we ever allow the people to be nationalistic. That is too narrow a thing for Catholics. Our very name means 'universal.' That is the opposite to 'nationalistic'—'and I do not mean that term in the restricted sense of Nazism, Fascism or Communism—though, it can lead, precisely, to the same or similar.' "

The Primate then summed up the findings of the day. He did it so quietly, so clearly and concisely, that a calm and even a real peace came over the assembly. They needed his kindness—for that is what it was; for most had come to Zagreb in a worried state of mind and with troubled hearts. Not one of them was without suffering. In every diocese there had been disturbing events; in some dioceses genuine upheavals. They knew not what tack to take. As they listened to their Primate they saw that he would lead them. He thanked them warmly for giving him what he sought: facts. They felt almost embarrassed by the way he expressed his gratitude to them;

for all they seemed to have given him were troubling facts. Yet they did not seem to trouble him. He spoke of God's permissive will in such a way that some felt ashamed of their little Faith and their smaller trust. His words were renewing both as he went on.

When he came to practicalities they were in admiration of the clarity of his vision, the fittingness of his plans, the depth of his insight into the problems, and the promised effectiveness of his measures. But before he concluded they were amazed at his tender considerateness for others. "That is true humanism" whispered one Bishop to a colleague, "because it is so divine."

Stepinac, after listing the facts, spoke movingly of Christ's prayer at the Last Supper for "one fold and one shepherd." But he immediately reminded all that wolves could come into the fold with sheep's clothing. Yet, he removed all possibility of misapprehension and any misconstruction of his words, by reminding them that sincere men could be in error, and that while the error must be corrected, the sincerity must be appreciated. He insisted on genuine personalism; that is, authentic respect for every human being as a person. Then he spoke of "freedom of conscience" and stressed the reverence each must have for this realm which must be left for judgment to God alone, and which none may violate.

"There are holy men among the Orthodox," he said. There are truly holy men among the Muslims. Revere them. Respect their consciences. 'Deus est qui judicat' as St. Paul tells us. Yes, it is God alone who can judge aright." Then he went on to speak of mistakes, especially concerning the "Uniates." He pointed out that they belonged to Rome, that Rome had allowed them their own Rite, and that no one of the Latin Rite should ever have anything but admiration for men who used the Oriental Rite.

Then he asked their opinions concerning his plan. He would write first to pastors and priests laying down the basic rules for reception into the Church. No one could be received into the Church who was not convinced of the truth of the Catholic Faith and its necessity for salvation. "Religion," he insisted, "is an interior matter of a free conscience, and the decision in favor of Religion excludes all dishonest motives."

On this matter of motives he stayed for some time, and showed that he knew human nature intimately. He had great respect and even admiration for its strengths, but he was anything but ignorant of its weaknesses. "The clergy must proceed in these delicate matters of the human soul strictly in accord with the principles of the Church, careful of its dignity and its good name, and, consequently, must refuse to admit those who would like to be received into the Catholic Church without the correct motives, looking only to the protection of their material interests and their own selfish ends."

He was stern at this juncture, but immediately softened as he said, "A great deal of understanding must be shown those who, during the past twenty years, under the direct or indirect pressures of the authorities—who at every step favored the non-Catholics, especially the Orthodox—in moments of weakness did violence to their best religious convictions and renounced Catholicism out of desire for honors, a career, or other personal interests." He paused here to say that it was estimated that between 1918 and 1941 there were close to two hundred and forty thousand individuals who had yielded to such pressures. He did not condone their renunciation, but he did not roundly condemn them either. He knew what pressures these poor people had been subjected to. He went on to say to his fellow prelates: "Such persons merit still further special attention if it is proved that one of them, during the time of his apostasy, had relations with the Church in so far as he was able, and even brought up his children in the Catholic spirit. There are, alas, several thousand apostate souls of this sort and their families, and it is necessary to show them special love, and to do all that is possible to bring them back into the Church and thus save them and their children."

Then His Excellency became more specific and even more practical. He promised that the Archiepiscopal Court would appoint to each parish a team of catechists who would be well prepared for this delicate undertaking. They would not only know the doctrine of the Church, but also how to propose it. Further, they would be instructed on the respect due to each person and the reverence due each individual conscience. These teams would never be independent of the separate parish offices, but would report to them, learn the place, time, and circumstances surrounding their work, and report back to them. Decades before the C.C.D. program had been set up in any country, the Primate of Croatia had it working in his. He even stipulated that there be what we now call "adult education" classes, "study groups," and wisely insisted on small numbers for each class, ten to twenty at the most; "so that able catechists may solve every difficulty of each individual." Should some favor "private instructions" he had no objections, but he ruled that such persons pass "a definitive examination before the pastor and his assistant."

It was a detailed plan drawn up, seemingly, there

and then at the meeting of the hierarchy. So much so that some of the bishops marvelled at the speed and thoroughness of the plan. But they failed to realize that His Excellency, busy as he was with a hundred, and even a thousand, different matters almost daily, was always thinking of souls, and most frequently on an individual basis, looking deeply into the faculties of those souls, and devising ways to nourish each mind and will and memory with the very life of God.

As the meeting broke up one Bishop was heard to ask another: "Which is to be the more admired in that man: his head or his heart?" only to get as reply: "His holiness."

Another asked: "How does he stay so calm in these chaotic and catastrophic times?" When a Bishop from Bosnia said something about "He's not in the midst of turbulence such as some of us are," and had received a nod of agreement from a Bishop from Hercegovina, and another from a Bishop of Dalmatia, the Secretary of the meeting, turned and asked them if they had heard anything about what had happened on *Vidovdan*, the Serbian national holiday, June 28, right here in Zagreb. Their blank faces gave a negative reply for them. Then the secretary quickly recounted how the Serbs, living in the city, rose up that day and attacked defenseless Croats with a ferocity that was unbelievable. There were many deaths in Zagreb, and no one of them could be called "easy." The *Ustashi* retaliated with somewhat similar ferocity. But it was the *"Nastashi"*— the "Upstarts"— who used this occurence as defense for their fanatical attacks on Serbs not only in the city, but all over the State.

"You may think that we in Zagreb are sitting in the eye of the hurricane. Maybe we are. But if we are, let me assure you that 'eye' not only sees all that is whirling

111

about it, it feels it as well. His Excellency has been made to feel all that you in the more distant parts may have seen. He is pressured from all sides. How he stays upright is beyond me. It is more than human nature can stand. Yet he stands it."

As the secretary hurried off, the Bishop of Mostar who had joined the group and listened to the secretary's 'quick resumé', quietly said, "My conclusion is that while we have our mottoes blazoned on our coats-of-arms, he lives his." There was silence after that comment. Then Bishop Misic added, "Yes, *In Te Domine Speravi*, sums up our Archbishop's life even as it tells how he lives day in and day out. There is no other explanation. He should have had a mental breakdown years ago, but you saw and heard him today. The calmest, and yet the most astute and acute in the whole assembly of Bishops."

Three Circular Letters went out from Zagreb in quick succession after that meeting. Each dealt with conversions. Each had a very specific phase of conversion. Motives for coming into the Church were stressed in the first two Circulars. Solid conviction was what the Archbishop demanded. Base motives were what he would have his priests recognize and repudiate. But then, as if he had reflected further on the matter, and taken the weaknesses of human nature more fully into consideration, he wrote a third letter to his priests. In it he told them that "if those preparing to embrace Catholicism have any secondary motives, these will not be an obstacle to conversion, provided they are not sinful in character." But that these *were* secondary motives, and to be recognized as secondary, is evidenced by the Archbishop's next sentence: "If the spiritual father, despite all his instructions and good will, cannot in a sufficient measure create this first and most necessary preliminary for reception into the Church—namely, pure intention, no dishonest motive, and conviction of the truth of the Church—then he must not present the petition for conversion, although he should still work with his aspirants in a suitable manner if there is any hope whatsoever."

The fourth and final Circular Letter was the longest of all. It showed much careful preparation by experts in the field of canonical legislation on the validation of marriages of those who wished to enter the Catholic Church.

Having taken care of his own in the Church, the Archbishop now turned to those in the State. He addressed Pavelic. Again it was a long letter, for His Excellency covered all the matter seen in the meeting of the hierarchy, gave facts, cited specific places, named individual officials, and then made suggestions and demands.

He bit right into the heart of the matter by saying: *Poglavnik!*

The source of these errors lies in the fact that work concerning conversions has not been entrusted to the authority to which alone, according to Divine Law and canonical regulations, it ought to have been entrusted; that is to say, to the Croatian Catholic Bishops, who alone are called to give this work an apostolic character of holiness and charity, to direct its effort toward the well-being of the Holy Roman Church and the Croatian nation. These conversions have been managed by men who frequently acted as if the ecclesiastical authorities did not exist. Because of that, mistake followed on mistake.

In the first place they did not keep in mind the fact

113

that the question of rites in Croatia is not a dead issue, nor a mere formality which one can easily forget. There are customs which do not date from yesterday, but from the first centuries of Christianity. They have lived in the souls of men for more than sixteen hundred years; they give form to piety and to the whole spiritual life, often more so than the truths of the Faith themselves. For this reason the Sacred Congregation for the Oriental Church ... 'draws attention to the fact that it is necessary for Roman Catholic pastors in Croatia to be advised by their Bishops not to prevent the Orthodox from their natural return to the Oriental Rite of their conversion. . . .'

This means that the psychological aspect of this problem is vital. It is necessary above all to know the man whom we approach with the Catholic truth. It is necessary to know his past, his traditions, and his feelings. It is particularly necessary to know the Orthodox religion, its structure in the past across the centuries, and at the present. It does not suffice to know only the dogmatic differences and explain them at the time of conversion, but it is also necessary to recognize what effects these differences have had on the souls of the Orthodox. It is indispensable to understand the Orthodox religion in its social, political, and cultural aspects. Its errors have exerted a profound influence, and Communism has found nourishment and encouragement in the Orthodox religion. This schism was inspired by opposition; and this opposition, through the centuries, has produced bitterness and hate—a hate which has gnawed at souls and minds, and whose fruits have been negation, revolution, nihilism, and destruction. This is demonstrated in Russian Bolshevism, and in the religious struggle in Russia between the old traditions and the new trends.

We must not deceive ourselves with illusions. The Orthodox religion has forged a type of man who cannot change his way of thinking over night, mechanically, as if he were a machine. It is precisely this mechanical way of proceeding that has had disastrous consequences. That was evidenced at the time of the conversions in Poland. All that was erected artificially, without a profound spiritual basis, fell in ruins at the first opportunity, like a paper house. We have witnessed the experience in Spain, where disconcerting examples of conversions without convictions threatened not only Catholicism but the Spanish nation itself. This experience characterized the Latin Empire at Constantinople. This mechanical process carried with it a hate which concealed itself for a time, but at the propitious moment, burst into a flame of passion. This unfortunate method of building is fragile; on sand, and not on rock, and when the storms and winds come, nothing remains but ruins.

After that lesson in history and true depth psychology, the Archbishop went on:

The second fundamental mistake in relation to the conversions is that local authorities and *Ustashi* officials frequently forbid, in their own name, despite the NDH circular letter of July 30 of this year, any reception of Orthodox converts into the Greek-Catholic Rite. What is even worse, they forbid such conversions in regions where those who are Orthodox today were for several centuries united with the Catholic Church, and were turned away from union and from the Croatian nation for a time by Serbian propaganda and force. It seems that these conversions have been forbidden because of certain apprehensions of a political nature which, however, have no foundation, for the Greek-Catholic clergy have shown their pro-Croatian sentiments over a period of three hundred years in the face of the most difficult circumstances. The work of this clergy has been crowned with success, as is attested in the vigor of Greek-Catholic intellectual life and the strength of the faith among the masses of peasants in the Zumberak and elsewhere.

Cannot this Greek-Catholic clergy from the Diocese of Krizevci accomplish the same thing, with the same good results, in other regions in view of its experience and its three-century-old tradition? Instead of giving freedom of action to the Diocese of Krizevci in conversions in the spirit of the circular letter of July 30, the Greek-Catholic priests were overwhelmed by threats as, for example, Alexander Vlasov of Disnik in the Garesnica district who was bringing about the conversions in the territory of his parish, in complete accord with the regulations in the circular letter. He was told that he would be driven out of the country as an 'undesirable,' in spite of the fact that he was a citizen of the NDH.

In other regions, as in Veliki Zdenci in the same district, conversions from the Orthodox to the Catholic religion according to the Greek-Catholic Rite were simply 'annulled,' although they had been realized not only in conformity with ecclesiastical regulations, but also with the regulations of the civil authorities then in force, and with the special permission of the Ministry of Justice and Religion.

He went on with a few more specifics, then ended his long, forceful letter with:

Poglavnik! No one can deny that these terrible acts of violence and cruelty have taken place, for you yourself, *Poglavnik,* have publicly condemned those which the *Ustashi* have committed, and you have ordered executions because of their crimes. Your effort to insure the reign of justice and order in the country merits applause.

The Croat nation has been proud of its thousand year old culture and its Christian tradition. That is why we wait for it to show in practice, now that it has achieved its freedom, a greater nobility and humanity than that displayed by its former rulers.

The Church condemns all crimes and outbursts of passion on the part of irresponsible elements and inexperienced youths, and demands full respect for the human personality without regard for sex, religion, nationality, or race; for all men are the children of God, and Christ died for all, *qui vult omnes homines salvos fieri.*

We are sure, *Poglavnik,* that you hold the same position, and that you will do all in your power to restrain the violence of certain individuals, and to allow only the rule of responsible authority in the country. If the contrary were true, all the work for

117

the conversions of schismatics would be illusory.

It was a long letter. It was a strong letter. Pavelic had been receiving similar letters from the Primate ever since he was put into office. We may wonder what impression they made on him, and ask ourselves what the Archbishop was accomplishing with his many spirited protests. Perhaps the best answer at this juncture is contained in a letter from a pastor in Glina. It runs:

On August 29, 1941, Second Lieutenant Rolf, with about twenty young *Ustashi*, came to Glina. He immediately arrested all Serbians, for the most part widows of those who had been massacred on May 12, 1941. He showed mercy to only a few who had contacts with the Bank of the then Minister, Dr. Puk, in monetary matters.

As I was returning from the Bureau of Taxes, I met in the street a group of those who were being arrested. They said to me, crying, 'You told us, when receiving us into the Catholic Church, that we would have nothing to fear.' I replied at once: 'I will take your case to the Archbishop.'

I left for the District government, and I requested of the officer in charge of the District, at that time, Imper, to take care that these people were not killed. He replied: 'What can I do when Second Lieutenant Rolf has taken over command of the District? And beside that, you know that I can do nothing against Puk and Jerec' (who was a Prefect at Petrinja, a drunkard, a runner after women, and a cheat).

I then went to see the Second Lieutenant of the *Ustashi*, Rolf, (a man about fifty, completely grey),

118

and I said to him: 'The women and the children you have arrested today have been converted to Catholicism. The Minister of the Interior has decided that such persons have the same rights as other citizens, and His Excellency, the Archbishop of Zagreb, has personally obtained from the Minister an attestation of that decision. The Church would be betrayed if any harm should come to those who were arrested.' I noticed, from Rolf's expression, that these remarks were displeasing to him. He said to me: 'I have only the mandate to arrest them and bring them to justice.' I saw that he wanted to get rid of me as soon as possible.

At the Court, where I next introduced myself, I was told that nothing at all was known of the case, and that Rolf was using the jail as his headquarters.

After all that the *Ustashi* had done here under the aegis of the infamous Puk and Jeric, I clearly foresaw that the following night all the arrested persons would be taken off somewhere and killed, so I went back again to the officer in charge of the District, Imper, and asked his permission to use his telephone to call the Archbishop. He allowed me to do this, remarking that I should be careful of what I said because a *Ustashi* was seated next to the telephone switchboard in the Post Office.

I called the Archiepiscopal Court. The Porter answered the phone, and I asked him to call the Archbishop's secretary. In a few moments someone came to the phone, Dr. Stepan Lackovic, I think, to whom I explained the situation, for the most part in Latin, on account of the *Ustashi* seated next to the switchboard in the Post Office. The secretary replied that

119

His Excellency, the Archbishop, was not at home, but, that since it was a case of such delicacy, he would go look for him, and that I should stay close to the phone.

That was at noon, and I had at my house J. Crnkovic, then Administrator of the parish of Crkvena and today assistant at the parish of St. Mary; my father, Joseph Zuzek, now catechist at Kranj; and my assistant, Francis Bratusek, of the Levantine Diocese. That is why I left for my house after having asked the employee who was on duty that day, Stepan Klobucar, to advise me when the Archbishop's secretary called— the rectory is only a few minutes away from the phone.

We had just sat down to lunch when there was a knock on the door. Second Lieutenant Rolf entered alone, and giving me a piercing glance, said: 'I have just received orders from the *Poglavnik* that all persons who have been converted to Catholicism are to be set free. You, Pastor, will come at two o'clock, with the District officer, Imper, to the jail and read the names of the converts. You will give them a talk, and tell them to be very careful; because as soon as anyone opens her mouth (*ipsissima verba*), she will be arrested, and then no intervention will help her.' (He was thinking, naturally, of His Excellency, the Archbishop.)

At two o'clock I went with Imper to the jail where I told those who were gathered there whom they had to thank for their deliverance, and, while Imper went to look for some cigarettes, I opened the large outside door and released nearly all the arrested women who were crying with emotion.

That evening, Krnic, the Jailor's son, my pupil in

the High School at Glina, brought the others whom we had not been able to release at once, since they were Orthodox, to my house. My sister and I hid some in the cellar, others in the attic, and at about eleven o'clock that night, sent them off in a direction where there were no *Ustashi* soliders. And thus the arrested were restored to their homes, and since there were many Orthodox among the arrested, there were, together with those from Glina, about one hundred and fifty all told.

The next day an envoy from Puk and Jeric came to my house, the infamous Vidakovic, brother of the murderer who had killed the Administrator of the Bucica parish, Vedrina, and said to me brusquely: 'Yesterday you emptied the jail. You will be responsible for that, especially since you have no rights in the Independent State of Croatia, since you are Slovenian.' I replied to him: 'Know well that I was driven from Istra in 1923 because of my pro-Croatian sentiments! Shall I be repaid by Croatia in such a way? In any case, I am nothing. Let the Archbishop answer you!'

And that is how there are in Glina and surrounding villages, today, women who are still alive, who were saved by the intervention of the Archbishop, Dr. Aloysius Stepinac, and who will always remember with gratitude him to whom they owe their lives.

All the above (*ut supra*) can be attested by J. Crnkovic, parish assistant at St. Mary's.

(signed) Fr. Zuzek, Pastor

It was wearying work, and yet the Archbishop never seemed to weary. He was constantly under pressure, yet seemed always available. No sooner had one crisis passed when two or three others took its place. He had won in the case of the Nuremburg laws against the Jews. By 1942 it was evident that he had also won against the *Ustashi* movement for mass conversions and persecution of the Serbian Orthodox; for "rebaptism" along *Ustashi* lines stopped abruptly. But these victories gave the Prelate no elation; for he saw the realities of the situation with unblurred vision. It was not from conviction on the part of Pavelic, or on the part of the *Ustashi* that this mad movement had been stopped; it was from the realization that they had an opponent who would face them with truth and demand justice at every turn and for everyone be he Serb, Jew, Gypsy, man, woman, or child. And that this fearless and forceful opponent had behind him the mass of the people. These facts set many in the Pavelic government thinking on ways and means to silence Aloysius Stepinac who was not only acting like the Good Shepherd, but also as Good Samaritan. He was not only a challenge to those in power, he was a living condemnation; for many in office had already done, and wanted to continue doing, what the priest and the levite in the parable of the Good Samaritan had done—pass by, leaving those who were "half-dead" to die. The Archbishop knew he was not making friends by his protests. He also knew that God expected him to be both Good Shepherd and Good Samaritan. He would labor to measure up to God's expectations.

5 Good Shepherd and Good Samaritan

LIFE WAS NOT EASY for anyone in Europe in 1942. The Nazis had turned from a Western Europe, which they had practically subdued and were now dominating, to the East, and were now fighting the Russians with what looked like assured final success along a two thousand mile long front. But if life was hard in other parts of the continent, it was particularly difficult for anyone living in Zagreb, and, for that matter, in any part of the Independent State of Croatia.

The ordinary citizen, honest people, genuine patriots, were confused by what they saw going on all about them.

Jews, innocent though they were of any crime—save that, in the eyes of the Nazis, of being Jews—were arrested on all sides, rounded up like cattle, and shipped off to God alone knew where: concentration camps at Dachau, Auschwitz, Jasenovac, Jadovan—and many of them to death. Serbs were being persecuted by some of the *Ustashi*. Catholics were being butchered, wherever possible, by *Chetniks*. And to further confuse, and intimidate, the people, there was the growing movement of the *Partisans*.

Ideologies as disparate as the materialistic atheism of the Communists, the arrogant apotheosis of Aryanism of the Nazis, the pompous neo-Caesarism of Mussolini and his Fascists, were being bruited about along side of Ustashiism, Pan-Serbianism, and the Freedom of the Western Democracies. Above all the clamor was the steadying, yet sad and somewhat reproachful voice of Pius XII pleading for peace, brotherly love, common sense, an end to brutality, and a return to Christ.

The ordinary people looked on with amazement, then with fear, at the power and the progress of the Nazi regime. It looked as if Hitler would soon dominate all of Europe, and bring into being a "new Continent"— over which he would be Dictator. It was no pleasant prospect for a Croat or a Catholic. Then there was Mussolini, who did not have anything like the same power as Hitler, but by siding with the *Führer*, was far from powerless. Then there was Pavelic—a patriot certainly; a Catholic unquestionably; a Croatian to the core. But, because of the *Ustashi*—and especially the *Nastashi*—and the tie-in between his government and the Axis, did he merit trust?

Neither the Press nor the Radio helped any of the

ordinary people to clarity of concept, understanding of events, or to the possession of truth. Even the Catholic press, at times, was ambiguous and ambivalent.

But there was one voice in the city and the nation that comforted the bewildered populace—that of their Primate. He was always clear. His logic, compelling. His truths, convincing. And he was ever consistent. But what heartened the near despairing was the burning sincerity of the man combined with his utter fearlessness.

His sermons were not only heard; they were printed and reprinted, and circulated all over the land. Spoken publicly but once, they were read and reread, thanks to what was equivalently an underground press. They served as a constant spur to the people to hold fast to their Catholic Faith and to oppose, when necessary, Nazism, Fascism, Communism, and even Ustashiism.

But, while endearing him to the ordinary Croat, these same sermons did anything but endear him to any of those with power. Even those in power in the State began to think on ways and means to weaken his hold on the masses. Pavelic himself entertained some ideas on how to silence him. It would have been suicide for him and his party. Yet, in the turmoil of the times, the sanest of men do lose their common sense. The *Poglavnik* was on the verge of arresting the Primate when one of the cooler heads in the Government showed him the edge of the cliff on which he was about to tread and the depth to which he would plunge were he to alienate the masses by such a move.

Little wonder the masses held him in such high esteem. They knew he was obliged to be a Good Shepherd because of his priestly vocation and his appointment to the prelature. But what set them marvelling was the way he played the Good Samaritan. They saw him protecting the persecuted no matter what their race or religion.

He seemed to have a particular affection for the Jews. Whenever other means failed, he did not hesitate to hide some in his own rectory and urge other pastors to do the same in their own homes. He adamantinely refused to give the names of Jewish refugees to the Germans who knew only too well the numerous members of that people who had been protected by his *Caritas* and "Relief Committee." They even knew that he had applied for, and obtained from the Papal Secretariat of State numerous passports and visas for South American countries. They suspected, and rightly so, that he was smuggling out hundreds of Jews from the city, moving them to ports of embarkation, and seeing that they got safely away. But they could not stop him, intimidate him, or get any real information from him.

When the staff of the Schwartz Home for Aged and Sick Jews was arrested and imprisoned before he could intervene successfully, he ordered his Catholic nuns to take the Home over and to give exceptionally tender care to each of the residents.

Then there were the children. . . . He saw them everywhere, sad-eyed, hungry, homeless. Into his orphanages they went. When these were overcrowded, as they soon were, he commissioned nuns to take over other buildings belonging to the Archdiocese and make them into homes for the homeless. Never once did he question about the race, the religion, the political affiliation of the parents of these waifs, nor of the leanings of the children themselves. They were homeless. That was enough. He would give them a home. Many of these children were offspring of *Partisans*. These, it seemed, received more attention and greater affection from the Archbishop than did the children of Catholic Croats. One day he heard of four hundred Orthodox children who had been "orphaned" by a Nazi order which tore these children from their mothers who were then sent to concentration camps or forced labor camps in Germany. He went to the officials in charge and argued, cajoled, threatened and finally won permission to care for these little Orthodox children. Into another one of his "homes" they went, and there received care that was truly maternal.

None of this surprised his workers in *Caritas;* for all had heard his principle: "We must help our neighbor whoever he be, where and when we can, to the utmost of our abilities." But what did surprise even these workers was what appeared to them like his "omnipresence." He was at home in the *Kaptol,* the Archbishop's residence in Zagreb. He was in the offices of the *Ustashi;* in those of the German commanders of the occupying forces; in those of the Italians; in the orphanages and homes he had erected; in the house of his *Caritas* helpers; in the streets of the city; in the homes of the poor; in the pulpit of his Cathedral; in the roadbed of railroads where troops or prisoners were passing; he was in the country setting up branches of *Caritas;* he was on the very wagons heaped high with food and clothing he had asked his people to donate, carrying both commodities to Jew, Orthodox, Moslem, and his own.

Once, when word reached him that a train with eighteen hundred Jews aboard was to pass through Novska on its way to a concentration camp in Poland, he fought refusal after refusal, demolished subterfuge after subterfuge, and finally won his way to the side of that train to pass out supplies and food to give whatever

127

comfort and courage he could to the hapless victims. Two weeks later he did the same thing for two thousand Jews who were being transported from Greece to Germany.

To Italy, to Germany, and the concentration camps in his own Croatia went his secretaries to study conditions, report back to him the facts. These he weighed, sorted out, and then presented to the authorities demanding alleviations—and winning them. But, perhaps, the heart and soul of the man and the priest who was also prelate and patriot is best shown in the letter he wrote to the Croatians in a Forced Labor camp in Germany just as 1941 was coming to a close:

My dear Croatian Brothers and Sisters:

I consider it my sacred duty to say a few words to you who will celebrate this Christmas Day far from those whom you love and cherish; to you who will not, perhaps, have a chance to sing our beautiful Christmas hymns in church; to you who are forced by circumstances to think, even at Christmas time, how you can keep yourselves alive—how to get your daily bread.

But if you are far from your loved and dear ones, far from your Croatian fatherland, know well that God is not far from you. His Paternal eyes watch over you even there, His Paternal love surrounds you, and His arms protect you. Show yourselves abroad as true children of God, and as true children of your Croatian fatherland.

The first demands that you do not forget your soul, or soil it through sin, since it is created in the image of God. Since sin has existed in the world it has made no man happy, but caused the ruin of many. 'Does man gain anything else from vice,' asks St. Gregory, 'than that he makes his own heart a prison, where he is tortured by remorse, even though no one else accuses him?' Did the sin of the first man, Adam, bring anything but remorse and an immense sadness for his lost happiness? Did the murder of his brother, Abel, bring to Cain anything other than the infamous print of a fratricide which would not leave him in peace day or night? The adultery of David, did it not bring to the king a remorse which pushed him into an even greater sin—the murder of him who kept him from being able to sin without self-reproach? Drunkenness, adultery, and other vices, do they not bring to men only sadness and unhappiness for which, very often, there is no remedy?

So that this does not happen to you as well, do not forget your duties as Christians to your Heavenly Father. First, do not forget to pray. When a small child awakens in his crib he first looks all around searching for the eyes of his mother. As soon as he finds her he is glad, but if he does not find her, he begins to cry. We are all children of our Heavenly Father; for Christ has taught us: 'Our Father, who art in heaven.' Look therefore every day to your prayers to Him, our Heavenly Father, who is better to you than an earthly mother, closer than any friend, and able to help you when no one else can. God has shown His great mercy in the fact that He hears the humble prayers of His children everywhere. This, above all, is a great consolation to you who do not have, perhaps, the opportunity to go to church when you so desire. St. Paul prayed in prison and obtained the help and conversion of his jailor. The sick king,

129

Ezekiah, prayed in his bed and obtained, as a result, a fifteen year prolongation of his life. The thief prayed on the cross and obtained grace for his conversion, the salvation of his soul, and was the first to enter, with Jesus, into Paradise. The Prophet, Danie', prayed in the lions' den, among the lions, and remained unharmed so that not a single hair of his head was touched. The Prophet, Jonah, prayed in the belly of a whale and obtained deliverance. Job patiently prayed to God, seated on a dunghill, separated from the world, and regained anew his health and all his wealth that had been taken from him.

Pray, then, all of you, if you wish the blessing of Heaven to accompany you in your work, and to pass happily through the tempests of life. God does not wait for an elaborate prayer from you. The more simple it is, the dearer it is to Him. For the leper in the Gospel did not pray otherwise when he cried out: 'Lord, if you will, you can make me clean.' And he was made clean. His prayer was answered. If, then, you pray as a child to your Heavenly Father, He will do His duty as a Father, since He Himself has promised: 'In truth I say to you, says Christ, 'all that you seek from the Father in my Name, believe, and it shall be given to you.'

Show yourselves abroad, as I have said, as true children of the Croatian fatherland. That will not be hard for you if you succeed in the first; that is to say, in your duty to God. Let them say what they will, to me it is certain, that there is no greater patriotism, no greater love for country, than the leading everywhere, in all places, of a life without sin, honest and sober. It is not drunkards, nor murderers, nor thieves, usurpers, fornicators, nor card players who form the firm foundation of the fatherland, but hard-working men, sober and conscientious. No one has ever heard of a grape grown on a thorn-hedge.

I believe, moreover, that none among you have succumbed to the deadly theory of international communism, which denies all obligations to one's own people and country. The nation is one large family, created by the will of the Creator, in which each individual has his duty to the community, and the community its duty to him.

Appreciate, therefore, even from abroad, your Croatian fatherland, but do not despise other nations. And you can honor it in the best way by leading an honest life and doing honest work. For you know our national proverb: 'A good man is worth more than riches.' And one of the most beautiful possessions of your fatherland is the Catholic religion, upon which rests all our beautiful and honorable heritage. Confess that religion in public abroad as well as at home. I am convinced that no honest man will scorn you for that; for it is only thieves and traitors who merit scorn, never heroes.

I hope that these words of mine will find an echo in your hearts, since they come from the heart, warmly greeting you all. I wish for you all the abundant blessings of God and the peace of Christ who descended to earth on the holy night of Christmas accompanied by an angel song: 'Glory in the highest, and on earth peace to men of good will.'

Your Archbishop,
Dr. Aloysius Stepinac

It is always refreshing and reassuring to have historical documents for historical facts. The life of this Prelate would be unbelievable without such unassailable testimony. And what was his reward for such selfless devotedness? Abuse! And from all sides.

Toward the end of 1941, just as the Archbishop was penning the above letter, there came to him one Captain Rapotetz, as emissary from the Yugoslavian Government in Exile (they were then in London.) The Captain was on a secret mission to Yugoslavia, but with special instructions that he contact Archbishop Stepinac. In the course of a six-month stay in the country, the Captain managed to see the Primate six times. His Excellency was acquainted with the nature of the secret mission, hence he arranged for the Captain to distribute to war victims, including all who were being persecuted for their political convictions, the money sent secretly from the Government in Exile. In the course of one of their last conversations the Captain let it be known to the Archbishop that some in the Government in Exile were severely criticizing him for not breaking openly with the Pavelic regime. His Excellency smiled and said, "That could very easily be done. But then I would have to retire to some monastery. And what would happen, not only to the Church in Croatia, but to the thousands on thousands of refugees, and the countless thousands of others who are being persecuted daily by the various regimes in our Croatia? No, I will not do that; for I believe with all my heart that most of these sufferers are dependent solely on the Church's representative in Zagreb."

Those phrases about "thousands on thousands" sound like an exaggeration; for what single individual can care for "thousands on thousands"? But again historical testimony bears the Archbishop out. Before me is a document signed by members of the "Committee to Aid Refugees," which we have met already, and among the signers is the signature of Dr. Francis Seper, then Rector of the Seminary of Zagreb, now Cardinal Prefect for the Doctrine of Faith, a rather reliable witness, you will agree. The Document is a report made by one Theresa Skringer, one time Secretary of the Committee to Aid Refugees. She writes:

It was in 1937 that Nazism began in Germany and Austria to persecute the Jews, the Catholic Church, and the Protestants. Little by little people fled to any place there was some hope of finding a safe refuge. At that time many came to Yugoslavia, that is to say Croatia, feeling themselves safer there than in Slovenia. Their center was Zagreb. The Jews were very numerous, but there were other persons who, unwilling to adhere to the Hitlerite doctrines and the Nazi dictatorship, had been forced to take flight. Many of them had recommendations from the Ecclesiastical authorities.

In view of the great number and misery of these people, and wanting to help the neediest, the "Committee to Aid Refugees" was formed under the protection of the Archbishop of Zagreb, Dr. Aloysius Stepinac, who served as intermediary with the Yugoslav authorities. The refugees received: Financial aid and moral aid; medical care and medicines; information in various languages; visit permits; approved as a result of the special intervention of the Archbishop;

133

the cost of travelling to different countries; a visa for the country of their destination, given on the recommendation of the Committee, etc.

Most of these people left for France, to go from there to America, England, or even to China or Japan. Among the thousands of these refugees was Dr. Gere, now Minister of Justice in Austria, and the Chief of the Secret Police in the Cabinet of Benes, who fled with numerous documents of the Czech Government. After his arrival in Paris, the Czechoslovakian Minister in France sent the Committee a letter filled with expressions of gratitude since, according to this same Minister, the Germans had put a high price on Dr. Gere's head.

Czech, and especially Polish engineers came *en masse* to our country. The Committee gave them aid at the railroad station, and gave considerable sums to the Friends of Poland. There are today in Zagreb doctors who were helped by the Committee to complete their studies. Assistance was given according to our means to all refugees without regard to race, religion, or nationality. A colony of refugees from Austria remains today in Zagreb that was formerly under the protection of the Archbishop.

We have received letters from abroad asking that we describe the constitution of the Committee and how we raised the funds for our work. Similar institutions were subsequently set up in London, Paris, New York, and Utrecht, but with the difference that Catholics were distinguished from the Jews.

The Zagreb Committee, as the nearest to the Austrian frontier, was the principal one that worked without interruption until the arrival of the Germans in Zagreb when it was forced to burn all its records so that all evidence of these people would be unavailable to the Nazis. The importance attached by the German Government to the Committee is shown in the arrest of Miss Theresa Skringer, Secretary, who was sought out by the Gestapo the very day of the German arrival. She was arrested April 15, 1941, imprisoned in Graz and Vienna, where she was condemned to death, but, thanks to intervention from abroad, was freed September 1, 1941.

The Gestapo intended to kill the Archbishop, according to the statement of a high Gestapo official. They wanted to arrest the other members of the Committee, but most of them fled.

Among those competent to testify as to the truth of this declaration are:

(Signed) Msgr. Milan Belukan, Canon of Zagreb, member; Dr. Francis Seper, Rector of the Seminary of Zagreb, member; Dr. Richard Lang, collaborator with the Committee; Dr. Desanka Stamper-Ristovic, collaborator with the Committee; Msgr. Dr. Svetozar Rittig, member.

Because of the Committee, the Archbishop was frequently the object of ridicule, and was attacked in the Press. But he continued his great work of mercy as long as possible.

(Signed Theresa Skringer, Former Secretary
of the Committee)

The conundrum as to the acquisition of the enormous funds necessary for such work is solved in part by a glance at the Report to the International Red Cross, made by Fr. Stepan Lockovic, the Archbishop's Secretary, regarding Relief in Croatia. In that Report you read such names and sums as: 2,000 Swiss francs (20,000 kronen) remitted by the Committee for Aid to the Poles of Fribourg; 60,000 kronen—sent by the tannin factory and the steam saw mill of Nasice; 10,810 Swiss francs—Christmas present from the Holy Father for the Poles in Croatia; 203,064.47 kronen—sent by the factory at Nasice; 300,000 kronen—received from His Excellency, the Archbishop; 400,000 kronen—from International Red Cross for Croatia. Obviously, His Excellency became something of an international beggar for the poor and the persecuted.

But good is never allowed to thrive in this world of ours unmolested. The first major move, perhaps, to thwart His Excellency was made by the Government—at whose instigation there is some question. More than likely pressure was exerted by the Nazis on the *Poglavnik*. At any rate, it was his Government that first ordered the Press, whether daily, weekly, or monthly, to stop printing any of the Archbishop's sermons. The Editor of the Catholic weekly, *Nedelja*, learned how serious this order was when, after printing the Archbishop's Christmas sermon of 1942, he was threatened with the gallows. Then shortly after that a well-known industrialist of Zagreb was found with a printed copy of the Primate's sermon for the New Year. He was arrested, sent to a concentration camp, and there he died.

Next the Press indulged in tactics too familiar to any who have followed the bold, and often brazen, methods of dictatorships. Smears of all sorts began to appear in the dailies, then the weeklies, and finally the monthlies. His Excellency was portrayed as being pro-Communistic, then pro-Nazistic, and accused of being a politician rather than a priest, and the most unpatriotic of prelates.

With a controlled press, and the journalese of propaganda writers, it was not difficult to "prove" any one of the above smears. That he was "pro-Communist" was unquestionable when the daily paper told you how he had intervened in the case of the Kuresh brothers, Communists who had been tried and condemned to death. Croatia's Catholic Primate intervened, and by some means or other, won a reprieve for these men.

As for being "pro-Serbian," who could question it when, day after day, the compelling evidence of his own letters, pleading for mercy for five Serbs who had been condemned to death? One day the papers would carry His Excellency's letter to the *Poglavnik*:

"I ask you, *Poglavnik*, to use your power to modify the death sentence for one less severe. I am convinced that your act of amnesty, coming at the time of the anniversary of the foundation of our State, would have excellent results.

"May I, *Poglavnik*, draw your attention to the circumstances in the case of Velimir Jovanovic, who is considered the most guilty of the group condemned to death. As a former Yugoslav officer and an Orthodox. . . ." There it was in the Archbishop's own hand: a plea for a Serb and an Orthodox. Who could question his leanings? He let no one have any rest in this case. General Adolf Sabljak, Commandant of the City of Zagreb, received this plea in Holy Week of that year: "I ask you, General, on Good Friday, when Christ prayed: 'Father, forgive them, for they know not what they do'—and on the Eve of Easter, day of life, to undertake all in your power to let these five condemned men live. . . ."

The papers did not even suppress the result of all this pleading. They were out to smear the Archbishop as "pro-

Serbian," so they rather exultantly published a letter from Lieutenant General Percevic which ran: "This office has the honor to reply to your letter of April 2, addressed to the *Poglavnik* on the subject of amnesty for Jovanovic, Bonacic, Krunic, Ilic, and Bukovac, that the *Polavnik* has granted a commutation of sentence to all the above-named: the death sentence changed to life." Here was a Catholic Primate of Croatia not only pleading for Serbs and Orthodox, but pleading effectively. Who could question his "pro-Serbianism"?

That His Excellency was antagonistic to the State was "proved" again from his own correspondence to the *Poglavnik*. Had he not written, even before the first convocation of the Croatian Parliament:

Poglavnik,

I feel obliged to address you as head of the Independent State of Croatia to clear up certain questions relating to the convocation of the Croatian Parliament.

During the past few days several priests have asked me if I would persist in my decision to exclude priests from political activities in the light of my Circular Letters to the Clergy in 1935 and 1938. I replied that those Letters were still in force.

Here is the problem: Just after World War I, though young and still a layman, I had the opportunity to note the unfavorable reaction to the Catholic Church caused by priests who appeared on the electoral lists of the various parties contending for power. This was not surprising; for a priest who had declared himself an active member of a political party could never, as a politician, be a consistent defender of the ideals

138

of the Church, however honest and dignified he was otherwise.

Again I remember well the peasants in my own district who, even before the great war, fractured the skull of a parish priest who, in the elections, had defended the cause of a party which did not merit their support. This was not the only case of its kind. What is worse is that among the priests belonging to different political parties, there was sometimes such hatred generated, that they would not speak to one another for years, though formerly they had been the best of friends; all this to the great scandal of the people. The situation became the more serious if they neglected their official duties because of political activities. They lost hours, even whole days, in discussions that led nowhere, and abandoned their schools, their sermons, the catechism, visits to the sick, and many other duties. All their political activity led to little good and much harm to the Church and the country.

Things became worse after World War I. Priests threw themselves into politics, joining the numerous parties, from those on the Right, through the Peasant Party, the Popular Democratic and Radical parties, and even the National Yugoslav Party, and the Yugoslav Radical Union; all that, again, to the great detriment of the Church and the country.

That is why, on becoming Archbishop, I resolved to put an end to all these abuses. The first to be dealt with was the pastor of Bednja, Matica, a former member of the HSS, the Croatian Peasant Party, and then a Minister in the Cabinet of Zivkovic. I notified him to resign either his post as Minister or his pastorate.

139

He preferred the post of Minister, so I removed him from his pastorate. Today he probably realizes that right was on my side.

On the eve of the elections in the year 1935, I sent the Clergy a Circular Letter in which I forbade them, under threat of Canonical discipline, to become candidates on any Party's list so long as they held an ecclesiastical post. A certain priest hesitated and asked whether, despite the prohibition, he could become a candidate. I let him know he could do so, but on the very same day he would lose his parish.

I published a similar Letter in 1938, permitting no one to become a candidate, or enter Parliament, were it even on the list of the HSS, the Croatian Peasant Party, although there was ill feeling against me because of this.

On the evening of the opening of the Croat Parliament, I must, *Poglavnik*, insist on this point of view. The small good that priests can achieve in politics does not justify me in tolerating the harm, twice as great to the Church and the nation by abandonment of their priestly duties, whether these priests are members of the HSS, or of the *Ustashi* Movement.

Times have changed completely. The population has become unruly, the scourge of birth control decimates their ranks, the people are weighed down by sin and vices of every sort, and there are so few priests. In my Archdiocese the loss of one priest is a severe blow, because we have a thousand priests too few to administer our parishes. But, even in theory, a priest cannot accept responsibility for political acts. It is the Apostle himself who says: 'No one who fights (for God) involves himself with the affairs of this life, so that he may please his Master, Christ.' Ecclesiastical Law confirms this when it exhorts priests, *'senatorum aut oratorum legibus ferendis, quos deputatus vocant, munus ne sollicitent neve acceptent.'* This is the opinion of every true and faithful Catholic, who expect their priests to care for their souls and not involve themselves in political debate. This principle is emphasized in nearly every modern Concordat, and that, usually, on the initiative of the secular authority.

I ask you courteously, *Poglavnik*, to understand with benevolence my point of view, and to relieve four of my parish priests from their duties as deputies. Superhuman efforts are demanded every day of my priests in the spiritual care of the people; I am sure that each of them will give me thanks for delivering them from this added responsibility. If, however, some should find fault with my point of view—which is completely in accord with the spirit of the Catholic Church—I prefer unjustified reproaches rather than abandon the true interests of the Church and the nation.

For working sincerely for "the true interests of the Church and the nation," this prelate was now held up in the Press as "antagonistic to the State." The smears grew in number and nastiness. Many close to the Archbishop begged him to reply. He remained silent until the closing of the Procession of Penance at Zagreb in October, 1943.

As he looked down from the pulpit of the Cathedral he was somewhat surprised to note in a front pew Dr. Julije Makanec, the Minister of Public Instruction for the

141

Independent State of Croatia. His eyes roved over the densely packed Cathedral and noted other members of the government and many he recognized as members of the press. Here and there he felt sure he saw agents of the Gestapo and the OZNA, the secret police of the ever growing *Partisans*. But for the most part he saw he had his own people. He had prepared his talk for this occasion and was, if anything, pleased that so many "outsiders," as he called them, were present. He began with a parable. He had learned his lesson well from long years of study of his Master. Jesus was fond of parables and had used them not always to keep those with eyes from not seeing, but most frequently to keep even the blind from failing to see. This last was the Archbishop's purpose this evening. It was a simple little story of a "peasant who every day brought five pounds of butter to a baker in his town, which the baker needed to bake his bread, and who every day would give the peasant, as payment, a five pound loaf of bread."

His Excellency had not finished his little story before he noted that three or four men close to the Minister of Instruction were very busy taking notes.

"Fine," thought the Archbishop, "I'll give them plenty of matter for public instruction." So he went into the heart of the story which was to serve as a paradigm for all he had planned to preach this night.

"It happened one day," said His Excellency, "that the baker set about weighing the butter and, to his surprise, discovered that the peasant had brought him only four and a half pounds of butter. He called the peasant to account for cheating. But the peasant very quietly answered: 'My friend, I am not guilty; for, although naturally I have a scale, yet I have no weights for it. Because

142

of that I always put your bread on one side of the scale, and on the other, my butter. I always put as much butter on the scale as the weight of your loaf.' The baker did not believe this. But, when he used a more accurate scale, he saw the peasant was right, and since that time this baker has given his customers an exact measure of bread."

He paused momentarily and smiled a tiny smile as he looked down and across his vast audience. He noted that the men next to the Minister were still scribbling notes. Then he went on, still rather quietly: "You will ask, perhaps, what has this to do with the Procession of Penance. I shall answer by applying this simple parable to our lives today." He could feel the stir in the crowd. He went on more strongly: "Whether people believe, or whether they do not believe, God is our Creator, and we are the wretched of the earth who owe to our Creator veneration and obedience. In other words, we are debtors to God. And yet, it is almost two thousand years already since Europe, as well as the entire world, has tried to appear more intelligent than God, and has refused to give God the veneration due Him."

Then the specifics tumbled out: "How can we describe the outrages to God in the newspapers and books of the past twenty years? How can we describe the criminal abortions over the years performed in the name of so-called science and social advancement? How can we describe the corruption in the lives of numerous husbands and wives? How can we describe the evil that the pagan fashions of the women of our day have brought? How can we describe the debauchery and immorality to be seen on the beaches and at the bathing places? It is enough to recall our own river, the Sava. But what good does it do to prolong this list? The Prophet summed up

143

all the vices of humanity in a word when he said: 'For my iniquities have gone over my head; and as a heavy burden have become a weight upon me' (Ps 37:5). It is thus that we have measured for God, our Creator."

He had stressed that word "measured." He now paused long enough for his hearers to catch the emphasis. Then he applied his parable: "It is completely understandable, then, that God has measured out for us just as did the peasant. For Christ Himself once said: 'with what measure you mete, it shall be measured to you again' (Mt 7:2). And God has meted to humanity a just measure. He reduces to ashes and dust the cities which have forgotten their duty of honoring their God. He reduces to dust and ashes the villages that take His most Sacred Name in vain and violate the Lord's Day instead of blessing Him for the bread He gives them to eat and the air they breathe. He reduces to dust and ashes men's works of art so that they might know that the most beautiful work of art is the human soul, a pure human soul, the temple of the living God, which so many people have turned, by their sins, into a robbers' den. It is today that the words of the Apostle, St. Paul, are realized: 'It is a fearful thing to fall into the hands of the living God' (Heb 10:31). Since, on account of our sins, we have fallen into the hands of the living God, who destroys not only individual cities and villages, but also entire nations, our good sense tells us that we must humble ourselves before God like the debauched Ninevites, and that we must repent with a sincere penance for our sins which cry to Heaven for vengeance, if we wish to save ourselves from total ruin. And these are the reasons for which we have prayed this whole month, and for which we have had our Procession of Penance."

144

The Minister of Public Instruction was seen to sit back relieved, and those about him seemed prepared to put away their pencils and notebooks. Many in the Cathedral thought His Excellency might stop there— a brief sermon, but a pointed one. A homely little parable, but one that not only went home, but one they could take home. For bread and butter to them were as familiar as the flowers of the fields and the birds of the air had ever been to the men and women of Christ's day. But the entire edifice was startled by the Archbishop's next words: "This provides the opportunity to reply in public to innumerable officious advisors of both the Left and the Right, who suggest to the representatives of the Catholic Church just how they should proceed so that the guilt for numerous crimes that have been committed does not fall on that Church."

Now not only the Minister and his aides, but the entire congregation sat up as if electrified.

"Some accuse us of not raising our voice in time against crimes which have been perpetrated in certain sections of our country.... We reply, first of all, we are not, nor do we wish to be, a political trumpet of any sort, blowing according to the desires and momentary needs of certain parties or individuals." The Archbishop's voice rose as he went on: "We have always asserted the value in public life of the principles of the Eternal Law of God without regard to whether it applied to Croats, Serbs, Jews, Bohemians, Catholics, Mohammedans, or Orthodox! We cannot physically force anyone to fulfill the Eternal Laws of God, because every man has free will, and each will answer for his actions according to the words of the Apostle: 'For everyone shall bear his own burden' (Gal 6:5). It was with vehemence that His Excellency all but shouted: "For this reason we are unable to answer longer for those hotheads and extremists among the clergy. The future will show that the Catholic Church has not failed in its duty; that will be demonstrated beyond all doubt when things can be discussed more calmly, and all the facts are in.

"But today we wish to propose a question to certain groups and national organizations: Was it the Catholic Church that provoked this war which has had such terrible consequences—or was it someone else? . . . Was it the Catholic Church which, year after year, created in the souls of men the discontent and brutality which has had such tragic results—or was it someone else? How many times in the past twenty years has the Catholic Church reminded all the representatives of the intellectual and political communities that they should cease trampling on human and national rights, that they should cease destroying the generous humanity and the genuine morality of the people through the press and the cinema? All in vain! The wind blew despite our efforts and became the terrible storm which all true Catholics regret profoundly, but which all our most loyal efforts could not prevent. And for that we reply to the first group of those who reproach us: It is in you that is realized the story of the peasant and the baker! . . . And if anyone thinks that the Catholic Church trembles before the future on account of its conduct, he is in error. The Church stands serene, with a clear conscience, ready to face any situation which may arise."

Before that strong and defiant statement had been fully assimilated, the Archbishop was going on: "We reply to those who accuse us of pro-Communism, and of alleged inaction, that the Catholic Church is not an institution that lasts from today until tomorrow, but an organization that has survived, and will yet survive, innumerable states, nations, and transformations. It is not an institution that would make an agreement with Communism today and tomorrow deny that agreement and fight a war of extermination."

Many faces lit up at that direct thrust at Germany. Others, however, looked around fearfully for Gestapo agents. The Archbishop had always been bold, but this sounded as if he was being too bold. But before they could discover the reaction of any of the Gestapo their attention was magnetized by the Archbishop's next thrust: "The Catholic Church, moreover, has made clear an indefinite number of times what it thinks and where it stands. The Catholic Church can never recognize a system that takes from the peasant his land; from the craftsman his shop; from the private person the fortune acquired through honest work; from the worker the fruits of his labor; and, in general, from man, his very soul." That last phrase rang out through the Cathedral—and chilled.

With the same heat he had been using, His Excellency went on: "If social reforms are indispensable, as they are; if a more just division of goods and lands is needed, and that is what we preach; then no one has proposed a better solution than Pope Leo XIII and Pope Pius XI in their immortal encyclicals: *Rerum Novarum* and *Quadragesimo Anno*. That is *our* social program! It is put to work to perfection in our religious communities, where such a way of life is uniquely possible because its basis is God, and the bond binding subordinates is Christian charity, sanctified on the Cross of Christ. And when I say we cannot recognize the system that aspires to take from the peasant

147

his land and render him a slave to the State, we rely on more than merely right reason; we rely on the experience which says that our peasant would prefer to die rather than let himself become a slave on his own land."

Nods of vigorous approval followed that statement. But the Archbishop had only begun his condemnation of Communism.

"We cannot tolerate a system that denies the family, which the Church sees as a divine institution and the fundamental unit of every nation. To wish to make a man and woman husband and wife only for the time sexual relations exist, to wish to take from the family its sacred sacramental character, to prevent it from being the source of life and the place for the education of the children, to wish to take the child from its parents and declare him the property of the State—all that means undermining the very principles of that Natural Law of life, and the destruction not only of the family but of the nation and the national community as well."

The vast throng was held transfixed by the slim figure in the pulpit and saw his pale face take on a thin flush as he now lashed out at the Communistic regime and its attitude toward Religion. "We cannot recognize a system that would deny God Himself, the Creator of the Universe, and reduce the profession of belief in Him to the interior of four walls, where no one could hear or see us. We cannot recognize a system which refuses to little children the knowledge of God which is given them by religious instructions in schools taught by priests. If the entire visible universe is the creation of God—and it is not the result of fortuitous chance, for chance is the god of fools— then the entire universe must revere God, it must revere Him in all phases of public life!"

Never was the Primate more vigorous than in his closing remarks in his reply concerning Communism. He gave now what was a personal Profession of Faith: "This is our point of view, from which we will not retreat even at the cost of our life! And the future will show, as always, that the Catholic Church has been right, and that it cannot be otherwise. We do not profess these principles from today to tomorrow; we do not profess them through fear, or out of personal interests; but only because of interior necessity, conscious that this profession conforms to the Will of God, the Creator."

The Primate paused, surveyed his audience with a rare intentness. Then went on: "This is our reply to the charge that the Catholic Church is disposed toward pro-Communism, or is, perhaps, partial to it. But those people who reproach us in such a manner would, perhaps, do better if they would knock on the door of their own consciences and ask this question: Are there not a great number of people who took refuge in the forests, not because of a conviction of the truth of Communism, but very often out of despair, on account of the brutal methods of a few thoughtless individuals who thought they could do anything they liked, and that there was, for them, no law human or Divine? Is it not here that the story of the peasant and the baker is illustrated? Was the Church able to prevent this terrible destruction, although it condemned it, when its teachings were so cynically spurned?"

That query was for the *Ustashi* beyond doubt—and what a piercing point it made these days when the ranks of the *Partisans* were swelling. But before the congregation could recover from this direct attack on the ruling powers, they heard their Primate attacking another charge and another enemy. "Finally," he was saying, "we will answer those who accuse us of favoring racism, because, as you know, in the minds of some people, the Catholic Church is capable of anything. We have defined our position concerning racism ever since it existed, and not merely now. That position is brief and precise. The Catholic Church knows nothing of races born to rule and races doomed to slavery. The Catholic Church knows races and nations only as creatures of God, and if it esteems one more than others, it is because it possesses a more generous heart, not because it may happen to have a stronger arm. For it, the Negro of Central Africa is as much a man as is the European. For it, the King in a royal palace is, as a man, exactly the same as the lowest pauper or gypsy in his tent. It sees no difference between them. Both possess an immortal soul, both have the same royal origin, finding their source in God the Creator. That is the racial doctrine of the Catholic Church, and anything else is vulgar speculation and mean innuendo."

Now he sounded almost angry as he thundered: "The Catholic Church cannot admit that one race or one nation, because it is more numerous or better armed, may do violence to a smaller nation with fewer people. We cannot admit that innocent people may be killed because someone, say a frontier guard has, perhaps, killed a soldier, even if he is of a more noble race. The system of shooting hundreds of hostages for a crime, when the person guilty of the crime cannot be found, is a pagan system which results only in evil. It is absolutely certain that if order is sought with such measures, many people who up to now have obeyed the voice of the Church, although exposed to terror, will finally attempt to find safety in the forests. Is it not again, then, the realization of the story of the baker and the peasant?"

The hearers knew well to whom and to what the Primate was referring. Villages had been burned, and all the villagers killed, because a single German soldier had been shot by someone near the village. And even the *Ustashi* seemed to have indulged in the same terroristic tactic from time to time. Heads were nodding in agreement: "with what measure you mete out. . . ."

But now the Archbishop was concluding. "Finally, I realize the question in the minds of the thousands listening to me is: What order does the Catholic Church propose at a time when the whole world is fighting for a new order? I will tell you. . . .

"We condemn all injustice; all murder of innocent people; all burnings of peaceful villages; all killings; all exploitation of the poor. We sorrow for the miseries and the sadness of all who suffer today unjustly, and we reply: The Catholic Church upholds that order which is as old as the Ten Commandments of God. We are not for that order which is written on perishable paper, but for that which is written by the hand of the living God on the consciences of men.

"The basis of this order is God, our Lord, who does not lose Himself in rhetoric as do earthly lawgivers, but has summed up the whole order in the words of the Ten Commandments. We must give honor and glory to God, since He is our Maker; to our parents, superiors, and to our country—love, obedience, and sacrifice if that is necessary. Our neighbor, no matter what his name, is not a cog in the machine of the State, whether he be colored red, black, grey or green, but is a free child of God, and our brother in Christ. That is why we must recognize in our neighbor the right to life, to fortune, and to honor; because it is written: Thou shalt not kill; Thou shalt

151

not steal; Thou shalt not bear false witness against thy neighbor! We must respect his family, because it is written by the hand of God: Thou shalt not covet thy neighbor's wife; Thou shalt not covet thy neighbor's goods! We must respect ourselves, because it is written: Thou shalt not commit adultery! It would be a very grave mistake to think that in this order there is no Last Judgment for those who violate it. All this frightful chaos which the world is now enduring is only punishment for the violation of the Ten Commandments, and because of contempt for the Gospel of Jesus Christ. And if humanity does not wish to recognize again the Divine Authority which is above it, then it is certain that the hand of God will strike again and even more rigorously.... Is it not, again, the case of the peasant and the baker?"

It had been a thunderous sermon. The prelate's words reverberated around the walls of the ancient Cathedral, and held all in the audience literally spellbound. But not all from approval of his words! Most thought he had ended his reply to his critics, and were on the verge of moving toward the aisles. He had rounded off his sermon perfectly by bringing them back to the parable with which he had opened. But His Excellency had not yet left the pulpit. He was looking down over the vast audience with a more benign expression than had been on his handsome features all night. His tone of voice changed, and his whole person and personality seemed to take on a totally different attitude as he said: "My dear brothers . . . our Procession of Penance comes to an end. When Jesus, our Savior, passed by the town of Jericho, two blind men cried out to Him: 'Jesus, Son of David, have mercy on us!'—'What would you have me do?' asked Jesus.—'Lord, that we might see,' replied the blind men. And we end our Procession with the ardent prayer: Lord, let all those who are blind see, and let them realize that there is neither peace nor happiness for any man, for any family, for any nation or state without You, God the Creator. Because it was written for today, and forever: 'If the Lord does not build a house, in vain do they labor who would build it'; and, 'If the Lord does not watch over a city, in vain do they watch who would guard it.' Let all men learn to know that You are our Father, and that we all, regardless of color, language or shape, are your children, and among ourselves, brothers. If we have erred up to now in taking roads that lead to ruin, let us return to the way of Your Commandments, to the path of the Gospel of Christ, which to the blind may seem hard and bitter, but which alone can make happy all men and all nations. Amen."

The mighty throng was slow in dispersing. Knots gathered here and there outside the Cathedral and in front of the *Kaptol* discussing the tremendous address. All had been stirred. The truths told had not been new, but the way they had been told was mighty new. As the Minister of Public Instruction's car pulled away from the curb many recognized him and wondered what the reaction of the government would be. Others spotted members of the Gestapo, and of the OZNA, and wondered just what the Occupying Forces would have to say—and what they would do. And what of the *Partisans*? For no one could miss the targets His Excellency had seen fit to shoot at, nor the accuracy of his shooting. That he had demolished all the charges made against him and against the Church no one doubted. But many wondered aloud just how the frontal attacks he had made on everyone in power of any kind in Croatia would be met.

In the office of *Hrvatska Strazha,* the Catholic daily, there was ambivalence. Monsignor Shimrak burned with desire to print the sermon *verbatim.* His assistant editor kept reminding him of the prohibition of the government. "If he can be so fearless, shouldn't we be ashamed of our conformity?" was the Editor's argument. But his assistant kept urging prudence, and insisting that their paper was only a paper and not the Primate of Croatia. They could be suppressed by Government order; the Primate was almost untouchable because of his position and his popularity with the masses. He had international standing because of his prelacy, and had the respected and feared Vatican behind him. What did they have? The discussion was heated, but the assistant finally won his point.

"You've heard me refer to the necessity for asbestos for His Excellency's early pronouncements, but let me tell you our presses would turn to masses of melted metal if we ever tried to put that sermon on them," was his admiring remark and his effort to set his superior's face smiling.

In another office, not far away, another argument was in progress which would end in no smile. The Minister of Public Instruction was adamant: something had to be done—and done quickly. He had privately taken the *Poglavnik* to task for not having followed earlier advice to silence the Primate. Now in public he was urging his writers to get to the task of tearing His Excellency apart— somehow—he did not care exactly how. If they could not do it, he would do it himself.

Six days later, on November 6, 1943, the results of that conference were in the hands of the public. *Nova Hrvatska,* a daily with wide circulation, carried the bold, black, heading THE COMPETENT AND THE INCOM-

PETENT over a long article with the imposing by-line: Dr. Julije Makanec, Minister of Public Instruction.

It was a cleverly written article, but no one could fail to recognize it as a direct attack on the Archbishop and his sermon. It began with a laudation of Europe and Europeans: "Europe is the continent where the human spirit has attained its highest level," was the opening sentence. Not many Europeans would be inclined to question that statement. But any good rhetorician would recognize it as an effort *"reddere eos benevolos."* "To render your audience benevolent" is the rule for any good introduction. Mackanec, if it was he who actually composed the piece, knew his Rhetoric. His next sentence, however, could and would be disputed. But it was the sentence which set the tone for the rest of the article: "If man is the image of God, then European man is so to a special degree."

He was not long in letting his reader know the point and purpose of his article; for early in this opening paragraph he lifted words right out of the Archbishop's sermon as he asked: "What would the world be today without all that the European spirit has created? The European man is without doubt more an image of God than is a Negro in Central Africa. A Gothic Cathedral surely reflects eternity in a more intense and sublime manner than a Negro's filthy hut, or a Gypsy's tent; the Ninth Symphony is certainly nearer to God than the howling of a cannibal tribe of Australia."

Not many readers would ask themselves if there were any cannibals in Australia. But no reader would ask if the Minister were getting bitter.

"Nationalism is the child of the European spirit," was the topic sentence in the next paragraph, and no one

155

with a nose could fail to smell Naziism, nor, as he read on in this second paragraph fail to measure the towering height of the *hubris*—that satanic pride—which had made Naziism. For Mackanec sounded worse than Hitler as he went on: "It is only the European mind that knows large groups of people united, not for any material profit, but by a belief in a higher common vocation and the feeling of a need for its own common expression. Only in Europe are there nations formed as moral and political units, whose life is directed to a higher spiritual goal. If national movements have appeared elsewhere outside of Europe, they are direct or indirect consequences of European influences.

"This sublime thought, that every wholly valid nation is a special idea of God, that it incarnates in itself, in a singular and peculiar manner, the idea of humanity, and is, for that very reason, indispensable to humanity—this thought was born in Europe." The Minister was sounding lofty. But what was he actually saying? What was he trying to sell? It was not undiluted Naziism. Nor could it be Communism. For already he had used the word "spiritual" and had just now spoken of *God*. But what is all this about a nation being "indispensable" to humanity? But not many readers could stop long enough to ask what the Minister was saying. They rushed on to see what he had to say.

"Every civilized nation takes for one of its highest duties the preservation and development of its individuality. The final goal of each national struggle is the preservation of the national individuality, the national immortal soul, which God alone has instilled in the nation. And on account of this, each thinking member of society considers it his sacred duty to collaborate in this struggle.

156

And rightly so, because it is directed toward the preservation of those things the nation regards as its highest values and which alone gain for it the character of a sacred thing—and every struggle one wages for a sacred thing is holy."

Hurried readers might begin to consider their Minister of Public Instruction something of a mystic. He most certainly was God-conscious. Just look how he uses those words so familiar and precious to Catholics: God, image of God, immortal soul, sacred duty, etc., etc. But the unhurried might stop there and say: "Pseudo-mystic—and like all 'pseudoes' quite superficial when sounding sublime, and totally mistaken while sounding so sure. Yet the next sentence would catch the eye of all: "To preserve its own individuality, received from God, is one of the highest ethical, even religious duties of a nation; because, in this struggle for personal spiritual preservation the nation fulfills the Will of God."

The article went on for some time with this kind of special pleading for the nation as an idea of God, spoke of the blood spilled and sacrifices made to preserve the national individuality, and quite a few of the readers could thus early and quite easily have wearied of the welter of words had not the Minister—or his writers—suddenly stated: "He cannot be national who does not understand the value of the national state with regard to national freedom and independence, or, at least, esteems it too little, and speaks of it as something ephemeral and of small importance.

"If its own national state, to which a nation has a right according to the Will of God, is the most important and sacred thing for every living nation, then its greatest enemy is he who wishes to rob it of that national state.

157

Anyone is an unworthy son of his own nation who respects too little or disdains this national struggle for a national state, who holds himself aloof from this sacred struggle and who even appropriates to himself the right, being on the side lines out of danger, to cast words of reproach against those who suffer for their nation pain and bloody wounds, but who completely forgets to blame those who destroy his nation, his home, tear down his house, his state, and force it into a life without honor, unworthy of a servant or a slave."

There seemed to be too much talk about God and His Will, about the sacredness of the struggle and the nations, commingled with passion, bitterness, and even brutality to make this article palatable to the discerning. But in disturbed times not many are truly discerning. So most read on avidly.

"The reality in which we live is hard and cruel. And the Croatian people are placed in this reality. This reality does not conform to our thoughts and our desires; it is what it is. We must preserve ourselves in it if we wish to fulfill our duty to ourselves. Combat, blood, suffering, misery are not novelties to the Croatian people who have bled for thirteen centuries in our geopolitically dangerous territory on which we live. Whence come these sufferings, this blood, these pains? Are the Croatian people so wicked, so vicious that they must regard in these secular trials the punishment for the violation of the Ten Commandments of God?"

Those who had been in the Procession of Penance and had heard the Archbishop recognized that last thrust. They had to conclude that either the Minister had been there himself, or that he had some superb reporters. They became more interested.

"Are the Croatian people in their depression and penitent discouragement now going to grovel upon the earth like worms, begging mercy from their enemies, because they are so wicked and corrupt? Is it not in this way that they would reap only the disdain and repugnance of all their neighbors and of all the strong nations that exist and that have steeled themselves in struggles and sufferings?"

Not many readers caught the twist Makanec had given the Archbishop's words. He had never asked anyone to beg mercy from their enemies; he had told all his hearers—and through them, the State—to beg mercy from God. But if anyone had caught it, he would soon forget it as he was swept along by the Minister's next appeal to Croatian dignity and pride.

"The Croatian people are too proud of their own value and of the justice of their struggle to accept the philosophy of a worm crushed underfoot. The Croatian people believe in the ethics of suffering. They know the Almighty often strikes hardest exactly those whom He loves the most, exactly those whom He has chosen for the greatest things. He strikes them with harsh trials and miseries to see if they will persevere courageously in the trials, and thus show themselves sufficiently worthy of the vocation He has reserved for them in His great wisdom."

Every priest who read that article had to be angered at the way this man was twisting theological truths; angered the more as they realized that many an uneducated Catholic would hear echoes of the Bible, God's inspired word, in the rantings of this official. How many of the peasants would be able to distinguish between those God loved and tried to make more lovable, and those whom He justly punished for their sins, by these

159

trials? The priests had to admit the article had been written with diabolical cleverness; so diabolical it was almost blasphemous, as they saw in the next short paragraph wherein the Minister had said:

"It is with such a feeling, and with such a conviction, with such a philosophy of an heroic and righteous man that the Croat suffers the Calvary of today, and not with the philosophy of a being who has neither pride, nor backbone, nor faith in his own value and in the justice of his deeds—the philosophy of a worm."

The Minister now grew vitriolic as he cleverly retorted the Archbishop by using His Excellency's own words and phrases.

"Who appears on the scene today as an enemy of the Croatian people and their State? Who has brought to Croatia these terrible blows which bleed it today? Is it not those who wish to 'take from the peasant his land, from the craftsman his shop . . . and from man in general his soul'? Is it not those who wish to take 'from the family its holy and sacramental character and to prevent it from being the source of life and the place for the education of the children'? Is it not those who desire 'to shake the very principles of the Natural Law of life'? Is it not those who wish to 'forbid little children the knowledge of God' and generally to stamp out the image of God in the human soul?"

That was a frontal attack on Communism, but that it was also a frontal attack on the Archbishop was evident from the next line: "The Episcopate of Spain may serve as an example and model to all others respecting the just appreciation of the danger that comes from this adversary of the national liberty of the civilized life of every nation in Europe, as well as the very principles of Christian civilization. In the fight against this adversary it has not stood to one side, nor has it adopted a lukewarm and vague attitude." Then came an emotional appeal that blew hot with hate and love. . . .

"In the bloody and inexorable fight against these satanic adversaries Croatian lives are snuffed out every day, and the best sons of Croatia are dying. All their sacrifices—do they not merit a single word of eulogy and recognition? Do not men who find themselves in danger every day in the fight against this serpentine and heartless enemy, men for whose lives their dearest ones—their wives, mothers, sisters, and defenseless children—tremble every day; do not these heroes and unhappy men, these soldiers and martyrs who defend with their blood the sacred and just rights of their people, merit nothing else than that this man, who lives outside of all danger— thanks to their pain and suffering—should address them words of reproach and, instead of words of praise and recognition, speak to them just as he does to those who ravage and coldly, purposefully devastate our Croatian countryside in order to prepare for the final catastrophe of Croatian national freedom?

"Croatians are, for the most part, a Catholic people. They were always good sons of the Church and they want to remain so in the future. They see in a Catholic priest the servant of God who has his sphere of sublime obliga- tions, obligations which are not of this world. For the obligations of this world the Croatians have had secular leaders, and they have them today. It would not be at all opportune for men who neither know nor have a feeling for secular problems, who cannot accustom themselves to the harshness of this world, who are devoid of every political instinct and of every talent for penetrating to the essence of this fatal struggle of our day; it would not be opportune that such men, however unknowingly, spread political confusion and defection among the soldiers who defend with their lives not only the foundations of the Croatian State but also the Catholic Church against an enemy who would, without mercy, cut the throat of the organization of the Catholic Church as soon as there were no more soldiers, or as soon as they succumbed in battle. It is not necessary to particularly emphasize that all other sects recognized and defended by law would meet the same fate.

"Among all political faults, the worst is to cut off the branch on which one is sitting. God has destined for each class its sphere of obligations. That is why it is best that everyone remain in the field to which he has been called and in which he is competent. This is entirely valid for that high ecclesiastical dignitary who has, recently, in his sermons, passed beyond the limits of his vocation and begun to meddle in affairs in which he is not competent. He who does not understand the meaning of the political struggle, who has no comprehension of political values, and who does not know how to weigh and evaluate them, will always do his best to keep himself aloof from the political sphere, leaving these things to those more competent, to those whom God has destined for the struggle to be at the head of their people as the political and military leaders who carry on their backs the responsibility of the national fate. It is in this way that he would be most useful to the Catholic Church and the Croatian people, who will not allow themselves to stray from the road of honor and pride because of any trickery, and who will not do so after such an example as our neighbor to the west has given us. It is easy, being on the brink of a precipice, to fall into the abyss of dishonor and infamy, but it is very difficult to climb out again. He alone who knows very well the land to which the road leads, because he has travelled it frequently and has lived there, can successfully lead the people, but never he who is a stranger to this land. He cannot be guide there, but rather he needs a guide himself."

After reading that ranting, one might be tempted to say that the Minister of Public Instruction for the Independent State of Croatia had missed the whole point of the Archbishop's sermon; and in yielding to that temptation he would not be wrong. But when one reads the communication that came to the head of the Croat Government regarding the reaction abroad to the Primate's sermon, one sees that the Minister had reason to fear— yet no justification for the vicious attack. He had missed the point. The Good Shepherd and the Good Samaritan had simply told the heroes of the land and the leaders of the State, as well as the erring among the Croats, among the Nazis, the Fascists, and the Communists that there was but one way to honor, to dignity, and to peace: God's way. But the Minister could not hear him when such reports as this kept coming in even from abroad:

"The undersigned has the honor of communicating that the radio stations of the enemy are exploiting the notorious sermon of the Archbishop, Dr. Aloysius Stepinac, in a way that suits their purposes.

"On the twenty-eighth of this month the London station transmitted the following on a program in the Serbo-Croat language at 1:15 P.M.:

'In Yugoslavia the Germans are making their persecutions harsher in order to break the courage of

163

the Serbs, Croats, and Slovenes who are fighting for their liberation.

According to reports from Zurich, the most recent victims of the Germans are twenty-three priests whom the Germans have arrested in Dalmatia. The priests referred in their churches to a sermon delivered recently by the Archbishop of Zagreb. The priests said that the sermon of the Archbishop was in accord with the spirit of the Catholic Church. The arrest of these priests provoked great anger among the people. Their fate is not known, but more serious news is awaited.

Reports state that the Quisling press in Yugoslavia announced that the Archbishop had said: "The Catholic Church recognizes all races and nationalities as creatures of God, and all of them are equal in the eyes of the Church." The Quislings say that the Archbishop tried to justify the fight of the *Partisans,* and that he described the bombardment of Germany as Divine vengeance.'"

One will look in vain among the statements of the Archbishop for anything referring to the bombardment of Germany, or any direct mention of the *Partisans* as being justifiable. But not many listeners to the radio, and few readers of the press, would ever take time to search the writings of the Primate. Dr. Jules Makanec, Minister of Public Instruction, knew this. Hence the brazenness of his attack on Stepinac.

What effect did the attack have on the Primate? None at all if we are to judge from the steady stream of letters which issued from the *Kaptol,* addressed to German, Italian, and *Ustashi* Ministers. No slightest trace of timidity is noticeable in any of the correspondence.

To the German Minister in Zagreb he wrote: "About eight days ago the Vicar of the Parish of Kravarsko, Francis Genc, was arrested and taken away with twenty men of the same place, by individuals belonging to the German Army. At the moment they are all in Sisak, detained by the German Police.... I earnestly beg Your Excellency to take measures to release the above mentioned persons as soon as possible." Then a few days later, of the same General to whom he was sending the list of names of those taken from Kravasko, he asked: "Is there no way to avoid the rape of women and the murder of an old peasant who wished to defend the honor of his grand-daughter? The people have been plunged into black despair."

The result?—A letter from the Minister of the Interior of the Independent State of Croatia informing the Archbishop that a request had been submitted to "competent German authorities for the removal of this army division from the territory of the Independent State of Croatia."

Less than a month later von Horstenau was hearing from the Archbishop again about a similar incident in the village of Hrusevica. Fifty men were taken to prison. His Excellency simply said: "The wives and children of these unhappy families ask that they (the prisoners) be returned to their homes. Let only those be kept in prison against whom there is some proof of criminal action." The General made speedy reply and promised that the men listed would be liberated.

It would appear that the Primate paid no attention to Makanec's attack. But in a scorching letter to Raffaello Casertano, the Italian Minister of Zagreb, Stepinac seems to be referring indirectly at least to one passage in the attack which told him to stay out of political matters.

Italy had not only occupied Croatia along with the Germans, but had even annexed certain portions of the State. The Archbishop minced no words as he wrote to the Minister. The letter merits full quote.

Excellency:

With reference to my letter to you of Feb. 6 last, informing you of the excesses of Italian troops who, in a certain village of my archdiocese, have dishonored the Italian Army, I wish to transmit sworn statements regarding these acts. . . . This is proof that my letter was not written in undue haste or as the result of nervousness, but was the consequence of the facts, all of which have been fully confirmed.

Excellency, these excesses, as well as the treatment of Croats interned in concentration camps in Italy, are obstacles to the real friendship of Croatia and Italy. The Italian authorities have promised to repatriate the internees in Italy, a policy which fills our heart with joy and satisfaction. I hope that the Italian military authorities in Croatia, on the request of Your Excellency, have ceased and will cease from acts such as those described in this report.

This state of affairs has a religious as well as a political and national aspect. Natural Law is involved, which should be respected in conscience by all. There is the special factor that the Italian people is profoundly Catholic and has the great good fortune to have the Vicar of Christ in its capital. This makes all the more repugnant outrages and scandal on the part of those belonging to the noble and Catholic Italian people, especially when these acts are offensive to the rights of Croats living in occupied or annexed territory.

It is to be observed that in Croat territory annexed by Italy, there is a steady decline in religious life and a certain tendency to pass from Catholicism to the schismatics. The responsibility and guilt for this situation, before God and posterity, will be Catholic Italy's.

The religious character of the problem obliges me, as responsible for the religious welfare of Croatia, to write Your Excellency in this vein. I hope Your Excellency will take these comments in the proper spirit. I write not as a diplomat or a politician, but as a representative of the Catholic Church which must preach always and everywhere Truth, Goodness, Justice, and Peace.

I trust that Your Excellency has observed that I have striven to defend the rights of others as well as those of our own without distinction. I do so now, and will always in the future defend the rights of my people who for thirteen centuries on this Adriatic coast have contributed much to the common civilization—the Christian civilization—of Italy and Croatia.

I am always ready to discuss these matters of common interest and justice with Your Excellency personally.

With expression of greatest esteem, I am
(signed) Aloysius
Archbishop of Zagreb

By the end of 1943 Aloysius Stepinac saw that he and his people had another and more potent enemy to face. He would do it as he had always done: with Faith and Fortitude.

167

❖❖

6 The Irresistible and the Immovable

IN THE SUMMER of 1941 the eyes of the world were focussed on the amazing German Army as it opened a two thousand mile front from the White to the Black Seas. The eyes of the world blinked as that front, with blinding speed, blitzed its way through Lithuania, Latvia, Estonia up to the gates of Leningrad in the north. Then came winter.

But "when winter comes, spring cannot be far behind" so, in the summer of 1942 the world saw the Nazis do in the south what they had done in the north: from Rumania and Bulgaria they sped across the U.S.S.R. to Stalingrad.

Both cities lay under seige. The Soviet Government moved from Moscow to Kuibyshev. It looked as if what had happened in the west of Europe was to be duplicated in the east, and that Hitler would dominate the Continent. But then Franklin Delano Roosevelt and Winston Churchill promised to supply Russia with materials essential for the prosecution of the war. And again came winter.

But this winter was different from the last; for in it came the Russian counter-offensive. Leningrad, after seventeen months of seige, was relieved, while from Stalingrad rolled out an army that captured twenty-two Nazi divisions and pushed the once irresistible Germans back to Kharkov. By the spring of 1943 the Russians had recaptured 185,300 square miles of territory, and had killed an estimated half million Nazis. The world began to hope.

In the following summer the United States poured in supplies, especially planes, from every conceivable angle: through Archangel in the north, through Vladivostok in the far southeast, and even through the Persian Gulf and Iran. Meanwhile Anglo-American bombing was crippling German industry, greatly reducing the output of German planes. This unhinged the plane-tank combination of mechanized warfare which had so electrified the world and won the amazing earlier successes for the *Whermacht*. Before summer was out the Russians had deprived the Nazis of their superiority in the air. And the hope of the world rose higher.

In that same summer the Allies invaded Sicily. At summer's height Benito Mussolini was forced to resign and the twenty-one year Fascist rule was broken. By the fall of 1943 Italy had surrendered to the Allies. And hope rose higher still.

But as the world's hope rose and rose, in what was

170

known as Yugoslavia tensions rose proportionately. For in 1943 Drago Mihailovic, who in 1941 had been promoted to General and designated Minister of War by the Yugoslav Government in Exile, and in 1942 had been commended by the United States of America for the "magnificent resistance" he was leading against the invading Nazis, and in general had been looked upon as the "darling" of the Allied Powers, suddenly lost his place in the hearts of the Western leaders.

The first hint of his displacement came in a radio broadcast from London in which the Serbian's role in the struggle was greatly minimized while that of one Josip Broz Tito was correspondingly enlarged upon. In October of that same year, 1943, Mihailovic received his last shipment of supplies from the United States. Teheran had something to do with this, for there Britain and the United States strove to please Russia who was committed totally to Tito. Why not, wasn't he one of their own?

David Martin, in his book *Ally Betrayed,* says: "Tito was created, not by the political Left but by the political Right, not by the Labor Party and Roosevelt, but by Churchill, Leopold Amery, Brigadier Fitzroy MacClean, Setin Watson and the most conservative of the Yugoslav politicians." His statement gains credence when we hear Churchill himself saying in late 1943: "Marshal Tito has largely sunk his Communistic aspect in his character as Yugoslav patriot leader." The irony of that remark lies in the use of that word "character." Churchill was right, but in the directly opposite meaning of the word; for Tito had assumed a "character." He was play-acting all the time as he posed as Yugoslav patriot. So successfully did he "sink his Communistic aspect" that the Western World did not see him as he was—and is—until after

171

he had achieved his Communistic end. But there were those in Croatia who had sharper eyes, and none sharper than those of Archbishop Stepinac.

By the time of the Quebec Conference between Roosevelt and Churchill it was agreed that all personnel attached to Mihailovic should be withdrawn. Formal recognition of Tito came in November of 1943. The Yugoslav Government in Exile repudiated Mihailovic entirely, and the Allies recognized Tito's "National Committee for Liberation" as the *de facto* Government for Yugoslavia. Britain then sent a "Military Mission" to Yugoslavia headed by General MacClean. In that Mission was Randolph Churchill. They soon arranged for supplies to be sent Tito by air and sea. From then on Tito had things his own way.

But what about the Croatian people? The capitulation by the Italians had given them a breath of freedom; for the Occupational Army was withdrawn and the territory ceded to Italy by the Pact of Rome was recovered. Further, the Croats disarmed many Italian units and captured huge amounts of arms and equipment. But that breathing was not too deep, nor too free; for the *Partisans* had captured even larger amounts of arms and equipment—and set about using them immediately in a way that augured ill for the Independent State of Croatia. Yet strange things were happening among the Croatian people. Perhaps Ivan Babic, in his *Military History of Croatia*, has summarized it best. He says:

The war raged all over the country. It was typical and destructive guerilla warfare. Because the three domestic protagonists—the *Ustashi, Chetniks* and *Partisans*—were extremists, this warfare assumed the most

172

bloody and brutal forms. The atrocities of the *Chetniks* and the *Ustashi* were mostly the product of passion, mutual hate, and nationalistic hysteria; but they were, nevertheless, the work of amateurs. The atrocities of the *Partisans*, however, were the work of experienced, professional terrorists, and were planned with a double purpose: the extermination of all actual and potential contenders for future power, and the deliberate and cunning provocations of German and *Ustashi* repression of the helpless population, which then was forced to take refuge in the *Partisans'* ranks. Thus every instance of destruction and terror, from whichever part it came, worked to the advantage of the *Partisans* and helped them in their drive for power.

Archbishop Stepinac had said the same thing in other words in that sermon of his at the end of the Procession of Penance. He knew exactly what was going on, and did all in his power to alert the rulers of the country to the hard facts. But, as we have seen, they would not listen.

In early 1944 the Russians had penetrated Estonia and were on the borders of pre-war Poland. By summer of the same year the Soviets had reached the mouth of the Danube. Rumania capitulated and was followed a few days later by Bulgaria. Tito flew to Moscow just prior to this and concluded an agreement with the Russians which allowed the Soviets to enter Yugoslavia in pursuit of the common enemy. He stipulated, however, that the *Partisans* should retain political control and the administration in areas under Red occupation. The German army of occupation was continually harassed by the *Partisans* and was unable to halt the advance of the Russians.

173

On October 20 of this year Belgrade was "liberated." Two weeks later Moscow issued a statement saying that the Allies were agreed on having the Yugoslav peoples use their right to choose their own government at the conclusion of the "liberation." The handwriting was on the wall for Pavelic, the *Ustashi* and the Independent State of Croatia.

It was at this time that Archbishop Stepinac addressed a Circular Letter to his Clergy in which are seen the man, the priest, the patriot and the prelate again. He began by saying: "Reverend Brothers: For the past few months world events have been developing with the speed of lightning. The frontiers of states; the governments of nations; the social conditions of the world; the principles and precepts of world systems with their intellectual, social and political maxims, all have an uncertain future and are all subject to change since they are, according to their nature and form, temporal and human, hence ephemeral.

"Only one institution is eternal and imperishable in its existence, in its precepts, and in its judgment of the world; this because it is of divine origin and guided by the Holy Spirit. It is the Church of Christ and its doctrine. Its one Divine Founder has said of it: '. . . the gates of hell shall not prevail against it' (Mt 16:18).

"Although its mission does not consist in establishing the forms of states, directly determining their social intercourse, or judging the controversies of their subjects, its doctrine is of such a nature that it provides the principles and imperishable maxims concerning all phases of human society. It is necessary to warn everyone who seeks new ways to correct and regenerate humanity that the great Pope Leo XIII was right in saying: 'If one is looking

174

for the way to save human society he must know that it is to be found only in the Christian regeneration of public and private life. One should know the axiom that each society must return to its original sources if it wished to attain spiritual renewal' (Leo XIII, 1891, 12, 40). It is necessary, then, that society return to God and His Commandments, for, as the Church is a divine institution, it consequently has the same Creator as human society; but beyond that, it is, according to the divine order, the guardian and teacher of divine knowledge. The Code strongly emphasises that, 'The Church has the right and duty, independent of any civil power whatever, to teach the knowledge of the Gospels to all nations. All are obliged, according to Divine Law, to acquire that knowledge and embrace the true Church of God' (Can. 1322, No. 2).

"It is for this reason that the Church has precisely and irrevocably stated its opposition to every doctrine and theory contrary to its teaching."

Was the Primate already preparing for his collision with Tito? Did he have some special gift of looking into the future? He went on:

"In effect, the first and most important effect of the coming of Christ and His Church is the salvation of souls for eternal life, but His doctrine is so full of life that it is a rich source even for the temporal existence of men, individual, social, and political. The Church of Christ gives us our general directives and also sheds light on those questions which trouble the world today and in the chaos of war, a war that would not be if the voice of the Teacher had been heeded. The questions are these: a) the freedom and worth of the individual as an independent entity; b) the freedom of and respect for Religion; c) the freedom of and respect for every race and nationality;

d) the freedom of and respect for private property as the basis of the personal freedom of the individual and the independence of the family; and, finally, e) the freedom of and respect for the right of every nation to its full development and to independence in its national life."

That was throwing down the gauntlet to Tito and all others of his ilk. The Archbishop did not mean it that way. All he sought to do was recall to his own the truth by which they were to live, and the truth which gives life— not only to the individual, but to nations and states. It is interesting, and enlightening, to study the "freedoms" the Archbishop stresses and the famous "Four Freedoms" of Franklin Delano Roosevelt which became, thanks to a propagandistic press, the slogan for winning the war and, hopefully, "winning the peace." The Primate's are much more profound—and necessary—than the President's. His Excellency stated clearly the reasons he wrote this Letter. He said:

Reverend Brothers, I have several times emphasized the doctrines of the Church in my sermons and in my letters. I have, moreover, reprimanded, not only privately but also in public, all errors and transgressions against the principles of the Church no matter what Commandment of God they concerned. But I have especially condemned those transgressions which relate to the great law of Christian charity toward one's neighbor.

Now, as we approach troubled and uncertain times, I consider it my duty as Archbishop once again to draw your attention to these matters, especially when a great many priests are asking me for counsel and

176

instructions. In thinking of all I have just said, I ask you particularly, Reverend Brothers:

1) That the doctrine of the Church become more alive for us under wartime conditions, waged by the different modern theories, because in this chaos and conflict of diverse ideologies our uninformed faithful and even priests are easily led astray.

2) That individual priests allude to nothing in their writings, in their sermons, or by their actions which relate to things on which the Church alone and its highest authorities have the right and the duty to speak with competence and to pass judgment.

3) I warn you that it is only the Holy See and the Hierarchy which have the right to intervene in the relations that exist between the authorities of the Church and those of the State, and that other ecclesiastics must confine themselves strictly to preaching the Gospel, occupying themselves with spiritual work and the salvation of immortal souls, and leave the 'negotia saecularia' to others according to the words of St. Paul: 'Nemo militans Deo implicat se negotiis saecularibus' (2 Tm 2:4).

4) I warmly recommend to your heart and to your conscience that each one of you remain at his post and that this be a consolation and of spiritual utility to each one himself and to the people who trust in him; do this if there is no particular or personal reason or especially clear indication that it would be better to go in hiding.

5) I command that all sacred vessels, vestments, and other objects of value be put immediately into a safe place in those regions and villages where it is

dangerous or difficult to keep them where they are now.

6) Remember always that the Church has the right and the duty that God has given it to teach the Gospel truths and lead its people to the salvation of their souls, no matter what temporal or civil conditions are found in the world (Can. 1322, No. 2).

Keep always present in your minds in these terrible days the words: 'Your protection is in the Name of the Lord, who created heaven and earth.'

What was all this talk about "uncertain times" and "terrible days"? Well there had been an invasion of Normandy that summer, and Allied armies were racing across France. Hitler could not strengthen his eastern front while his western front was being pushed back toward Berlin, so Russia was rushing toward the same city. That meant that Croatia's *Poglavnik* and his Cabinet had some thinking to do. They did it. That is why the *Ustashi* Minister of Foreign Affairs, Alajbegovic, came to the *Kaptol* one day early in the spring of 1945, to inform the Archbishop that it seemed as if the Germans were determined to defend Zagreb against the onslaughts of the *Partisans* and the Soviet. This could mean the bombing of the city. Would he allow the historically valuable documents of the State, at least the archives of his own Foreign Ministry be kept in the *Kaptol*? The Archbishop saw the value of such documents immediately, and the imminent danger the city was in. So he agreed to keep them for the Minister. Then came a second request that the Primate could hardly have expected from the Pavelic Government: Would he agree to be Regent of the State while the Government went into exile?

"Are they planning to go?" was the natural question. Indeed they were—and soon.

The Archbishop made instantaneous reply to the suggestion that he take over full power of the State. How could he possibly consider such a thing after so often and so vigorously commanding his priests to stay out of politics? He was *spiritual* head of the people of Croatia. He would never even think of being their temporal head.

Of course the Minister pointed to his prestige with the people, their obvious love for him, their ready devotion. The Archbishop was immovable. When the Minister went on to point out the probabilities of the massacre of tens of thousands of citizens, not only from the incoming *Partisans* and Russians, but even from the outgoing Germans and *Ustashi,* the Archbishop frowned in heart-deep concern. Could he do anything to prevent such a horror? There was a possibility: would the Primate visit Machec, head of the Croatian Peasant Party? Machec was under house arrest at the time. The priest in Stepinac came to the fore. He would visit Machec, but visit him as priest, with hope of helping the people who were threatened from so many sides. He went, accompanied by the man who had the keys to Machec's house, the *Ustashi* General Moskov. He talked with Machec about saving the people from the massacres. Machec, naturally, promised to do what he could, and even told the Archbishop that he would remain in Zagreb. He did not do this. But the Archbishop did, despite an offer to get him away from the city before it fell into the hands of the *Partisans.*

Into the hands of the *Partisans* it fell, but that is a story of international power politics whose roots go back

179

decades, and even, in one sense, a century, but whose fruits are being garnered even today. It makes interesting, but not always cheerful reading.

It is quite generally said that Yalta gave Yugoslavia to Tito. There is truth in that statement, but it is not the whole truth. Long before Yalta Tito was—as he is today— a thoroughly committed Communist; as thoroughly committed as ever Stalin was. They split, it is true, but not as Communists. They split over tactics. Many historians will say that the split came on April 12, 1948, when Tito told the Central Committee in very plain language: "This is not a matter here of any theoretical discussion.... Comrades, the point here is, first and foremost, the relations between one state and another." It was an historical statement; because for thirty-one years it had been dogma that Communism implied unconditional support of the Soviet Union. Tito, by differentiating between ideology and independence, had shattered that dogma. He shattered it successfully. But to find out when and where the actual shattering began, we have to go back to the winter of 1941-1942, and enter the wild forests of Bosnia. It was then and there that Tito and his *Partisans*, all unaware, defied Moscow by refusing to cooperate with Mihailovic and his *Chetniks*. That unconscious defiance enabled Tito to seize power unassisted by the Soviets and brought him into head-on collision with the strategy Stalin had so carefully worked out for himself and Communism.

It really was all accident; for the *Partisans,* and Tito himself, were fanatically devoted to both Stalin and Russia at the very time this all took place. This is evidenced by the signs and slogans they painted and scratched on the walls of the towns they captured: "Long Live Stalin" and "Mother Russia." The historical fact is that with the invasion of Russia by the Germans communications between the Comintern and its agents in the field broke down.

Tito attacked Mihailovic, and his *Partisans* "liberated" some town in Serbia. Immediately they proceeded to destroy the administrative structures of those towns and set up an undisguised Communistic dictatorship. Thus, while the end was the same for both Stalin and Tito, the means differed. Stalin was for long-term strategy; Tito, for immediate tactic. Stalin would outwardly respect, conform and cooperate with all "patriotic forces" and thus spare the "prejudices" of the American and British allies. Tito wanted results whether they offended the British and Americans or not.

When contact by radio was again established between the Comintern and its agents, Tito learned that Moscow questioned his tactics and doubted that he was following the "party line." He heard over the radio that he should "take into account the fact that the Soviet Union has treaty-relations with the Yugoslav King and Government, and that anyone taking an open stand against them could create new difficulties in the joint war effort and the relations between the Soviet Union on one hand, and Britain and the United States on the other. Do not consider your fight only from your own national viewpoint, but also from the international standpoint of the British-American-Soviet coalition."

Small wonder Stalin is said to have been "stamping with rage" when he heard what Tito had done and was doing; for his carefully calculated strategy, which would have led him to complete domination of the Balkans had been upset by some guerillas in the Bosnian woods. Just before he set out for the Teheran Conference of the Three

181

Great Powers, Stalin received the news that Tito had been given the title of "Marshal" by the Anti-Fascist Council for the National Liberation of Yugoslavia, and that the Council would declare the Yugoslav Government in Exile illegal, and refuse King Peter permission ever to return to Yugoslavia. It was an "unusually angry" Stalin who appeared at Teheran.

But at Yalta things were a bit different—and Stalin got his way. Here Roosevelt, Churchill and Stalin pledged their joint efforts to assist "liberated" countries in Europe. Of course Yugoslavia had been "liberated." Churchill and Roosevelt pressured the Yugoslav Government in Exile to merge with the Tito apparatus in their country and add six new members to the existing Cabinet. King Peter was amenable and even went so far as to appeal to his people to join the "National Liberation Army." The King gave some recognition to Croatia, however, by appointing Dr. Ivan Subasic, then Ban of Croatia, as one of the new members to the then existing Cabinet. Subasic accepted and met with Ivan Ribar, leader of the Anti-Fascist Council for the National Liberation of Yugoslavia, to draw up a plan for creating a united Yugoslav Government.

This was strategy for Stalin, but Tito would turn it into tactic. Three months after Yalta King Peter again designated Subasic as Premier under a regency composed of a Serb, a Croat, and a Slovene "until the plebescite should be held." But already by March a temporary Government had been set up in Belgrade, but only after some shifting of personnel to satisfy the demands of Tito who was made Minister of Defense, while Subasic became Foreign Minister. In August of that year the National

Front presented its program for the new Yugoslavia. This organization was under the direction of Marshal Tito, and it made the usual claims the world has heard for decades about it being for a "National Democracy." It soon called itself the "Provisional Assembly," and blithely prepared for the "Constituent Assembly," which was to draw up the basic laws for the new Yugoslavia. Opposition to this Assembly was soon voiced. Milan Grol called for more parliamentarianism and greater freedom. He got nowhere. Several Croat members, among them Subasic himself, resigned. But that disturbed neither the Marshal nor the Assembly. On they went with their plans for the plebiscite. This was held in November, 1945 and, as was to be expected from such a "democratic" election, it heavily favored Marshal Tito. Whereupon it was declared that the Monarchy no longer existed, but in its place stood the Federal Peoples Republic of Yugoslavia. A constitution for this Republic was drawn up in January of 1946, modeled with scrupulous fidelity on that of the Soviet of 1936.

But long before this Croatia, the Catholic Church in that land, and the Primate had learned who was ruling that nation as well as all Yugoslavia.

Even before Belgrade was "liberated" Croatia had felt the tentacles of Communism tightening around her. Before World War II was ended the pressure of those tightening tentacles was enough to choke out life. The press and all organs of public communications were under control of the Communist Party. The Interior Department had been penetrated deeply. The Police were under the Party's thumb. Any and all opponents to the Party were terrorized or beaten into submission and acceptance. Soon a Secret Police, modeled on that of Russia's, was not only existent, it was all but omnipresent. Then "People's Courts" were opened, and all "criminals" hauled before them. In these the steps made so familiar by the Soviet were faithfully followed. As one of the Commisars of Justice put it: "In our People's Courts the procedure is simple, short, effective; without any delays oral or direct." In a Dalmatian paper this explanation was printed: "Instructions as to the work and organization of the Courts were given by the Anti-Fascist Council of Croatia. According to these instructions judgments are not to be given by trained jurists under the complicated laws hitherto in force, but are to be made by the best sons of the people, not by the dead letter of the written law, but by the proper, healthy conception of the people. The judges are to be chosen from among the people." And Belgrade Radio stated early in May of this year, 1945, "It is not important that the judges be professional; it is important that they have democratic ideas and are devoted to the Movement. . . ."

In such "Courts" and under such a "legal system," in a period of three days, one hundred and five persons were sentenced to death in Belgrade alone.

As is their wont the Communists went after the workers, the students, and the young. Their one real enemy, of course, was the Catholic Church. Long before the "plebescite" was held they were on the attack against the Church. The press was filled with calumnies against the Catholic Church, the Catholic hierarchy, and the Catholic clergy. When charges of criminality were levelled wholesale on all the above, the hierarchy met and, on March 24, 1945, under the Presidency of Archbishop Stepinac, issued a Pastoral Letter, which began:

Dearly Beloved,

In the past, we Bishops of Croatia, have made known to you our thoughts on matters of supreme moment for your spiritual welfare. In this tragic time of war we lack adequate means of contact with our flock, and it has not been given us in all places and in every parish to alleviate the very grievous ills which have afflicted the faithful of every diocese of Croatia. Because your sorrows, and those of the entire Croatian nation, have been multiplied by your anxiety for the fate of your country, upon which a deluge of falsities and calumnies have descended, we, empowered to act in the name of the Bishops of Croatia gathered in council, consider it our bounden duty to speak to you, most dearly beloved, to rectify certain calumnies and vicious lies which affect the most sacred rights and existence itself of the Catholic Church and the Croatian nation.

That was putting the purpose of the letter plainly enough. That clarity came from the pen of the Archbishop. What followed was the Primate at his honest and most fearless best. He exhorted all to fidelity to God's law and the care of their own individual immortal souls, urged them on to greater trust in God, charity toward their neighbor, and confidence in their Creator and Preserver. He went so far as to tell them they were to do this "even if it means the shedding of your blood." He was ever realistic. He had reason to mention the shedding of blood; for after asserting that "All criminals, of whatever political leaning, must be brought to justice and punished for their crimes," and adding: "If any priest, a rare occurrence, has injured others in their rights, we shall not

185

hesitate to impose ecclesiastical sanction against him even to deprive him of his sacerdotal or religious status," he went on:

But from the depth of our soul we protest before God and mankind against the systematic murder and persecution of innocent priests and Catholic faithful, many of whose lives excel in sanctity, upon whom the maddened enemies of the Church have brought death. The enemies of the Catholic Church, especially the followers of materialistic Communism, which the entire Croatian nation rejects (he who would dare to assert the contrary, would be lying to the whole world), have in Croatia exterminated by fire and sword priests and the more outstanding of the faithful.

It is apparent why they accuse all bishops, priests, and religious as war criminals; why they attempt to foist accusations upon them. In the civilized world, however, not a single person will be found to approve such flimsy and arbitrary charges, or believe that bishops, priests, and well-known religious communities are war criminals, worthy of capital punishment; as perpetrators of massacres. Perpetually shall the blood of these heroic martyrs cry out in accusation against those who use murder as a means to power.

The Catholic Bishops of Croatia are prepared and ready to have each individual case investigated by representatives of other nations and by an international committee. In this way the charge of war criminality will be proved a lie, and simply a means of exterminating those who oppose and want no part of Communism.

Wherefore the Croatian Bishops recommend that a committee be set up to examine all cases, to gather facts for presentation to an international commission. Thus the truth will become apparent, how lies have been made the instrument of an ideology, whose followers seek, in every possible way, to enslave the entire world, despite their numerical inferiority. In Croatia their number is literally microscopic.

That was too honest a solution for the Communists. That was too open a vigorous attack on them and their system. Feeling strong enough, even in Zagreb, they proceded to arrest the Archbishop and put him in prison. That was on May 17, 1945. For seventeen days, without any charge against him being formally presented, he stayed in that prison. Then, just as suddenly as he had been arrested without formal charge, he was as suddenly released from prison without any given reason for discharge. However, he was not free. He was under "house arrest."

Two days after his release from prison the reason for his "freedom" was clear: Marshal Tito was visiting Zagreb. The State authorities expressed a desire that, in the name of the Catholic Church, the higher clergy pay him a visit. The Croatian Government put automobiles at the disposal of the clergy, but no one invited the Primate, nor did any automobile await him at the *Kaptol*. He was under "house arrest." His "Government representatives" were members of the OZNA.

Since the "plebiscite" was still half a year away the Marshal was only Premier of Yugoslavia, but Vladimir Bakaric, then President of the People's Republic of Croatia, had no delusions about who was running the country, nor who would be, after the "plebiscite." Josip Broz Tito was already Communistic dictator—and Bakaric took his dictation. That is why it was the Vicar-General, Francis Salic, one of the Primate's secretaries, who met Tito and told him that he himself was "not competent to give in the name of the Church a statement of any validity, for it is only the Ordinary, Archbishop Stepinac, who can do that, but he has been deprived of his freedom." Tito could only smile to himself at such a statement. He knew where the Archbishop was, and why he was there. This primary meeting with the "Higher Clergy" was but a prelude to the real meeting between the two "Primates" of Croatia. That would come only after this bit of stage-setting had been completed.

Dr. Salic did tell the Marshal that he hoped 1) that the Catholic Church would have complete freedom in carrying out its mission; 2) that it would be able to teach religion freely in all classes; 3) that it would continue to have its Catholic High Schools and Boarding Schools; 4) that Catholic Action and other religious associations would function freely; 5) that it would continue to publish its newspapers and journals without interference in the new State. He ended with: "On this basis a cordial understanding between the Church and the State can develop."

Then Tito, in true Soviet fashion, assured him that he wanted the greatest possible freedom for the Catholic Church in Yugoslavia in regard to Rome, but he also wanted the Slav idea to be propagated. He added that he was not satisfied with the attitude of the Church and the clergy to date. Then he suddenly said: "You would, doubtless, like to know something about Archbishop Stepinac, but I can say nothing about him, since he is where he is at present."

Maybe the Marshal was baiting them, but maybe he was surprised with what he caught. For immediately he was told by the clergy that they looked upon the Archbishop and that he actually was—"the greatest Croatian alive today and a devoted worker for the nation."

When Tito looked his surprise and question, he got his reply. He was told that there were certain members in his own government whose lives had been saved only by the intervention of the Primate; that, during the war, the Archbishop had fed some seven thousand *Partisan* children; that he had defended the Jews, Serbs, Gypsies and saved the lives of many of them; that his was the one strong voice in the nation that protested effectively against racism, hypernationalism, brutality and violence; that even at the time when Pavelic and his police were making every effort to remove him from his position as Primate, the Archbishop went on fearlessly intervening with the same Pavelic on behalf of the poor and those in misery. On and on went the laudation with incontrovertible facts. Then the clergy ended with "We hope with confidence, Marshal, that you will set him free so that he can continue his work for the people and the nation."

Tito looked sober and was silent a moment then made the observation that many priests had been *Ustashi* and even *Ustashi* officials, and added that they had fled the country with the *Ustashi*, but that some had been captured and were now in concentration camps.

The Vicar-General was not intimidated. He told the Marshal that true Croats had always yearned for independence, that when Pavelic and the *Ustashi* took power many believed that they were the instruments who were fulfilling the life-long dream of the Croats and had joined the Movement. But once they saw what the *Ustashi* were doing, they left the Movement. It was true that some had fled the country but there was an explanation for that:

189

some priests were Chaplains in the Army and felt obliged to take care of the soldiers even in exile; that some had been taken away by force; and that others had fled for fear of their lives at the hands of the *Partisans*. When he saw the Marshal bridle a bit at the mention of *Partisans*, he had courage enough to say: "We take the liberty, Marshal, of warning you that the concentration camps, filled with innocent people, will engender unrest and discontent which in no way will be beneficial to the State."

Tito then became suave and assured the clergy that he did not ask everyone to hold the same opinion in politics that he did, but that he did demand that no one interfere with him in his work to consolidate the State. He even admitted that Religion was a very important factor in the life of the people, and promised that nothing would be done by decree of the Government, but only by agreements. Then he stated that he was going to have a speedy investigation made of all who were interned in the camps and free all whose hands were unbloodied.

It was a conciliatory little speech and it emboldened Dr. Salic to call Tito's attention to what the *Partisans* were doing in Zagreb. Salic was diplomat enough to introduce his remarks with: "We are convinced, Marshal, that you neither know nor approve of their outrageous actions, but the fact is that some *Partisans* are going about the city armed with revolvers, preventing nuns from praying with their children, and even transforming some convents and chapels into dormitories for themselves and other people, and removing crucifixes."

Tito immediately replied: "You are quite right: I neither knew, nor approve of this." Then, turning to the President of the Croatian Republic he almost barked: "Bakaric, write all that down."

190

The next day Archbishop Stepinac was released from "house arrest." On June 4 he was face to face with Tito. Count O'Brien tells us that the Primate's opening words were: "I did not come here to ask any favor of you. I came here because you sent for me. You have taken me out of prison for a purpose. Let me remind you what I stand for: I insist upon freedom for all the people. You have given no sign that you intend to respect the Constitution. I am going to resist you on every move in which you disregard the Constitution and the people."

I have no written testimony to prove those words true. But they are "in character." Dr. Bakaric was present at the meeting. His transcript does not carry O'Brien's words, but it does show Stepinac presenting his case for the Church and the people with as much force and clarity as the Count's words indicate. Bakaric states that the purpose of the meeting was to find a common basis for the clarification of the relations between Church and State, and thus prevent, as far as humanly possible, conflict and tension.

The Archbishop accepted that statement at face value and immediately reminded both the President and the Premier of the French proverb: "When there are dissensions in a country, things go badly." Next, that a State is secure only when its citizens are secure, but that citizens can never feel secure unless their rights to freedom of conscience and the practice of their Religion are respected. The Primate touched the nerve center when he informed the Premier that it was the Holy See alone that had competency to settle matters, and that the best way to establish proper relations would be through a Concordat, but that other means were available such as the *modus vivendi* established in old Czechoslovakia. Then he re-

191

minded Tito that the Catholic Church was an organization that numbered more than four hundred million people who, though all did not live up to their religious commitments, exercised, nevertheless, a tremendous impact on public life and public opinion, and that all would be watching the new State to see what its relations would be with the Holy See.

Tito admitted that he understood the importance of the matter and was, in principle, ready to settle it. But he expressed fear over the Holy See's seeming lack of benevolence toward Slavic peoples, and particularly toward the Yugoslavs.

That brought immediate reply from the Primate. "So far as I can see, your fear is utterly without foundation. During the war the Holy See, in a very concrete manner, has shown itself most benevolent. For example, in the question of the Medjurje, a very delicate question for the Croatians, the Holy See did not for a moment give in to the offensive of Hungarian diplomacy; with the result that the Archbishop, though completely alone in facing the Hungarians, was the sole holder of ecclesiastical jurisdiction in the Medjurje during the entire four years of the war, even though Hungarian troops occupied and even annexed the Medjurje. Cardinal Maglione, the Vatican Secretary of State, gave me his word of honor that there would be no change of the *status quo* there so long as the war lasted. That word was kept despite the many difficulties the Hungarians made for the Holy See. And you say the Holy See is lacking in benevolence toward the Yugoslavs?"

When Tito made as if to answer, the Primate went on: "There was a similar question in Dalmatia when the Italians were occupying it. Not for a single moment did the Holy See think of taking the Croatian dioceses there from Croatian Bishops and give them to Italians." The Marshal made as if to interrupt, but the Archbishop went on: "Also, in a general way, the Holy See has shown great respect and friendly feelings toward the Slav nations. All you have to do is recall Leo XIII when Strossmayer had entered into conflict with the Imperial Austrian Court on account of Russia. Then one must never forget that Pius XI founded a special institute in Rome under the name of 'Russicum.' Why look, today, the head of the Sacred Congregation for the Oriental Church is a great friend of the Slavs, Cardinal Tisserant, a Frenchman."

It can be doubted that Tito knew much about the examples the Archbishop had cited. But the Marshal could not doubt about being in the presence of one who knew exactly what he was talking about, and would talk about them forcefully. Josip Broz had faced some forceful men in his rise to power. He had stood eye to eye with Mihailovic. He had stood before Stalin. But he had never confronted anyone stronger, more resolute, more fearless, or more forceful than Aloysius Stepinac. Yet, if the Archbishop appeared resolute, he was talking with a man who was anything but vacillating. Tito thought he could win a point by being specific. He told the Archbishop that the Church should give its support to the State authorities in Istria; for, he rather vehemently insisted, Istria was one of Yugoslavia's provinces.

"If Istria is Croatian, and, hence, Slav," fired back the Archbishop, "it is so only because of the Catholic Church." Surprise showed on Tito's countenance. "Look at the facts," the Archbishop commanded. "All the intellectuals had either fled long ago, or if some stayed, they were denationalized, with one, single, sole exception: the Catholic clergy. These, under an occupation that lasted twenty-five years, not only stayed, but in the face of brutal opposition, kept their native tongue. It was on account of these men that the Holy See had endless difficulties with the Italian Government. I'll give you just one case: that of Monsignor Fogar, Archbishop of Trieste. He was so impartial, and even noticeably friendly toward the Slavs, that he was pressurized by the Government constantly, until finally, they made him resign."

When Tito sat there speechless before the onslaught, the Archbishop grew incisive. "Benevolence toward the Southern Slavs has never been wanting to the Holy See. Why it let it be known informally that it would enter into a Concordat with the last Government of Yugoslavia. But the stupidity of the leading negotiators from Belgrade made a fiasco of this most favorable opportunity. Benevolence? Look at this final fact: All over Yugoslavia wherever you go to church you can hear the Paleoslavic language being used in worship. That is a privilege not shared by the greatest nations in the world. Not by France, not by Germany, not by England. And you speak of benevolence?"

Since the Marshal sat there seemingly in deep thought and somewhat subdued, the Primate took a different tack. "Until now," he said a bit more quietly, "I have been speaking to you as an Archbishop. Let me now add something as a man, a man who considers things in an objective, realistic manner." Tito's head came up. His eyes lit with keener attentiveness. "If you really wish to consolidate the situation here as quickly as possible, you ought, frankly and courageously, meet with the representatives of the Croatian Peasant Party, and with the honest—now note that I say 'honest'— adherents of the

Ustashi Movement." Tito stiffened. "You do not have to make any decisions or compromises, but you can talk with them, all of them. Those who sincerely wish to work for the reconstruction of the State can be welcomed as collaborators. Should they refuse to collaborate, the fault, then, will be theirs, not yours." Tito was frowning. "Why not at least try such a meeting? You've got nothing to lose and everything to gain. Never forget that a wise statesman omits nothing that can possibly contribute to the welfare of his country, and to the happiness and contentment of his countrymen."

Tito nodded thoughtfully. Whether it was agreement or not, neither Stepinac nor Bakaric could tell. When no word came from the Marshal, the Archbishop closed his remarks by reminding Tito of something he most certainly knew; namely, that the Croats were a great people, with a stirring and noble history, but a people who had lost so many in the late war and its attendant circumstances, that another catastrophe could easily mean the extermination of the Slavic peoples in Southern Europe. Hence, the Marshal should make every endeavor humanly possible, to save every human life possible, and save each for the State.

The insistence on the State seemed to please the Marshal. Of course his concept of the State and Stepinac's concept differed as much as night and day. Josip Broz was thinking of Dictatorship; Stepinac, of Democracy. But the use of the word brought reaction from the Marshal. He assured the Archbishop that he would do all in his power to save human lives, but added: "It is not easy. For Justice must be satisfied for the violations— the gravest violations of humanitarian sentiments." Just what that meant, only Tito knew then, and only Tito

195

knows now. For the meeting came to an end on that note. But two "Primates" had met—and each had taken the measure of the other. It is tragically ironic that these two men, born in such very similar circumstances, having lived through all but identical experiences, should find themselves so much alike and so diametrically opposite. Each had been born in a small village of Croatia and into a large family. Each had the same early schooling. True, Stepinac went further in formal schooling. But they began life very much alike.

There is much mystery and more myth about the man the world now knows as Tito. But it seems safe to say that he was born in the tiny village of Kumrovec, the seventh in a family of fifteen, of a father who was Croatian and a mother who was Slovenian. Stepinac, you will recall, was born seventh in a family of twelve in the tiny village of Krasic, of a father who was Croatian to the core. Both Tito, who was then known only as Josip Broz, and Stepinac went to the local schools for their earliest education. But while Broz dropped out at the age of twelve after only four years of formal schooling, Stepinac went on to the Gymnasium.

That was the first break in a parallelism that is striking even though the divergence is even more so. Yet, even in that divergence there is a startling similarity. For if a saint is one who has had a vision, been entranced by an ideal, looked upon a shining star, and then committed himself headlong and wholly to the following of that star so as to achieve the ideal and fulfill the vision, then it can be said that both Stepinac and Broz became saints. But with what a difference due to the vision, the ideal, and the star. One is reminded of "Two roads diverged in a yellow wood"—ànd what has "made all the difference" is the fact that each of these men chose the different roads that diverged. And yet the parallelism remains. Look at it:

When each came of age, they were drafted into the Austro-Hungarian Army and fought in World War I; but Broz went to the Russian Front, while Stepinac was assigned to that in Italy. It was this that "made all the difference"; for while morale was high amongst the Croats who fought on the Italian Front, it was just the opposite among those who did battle near Russia. Both Stepinac and Broz were made prisoners of war; but again the similarity ended with the fact, not with what followed. For while Stepinac, with a strong sense of patriotism, enrolled in the "Yugoslav Legion," Broz practically defected, went into Russia where he remained through the five years of the turbulent Bolshevik revolution and watched the birth of the Soviet Union. By 1920 both were back in Zagreb, but while Stepinac went to College and contemplated marriage, Broz came back with a Russian wife and as a dedicated Communist.

By 1928 each had committed himself fully; for in that year Broz formally joined the Party, while Stepinac went to Rome to study for the priesthood. From 1928 until 1934 both were in comparative seclusion studying for their future roles; but while Stepinac was in a seminary, in the shadow of the Vatican, Broz was in prison. Yet, like Stepinac he had his expert teacher who tutored him most effectively; for, while in prison for his really Communistic activities in Labor Unions, Broz met Mosha Pijade, a brilliant Jewish intellectual from Belgrade, who completed the education Broz had begun in the shadow of the Kremlin. It can be said that each was engaged in a religious education; for Communism is a religion which

197

has as its Bible Karl Marx' *Das Kapital* with Lenin as chief commentator. While Stepinac studied the Fathers of the early Church, Broz was learning about and from the early fathers of Communism. Each had a "Pope": Stepinac had the Vicar of Jesus Christ, Pius XI, Broz had Marshal Stalin. Each looked upon the one and the other not only as having authority, but in cases, being "infallible."

By 1934 each was fully dedicated to a Cause and a Commander; for while Stepinac, in that year, was ordained priest of the most high God and commissioned to spread the Kingdom of God on earth, Josip Broz was made something of a "highpriest" in Communism and missioned to spread the kingdom of man; for, in that year, Milan Gorki, Secretary-General of the Communist Party had spotted Broz. Just as Ante Bauer had spotted Stepinac and had set about seeing to it that he would be his successor in the See of Zagreb and the Primacy of Croatia, so Gorki set about seeing to it that Josip Broz would be his coadjutor with something like "right of succession."

As you recall it was in 1937 that Ante Bauer died and Stepinac took over the Primatial See and began immediately to inject into the Clergy some of his own Apostolic spirit. That same year Milan Gorki died, but under quite different circumstances from those of Ante Bauer. Gorki had been in Paris, working, of course, for the Communist Cause. But suddenly recalled by his "pope" who was then purging his Party, he was unmasked as an "enemy" and summarily shot. Tito, as Josip Broz was now known, succeeded Gorki as Secretary-General of the Yugoslav Communist Party.

Just how Broz escaped the purge which saw more than one hundred Yugoslav Communists, and twenty of the Central Committee itself, done away with, is something of a mystery. But it is also a fact that he did escape it, and not only escaped it, but managed to profit by it. Like Stepinac, Tito set about injecting his own spirit into his closest companions and building up his Party. But while Stepinac did his reorganizing in the open, with love for every man as his motivating principle, broadening his *Caritas* organization for more help to the poor, and bringing into being his Committee for Aid to Refugees, Tito was doing all his organizing on the sly, and who can deny that "hate" for many a man, was—and is—the motivating force behind much of Communism. So the parallelism became more and more divergent.

When they faced one another in Zagreb in 1944 the parallelism and the divergence were at their apex. Each had a Leader who had died—but while Jesus Christ had risen from the tomb glorious and immortal, Marx and Lenin were rotting away in their places of sepulcher. For his Standard Stepinac had the triumphant Cross of Christ, a Standard that can never fall in anything like final defeat. Tito's standard was the hammer and sickle, which had known some temporary triumphs, but which, like all earthly standards is destined one day to fall, and wither away. Each had power; but while Stepinac's had come down from above and was derived from God Almighty, Tito's had come from below, and denied the very existence of God and was being used to blot out if possible all worship of Divinity. Each belonged to the hierarchy; but Tito's stopped at a man who was aging, Joseph Stalin, while Stepinac's went on to the God who is for ages unending. Each had a doctrine to teach and a movement to spread; but while Tito's was utterly materialistic and of this earth most earthy, Stepinac's was

199

from Heaven, and ultimately for Heaven. The end for Tito and his movement is a dead-end—some sort of a materialistic Utopia on earth. For Stepinac vistas open from the earth and time into an Eternity with One who is Life, Beauty, and Love. Towards those two different ends each would use quite different means. One would strive for spiritual perfection for the individual through recognition of objective truth, transcendent beauty, and enduring human and Divine Goodness. The other cared little for the individual as an individual, cared less for objective truth, and the only goodness and beauty he saw was that of the destruction of established society and civilization as we have known it and the erection of a civilization and a society that had no strata and little structure.

The "Archpriest" of Communism would look upon humanity as a great body which needed radical surgery and would readily admit that in using the scalpel membranes would have to be severed, some tissue destroyed, and much blood spilt. That could only mean, and for Tito it actually meant, that human individuals could be looked upon as so much expendable tissue on the body of humanity, some could be cut away, and others utterly destroyed. He would defend the spilling of all such blood as morally right since they furthered "history and society" —which, being interpreted, means "furthering the cause of Communism." The Archbishop of Zagreb would look upon humanity as a great body, but he would see it as the Mystical Body of Christ. Hence, he would find each cell precious, and even priceless, having been bought by "the mighty price" of the shedding of the Blood of Jesus Christ. Thus, Stepinac looked upon every individual human being with reverence, not only with respect. And he would think of himself as a Physician rather than as a surgeon, and would use everything at his disposal as preventive medicine when remedial medication was not called for. He would save every single human being—and save them for the furtherance of Christ's Cause. But for him the end never justified the means, as it does for Communism. So the striking parallelism is startlingly divergent, and explains the confrontation we have just seen and others we are about to see.

Stepinac had measured Josip Broz that day, and ably summed him up in one word: *Irresistible.* For he saw false religious zeal, false religious devotion, false religious fervor, which when coupled with political power was truly irresistible. He sorrowed as he realized that such a Communist had all the fervor, zeal and devotion of the early Christians, but what had been said about the Christians could never be said about these Communists: "Behold how they love...."

Josip Broz Tito had measured Aloysius Stepinac that day, too. And if he had to, could sum him up in a single word: *Immovable.* For he recognized a thoroughly committed man when he saw one. And he was angered to find that this man was a thoroughly committed man of God. But he well knew the power he held in his hands, and he knew how he would use it.

Two men of the twentieth century had faced one another in a room in Zagreb. And yet, it was but a confrontation that was as old as time: that of Good facing Evil. Let it be said without qualification it was the confrontation of Christ and anti-Christ; for no one can question that Aloysius Stepinac was not only for Christ, but actually was Christ inasmuch as he enjoyed and exercised the plenitude of Christ's own priesthood, having been ordained a priest and consecrated a Bishop. Nor should anyone question that Communism, embodied in such men as Josip Broz Tito, is in both the Joannine and Pauline sense anti-Christ.

Stepinac knew what the outcome would be in time, and was quite sure of what it would be for him in both time and Eternity. He would go on with Faith and Fortitude. He would live up to, and live out the motto he had emblazoned on his coat-of-arms: *In Te, Domine, speravi*— In You, O Lord, I have and will trust. He could have continued with the quote: "... *non confundar in aeternum!* I shall not be confounded in Eternity." Now let me explain just how he got that way.

·

7 The Secret

I AM NOT GOING to give you the secret of Josip Broz
Tito, for the simple reason that I do not know it exactly.
But I will say: Let no one sell him short. As pointed out
above this man because of his whole-hearted, whole-
souled commitment to a cause; because of his consistent
and persistent use of any—and every—means to attain his
end; because of his total giving of self in service for the
achievement of his purpose, merits admiration as an
individual. Had he chosen the proper Cause—the Kingdom
of God, rather than that of man—and most particularly
of Communist's man—he, because of his cast of character,

203

would have become a real saint. And let it be said here that, years back, Whittaker Chambers, in his truly remarkable book, *Witness*, told us the truth we need to ponder; this ex-Communist stated: "The Western world does not know it, but it already possesses the answer to this problem (the strangling of the greatness in the soul of man by the spreading Communist tyranny)—but only provided that its faith in God and the freedom He enjoins, is as great as Communism's faith in man."

I will hazard a few well-grounded suspicions as to Tito's secret of success. The first is that he showed wisdom in the choices he made early of the men, young men, all who would be in his inner circle. Already before Hitler's blitz into Poland in 1939, Tito had selected two Serbs, Alexander Rankovic and I. Milutinovic; two Slovenes, Edward Kardelj and Franz Leskosek; one Serb from Croatia, Rade Koncar; and a Montenegrin, Milovan Djilas, to be his closest co-workers. One can see in the selections of men from different parts of the country something of the outline already formed in Tito's mind of the future Yugoslavia. The fact that only three of this inner circle had ever been to Moscow, while the others had never been out of Yugoslavia, contributed in no small degree to their total devotion to Tito as leader, and the later creation of the Tito cult. Another element in his secret lies in the fact that perhaps no other Communist Party in any land had—or has—been so broadly based on students. It was these students who proved so valuable as vital cadres for the *Partisan* army, making excellent leaders. The final factor I add to Tito's secret is that, despite his acquired external charm, he is, at heart, as ruthless an individual as ever was Stalin.

He was the first among the so-called satellite leaders

to unleash a savage campaign of vilification against the clergy, which he followed by those utterly inhuman People's Court trials. He was the first to collectivize agriculture, and the first to take land from the peasants. As for his "purges," Rankovic himself stated in a 1951 session of the Central Committee that at least forty-seven percent of the arrests made by the dreaded secret police were unjustifiable. And Paul Lendvai, in his book, *Eagles in Cobwebs,* tells us that "Yugoslavia was second only to Poland in losses of population in proportional terms. No less than 1.7 million people, about eleven percent of the population, were killed, fled, or were deported."

Those facts and figures are not too well known in the Western world, nor are they reflected upon sufficiently by those in the United States of America, to whom Marshal Tito owes his position today. But his recent "purging" of Alexander Rankovic, who looked like his "heir apparent," and his exiling of Milovan Djilas, who was once second in command, have given the thoughtful clearer insight into the secret of Josip Broz Tito's success. With a total dedication to a cause, completely loyal collaborators, plus utter ruthlessness, almost any man could climb to power—and stay there.

Concerning the secret of Archbishop—later Cardinal—Stepinac I can be much more absolute, and thus show why I name him "the man for this moment." You have already seen him, alone, defy the seemingly all-powerful Third Reich, Hitler, and Himmler. You have seen him stand up, alone, to Mussolini and his mighty Fascists. You have watched him as he, single-handedly, resisted Pavelic and his *Ustashi* who had the backing of both Hitler and Mussolini during the occupation of the Independent State of Croatia. All the while he was opposing,

205

again practically alone, the *Partisans* who would emerge as full-fledged Communists under the leadership of Josip Broz who would later be known as Tito. Now Stepinac will give his energies to opposing Bakaric and the whole Communistic machinery as it worked away at the complete take-over of Yugoslavia. Small wonder he was once called "the von Galen of Croatia" at a time when von Galen stood out like "Athanasius against the world."

Whence such courage? It was genuine fearlessness, and not foolhardiness; for his bravery won many a victory as you have already seen. The odds against anything like success were literally overwhelming; and yet he often succeeded. It takes manhood at its best to fight in such circumstances; and Stepinac was always fighting. Completely unarmed he fought against those who had at their backs an arsenal such as the world, up to that moment, had never seen. It is amazing, and not a little puzzling. That statue of Judas, seen already on his desk, gives some inkling to this strength of character. For Stepinac knew himself a man. Hence, he knew himself as an individual with weaknesses. This knowledge turned him to the Source of strength. With St. Paul Aloysius Stepinac could say: "I shall be happy to make my weaknesses my special boast so that the power of Christ may stay over me, and that is why I am quite content with my weaknesses, and with insults, hardships, persecutions, and the agonies I go through for Christ's sake. *For it is when I am weak that I am strong*" (2 Cor 12: 9-10). He never did make that boast publicly. But that statue of Judas kept reminding him of that truth. It is the only truth that will make a man truly a man.

Aloysius Stepinac learned this truth when still young, but the full realization of its trueness came only with the years. This secret for success in life began in Krasic under the tutelage of Joseph and Barbara Stepinac in that first of all classrooms in the child's first school: the home. His family and his family life should never be called "pious," but it must be named "religious." From the dawn of reason each child in that household learned not only that there is a God, but that God is the one and only Father of each and every human being. It is the fundamental truth on which alone human life can be based; for on any other foundation a human may do a lot of living without ever knowing any human life. It was taught the Stepinac children in more ways than with words. In their own human father they saw what a father is and what a father does. He is the source of life and life's sustainer. That is why Joseph Stepinac worked so endlessly on his farm. That labor kept the roof over their heads solid, the walls of their home tight, the table in their dining room supplied, their bodies clothed, their hearth ablaze, and their hearts happy.

The step from the natural to the supernatural was easy for the smallest child. For the first prayer taught any of them was the one prayer taught to men by .God: the *Our Father*. Neither Joseph nor Barbara Stepinac could ever be called theologians, yet they were ever theological. That is why they, by word and much more by example, instilled into the hearts of their children the truth that each was naught but a child of God. From Him came their life. From Him came their sustenance for living.

A child's complete dependence on his earthly father made the analogy to every human being's total dependence on his Heavenly Father easy to understand. But what drove the lesson home unforgettably was the kind of life lived by the Stepinacs at Krasic. Every farmer soon learns how exact St. Paul was when he spoke of one planting, another watering, but God alone giving the increase. It is a priceless lesson in humility, but at the same time it is a stupendous lesson in nobility; for every diligent farmer who thinks correctly, and that means to think theologically, comes to realize that *it is God* who does give the increase. Therefore, all farm work is working hand-in-hand with God. The combination of humility and nobility so strikingly evident in Archbishop Aloysius Stepinac came from this realization garnered in boyhood as he worked with God: he knew himself to be in all truth a *son of God*. Being a son he had to say with the Psalmist: "What is man that You should think of him; what is mortal man that You should care for him?" (Ps 8:5). But, in the very next breath, because he was a son of God, he had to exclaim with St. Leo the Great: "No nobler privilege is man's than the right he has to call God his Father!"

No one who knew Aloysius Stepinac would ever question his humility. Nor could anyone ever question his striking nobility of carriage and character. But few could rightly explain the combination. But that is only because so few know what true humility is, and, consequently, so few ever come to see the only solid basis for genuine nobility. Humility enobles; for genuine humility is nothing but truth: the vivid realization that every living human being is but a beggar with hands outstretched to God, asking for the next breath and heartbeat, but a beggar who is the noblest visible creation in a bewilderingly beautiful universe that has come from and is ever held in the hands of an Omnipotent God. Man is an image of Him who is Truth, Beauty, Goodness, Love, and Being; not a passive piece of glass, but an animated mirror who, through his intellect and will, reflects in time and space the Eternal Mind that brought time and space into being, and the Infinite Will that sustains them in being. Man is the only creature in the visible universe who can freely mirror forth God and thus glorify Him with the glory He wants from His creation. From earliest childhood Stepinac was truly humble, and therefore consciously noble. He knew who he was, what he was, why he was, and what he must ever be: God's son. His one work in life was to please his Father by doing his Father's will. Life was that simple—and that sublime—for this son of a Croatian farmer.

But why not a figure of Christ, the true Son of God, on his Archiepiscopal desk, instead of that statue of Judas? It was there because Aloysius Stepinac was a realist. He knew himself to be a son of God, but he also knew himself to be a son of Adam. He realized that his one life's work was to become like Jesus Christ the only Son of God. For that was he born; for that had he come into the world; for that he must strive and even strain all the days of his life on earth. But he also knew he could become like one who had lived for years on the most intimate terms with Christ; had been singled out by Christ, not only to be a mere disciple, but one of the inner circle, "one of the twelve." Judas Iscariot had seen Christ face to face, had heard Him teach and preach; heard Him "speak as no other man had ever spoken"; saw Him do things no man had ever done; received His confidences and accepted His promises, especially that one of being "one with Him in His kingdom." Yet Judas Iscariot had betrayed Him. Aloysius Stepinac realized that, like every other human being, he himself could be like Judas. Judas Iscariot kept Aloysius Stepinac self-

209

conscious, Christ-conscious, and ever God-conscious. Hence, in all truth it can be said that Judas Iscariot actually saved Christ in Croatia; for it was Archbishop Stepinac's keen consciousness that he could become like Judas that enabled him to become so thoroughly Christlike.

Deep as we are into the secret of Aloysius Stepinac, we are as yet only on the surface. For long before "fulfillment" was an in-word, Stepinac was working for nothing else. But he had learned early what many of our later devotees of "fulfillment" seem never to learn; namely, that Paul in his Letter to the Romans has given the one and only correct prescription for human self-fulfillment: "Put on the Lord Jesus Christ, and take no thought for your lower nature to satisfy its lusts" (Rm 13:14).

With pity and amazement he saw men of his day move steadily toward what is the blasphemy of our day: the enthronment of man as ruler of the universe. He was not unaware of the marvels of science; nor was he unaware of the way man was looking on those marvels. Many, because of man's accomplishments, were beginning to forget that every man is but a subject of the one Creator, and the greatest genius nothing more than a mere human collaborator in the universe with the Universe's Omnipotent Divine Creator. But he saw many actually dethroning God, thinking that, because of the scientific marvels, they had no more need of Him; that they could, on their own, determine the destiny of the world. He pitied them, and prayed for them. He longed for the very power of Christ so that he could say with effectiveness: "*Ephpheta* —Be thou opened!*" He would have them see reality and recognize behind the mind of every great scientific discovery and advancement the mind of God.

Because of what he saw going on in his day he appreciated the remark Eugene Potier had made in 1871: "The world is changing its foundations." Stepinac did not like the "foundations" some men were laying for the world; for he saw them making the Useful take the place of the Beautiful; Industry take the place of Art; Political Economy take the place of Religion; and Mathematics supplant Poetry. Many considered these "foundations" solid because of their pragmatic values, but Stepinac saw them for what they were and what they were doing: destroying human dignity and human worth.

The Jesuits in the German-Hungarian College were honing the intellect of the studious Stepinac for ecclesiastical life and living. Their emphasis, of course, was on Philosophy and Theology, but they never neglected literature and science. That is how the aspirant for the priesthood came to agree with what Dickens had to say about the London of his day, with what Dostoevsky had to say of the St. Petersburg of his day, and what Victor Hugo had written about the France of his day. Each of these had seen the revolutions of their times not only as a thrust at, but as a very real threat to human worth and dignity. Since man would be Stepinac's concern throughout his priestly life, he weighed what these men had said, and was always on the *qui vive* to watch for similar tendencies in his own day. He discussed these literary works with his Jesuit Professors, and, with them, studied the trends of his time. It was education at its best: the shaping of the "perfectly rounded mind and man."

He often recalled the inventions that had so changed the world. Shortly before he had been born the telephone came into existence; not long after that came the internal combustion engine. That was just ahead of the hydroelectricity plants and the automobile. At his birth there were movies; just after his birth came wireless telegraphy, and before he was far along in boyhood there was the airplane. These inventions had had tremendous impact on mankind and world society. They had changed living; they were now changing life. He had not missed this fact; he kept watching this phenomenon.

One of his Professors told him about the Exhibition in London with its Crystal Palace in 1851, and recounted the remark Prince Albert had made at the time: "This Exhibition is evidence of human history's inevitable advance toward the unity of mankind." Stepinac knew that such a unity was God's plan and the very prayer of Jesus Christ just before His Death. But Stepinac saw that man was botching this plan of God, and never did he see this more clearly than during and after World War I; for it was then that he saw centuries-old empires collapse, dynasties disappear, and formidable regimes of hitherto unknown forms arise. He saw his continent, old Europe, totter even as he watched one new Power in the West arise, the United States of America, and another in the far East do the same: Japan. He pondered on these shifts of civilization and soon concluded that "progress," was not, as so many claimed, "an inevitable law of human nature" like unto the law of gravity, but rather merely a man-made idea, only an idea, and a comparatively new idea at that.

But as he saw his continent arm for World War II, as invention followed invention, stunning the minds of many men, the radio leading on to television, then during the war, science bringing on jet engines, nuclear fission, intercontinental missiles, and finally the bomb, he saw many men react and give in to the pessimism he recognized as being just as wrong as had been Prince Albert's optimism. He grew restive when he found so many thinkers ignoring or denigrating the very real achievements of the era just because they had been disillusioned by the fallacy of "inevitable Progress." He could understand their disillusionment, but he had little patience with their pessimism. He was happy to have so many awaking to the fact that every change does not spell progress and that the prophets of "inevitable Progress" had indeed been false prophets, but he would not have men over-react in their disillusionment and deny or debunk the very real changes that had brought betterment to the world.

Still, despite his appreciation of and even exhilaration over the many actual world-changing achievements of his day, he knew, deep down, a very real uneasiness about the "shift of the foundations" of the world. He saw man's outlook change from cosmological to anthropological. In the first, men had seen the universe as a unity, an ordered whole, and had recognized God as the Creator of that universe. In the latter, God seems to have disappeared, and men, while more aware of their physical solidarity with the universe, felt strangers to it. He understood the anxieties of such men and could foretell their frustrations. They had made man the focus of man's interests, and man the center of their search for security. Such a search could end only in frustration; for man can find little comfort in man and his humanness simply because his humanness gives no measure with which to gauge man's intrinsic and essential worth. For that, man needs the Absolute—the Transcendent God. But when he tried to talk to such men he found them shy and silent before the very possibility of the existence of God, the lone Absolute. Such shyness and silence disturbed Stepinac deeply; for he well knew that Western

Civilization has deep religious roots, and that without these roots it dies. He realized that man without God can never be man. His one life's ambition was to get man to know himself by knowing God—not the God of the Philosophers, nor the God of the Poets, but the God of Revelation. He wanted all men to come face to face with God who is a Person, in all truth, Three Persons; for that is the only way man can come face to face with himself, and know who he is, why he is, and where he is going. That is the secret of Cardinal Stepinac: he knew himself to be a son of God and that he could only live aright by living not only as God's son, but actually "in God's Only Son"—Jesus Christ.

To understand how he came to this realization, to adopt this "philosophy of life" which in all truth is a "Theology of life," we have to go to Rome and watch the Jesuits develop the whole man, not only his mind, but his heart as well. They did it more through the Spiritual Exercises of St. Ignatius than they ever did by formal Philosophy and formal Theology.

Thanks to these "Exercises" Stepinac relearned what he had already learned so thoroughly as a boy at Krasic, but in this relearning he went far deeper into reality than any young boy can ever go. St. Ignatius gives a "Fundamental Exercise" which contains a "principle and a foundation." It is all summed up in the fundamental truth that "man was created to praise, reverence, and serve God; and by this means to save his soul." As a "principle" it is a beginning for the *mind;* as a "foundation" is a beginning for the *will.* With this first principle, and for Stepinac it was first, he began all his reasoning about human life; from it flowed *the* truth about life, and Stepinac was seeking truth. From this same first principle, because it gave truth, there flowed to his will a foundation upon which he could build his moral life; for what is true is good, and what is good is true, and moral life is simply all about being and doing good.

Stepinac's first look at this "principle and foundation" almost blinded him. It was shining simplicity. St. Ignatius was making man look at God, not to learn who God is, but to grasp the truth about man, and truly learn just who man is! Aloysius Stepinac was set gazing at God as the Source of his own being, as the Shaper of his individual destiny. But this gaze was not for his intellect alone; it stirred the activity of his will. It was a gaze that was prayerful and filled with prayer; for Stepinac was gazing with mind and will on Him who had brought him into being and was sustaining him there. This gaze gave him vital understanding of that mysterious statement of St. Paul: "In Him we live, and move, and have our being" (Acts 17:18). This understanding set the young Stepinac breathing hard as he tingled with a joy and a gratitude that could be called ecstatic.

How could he fail to thrill to the reality of his own being? Ignatius had said: "Man was created." Stepinac knew that creation is the production of something out of nothing by an act of God. He was, then, nothingness, but he was simultaneously an act of God. Rising within him and suffusing his whole being was a reverential awe that set him praising the Omnipotent One who had made him, and at the same time the realization of who he was set him making an act of total surrender of his being to his Maker. He was back to the "know, love, and serve God" of his childhood days which he had culled from his Catechism, but now with a man's realization that the "praise, reverence, and service" he owed to his Maker could only be given in truth by becoming what he was: God's son.

"Man was *created*...." That last word had been burned into Stepinac's being long ago, but while making the Exercises, it took on higher heat and branded itself into his very soul. "Man was created...." He did not evolve. What a difference in personal dignity that truth gives to the human individual! Stepinac knew his body could have evolved, but never his soul; and he well knew that he was composed of soul and body, and it was this union of the two that made him a person. Aloysius Stepinac always carried himself with marked dignity. The foundation for that carriage can be found in the "Foundation" laid by St. Ignatius at the outset of his Spiritual Exercises. Therein Stepinac learned, as never before, his noble origin: he had been created by God— no one less than God! Indeed he was a noble being. But "*noblesse oblige.*" He had to live up to his dignity. He could be true to himself only by being true to God. But he could be true to God only by "praising Him, reverencing Him, serving Him" with all the powers of his God-given mind, heart, soul, and being.

This "Fundamental Exercise" explains Aloysius Stepinac as nothing else can. He himself not only thought and rethought it, meditated and remeditated it, but he lived · it day in and day out; for it had simplified all life and living for him. It is the fire-spawned granite of this fundamental truth that made the man, the priest, and the prelate the Gibraltar-like rock that he was.

People have marvelled, and people will yet marvel more, at the fearlessness of this Primate of Croatia—a fearlessness that stood out like a beacon on a mountain top in a world black with cringing fear. But people will never understand this fearlessness until they come to the realization that Aloysius Stepinac was steeped in one ever-present and always-penetrating fear. This fear came also from this "Fundamental exercise" in which St. Ignatius teaches that man, by "praising, reverencing, and serving God" is "thus to save his soul." The immediate illation is that man can lose his soul. That immediate illation fills any thinking man with a penetrating fear— and Stepinac was a thinker. He realized that his "praise, reverence, and service" had to be *freely* given. Consequently, because he was a *free* agent, he could refuse his service. But if he did refuse, his life would be an utter failure no matter what he accomplished while living.

That is why he heard in his heart: "If anyone wishes to come after Me, let him deny himself, take up his cross daily, and follow Me. For he who would save his life will lose it; but he who loses his life for My sake, will find it. For what does it profit a man if he gain the whole world, but suffer the loss of his own soul? Or what will man give in exchange for his soul?" (Mt 16:24-26). And also that other saying of Jesus: "Do not be afraid of those who kill the body but cannot kill the soul. But rather be afraid of him who is able to destroy both soul and body in hell" (Mt 10:28).

In the letters and sermons so far quoted you have seen something of the simplicity, in the strictest sense of that word, that is, the single-mindedness of this priest and prelate. That, too, has its explanation in this "Fundamental Exercise" of St. Ignatius; for the Saint had Stepinac look out upon the physical universe with its incalculable number of creatures, then into the universe of men, which bewilders so many who have never tried to reason out just why God did make such a world of beings. Ignatius of Loyola, though, tells those who make his Exercises that "the other things on the face of the earth were created for man's sake, and in order to help him in the prosecution of the end for which he was created." That statement of truth bewilders the man of no Faith, and stuns the man of little Faith; but for a man of Stepinac's Faith it swells his heart with love, and his being with love's fruit, which is joy. Stepinac could look on everything from an amoeba and a subelectron to Betelguese and the blazing sun, on everything from the galaxies in the Milky Way back to human cells floating in their protoplastic, translucent substance and realize that all—all had been made by his Father for him; made just to enable him to get back Home to his Father. But this wonder which led to worship also gave Stepinac reason to pause and ponder; for Ignatius immediately adds: "whence it follows that man is to make use of them only insofar as they help him to attain his end, and to withdraw from them insofar as they hinder him from that end."

It takes no great logician—and Stepinac was ever living logic—to realize that it is the neglect of this principle, disregard for this law of life, that is the basic cause for the multitude of miseries that plague mankind. Abuse of creatures accounts for God's greatest visible creature, man, knowing so many ills in his society and heart-breaking tragedies in his world.

But, as yet, we have not reached the bed-rock of Stepinac's personality; for we have not yet reached the bed-rock of Ignatius' "Foundation." That lies in the consequence he drew from the truths he had already told. The Saint goes on to say: "Therefore, it is necessary that we make ourselves indifferent to all created things insofar as it is left to our free will to do so, and it is not forbidden; in such sort that we do not, for our part, wish for health rather than sickness, for honor rather than dishonor, for a long life rather than a short life; and so in all things choosing only (*unice*) those which the better lead us to the end for which we were created."

Stare at those lines until you really see them. They require long and concentrated staring. That is what Aloysius Stepinac did. He saw that Ignatius had said "*must make* ourselves indifferent." He himself knew enough about himself and other men to realize that, by nature, man is anything but "indifferent" to such things as health, honor, and length of life. He saw, then, that Ignatius of Loyola knew man.

The word "indifferent," because of its connotations in English, is not the most felicitous word to use in an effort to convey Ignatius' meaning, or to give you the key to Stepinac's character. For neither the Saint nor the Archbishop did it mean anything like apathy, disinterest, mediocrity. Just the opposite. Only the strong man, one might even say only the heroic man, "makes himself indifferent" in the Ignatian sense.

Some have used the word "detachment" to explain the Saint's meaning. But, once again, because of connotations, this word is not too exact. In all actuality this doctrine of the Saint means "attachment"—attachment to the Mind and Will of God. That is why the Latin word *unice* was introduced and underscored in the text above. That is the word which explains Stepinac fully. There is an absoluteness to the word, and that explains the absoluteness of the man. It allows for no compromise. It demands utter exclusiveness. Ignatius is saying that the intelligent, honest man, the truly wise man will choose that which *alone*, that which *only*, that which *exclusively*, that which *absolutely* will better enable him to attain his purpose in life—which is none other than God Himself. The logic is inescapable, unassailable, irrefutable. Everything follows as inevitably as night following day or two and two making four. But it is one thing to learn a lesson, quite another to live that lesson; one thing to inculcate a truth, another to incarnate it. Cardinal Newman had something of the same in mind when he so precisely distinguished between a notional assent and a real assent. The one gives a nod of the head in agreement, the other sets the truth beating in the heart. When this *unice* of St. Ignatius becomes not only a verity but a vitality; when one lives this lesson day in and day out, then that one can be said to have fulfilled his humanity to capacity; for he lives not only for God alone, but with God alone no matter how immersed he may be in the events of his time or the society in which he moves. Such a man was Aloysius Stepinac. That *unice* gave "oneness" to his life; it also gave it "wholeness." That is why one is reminded of the words of Horace when he wants to describe Stepinac: *Integer Vitae.* He was a man of integrity and an integral man because he had taken *unice* as the guiding star for all his living, and throughout his life he never once took his eye off that star.

It was this *unice* which led him to the selection of and the placing of that statue of Judas Iscariot on his desk. Stepinac knew himself. He realized that he, as every other human being, could say with the pagan poet, Ovid: *"Vidi meliora, proboque; deteriora sequor*—I clearly recognize the better things, and I approve them; but it is the inferior that I follow." St. Paul had put it in other words when he wrote: "The fact is, I know of nothing good living in me—living, that is, in my unspiritual self—for, though the will to do what is good is in me, the performance is

220

not, with the result that instead of doing the good things I want to do, I carry out the sinful things I do not want" (Rm 7:18). But Paul ended this confession and lament with: "What a wretched man I am! Who will rescue me.... Thanks be to God through Jesus Christ Our Lord" (Rm 7:24).

Ignatius of Loyola, one of the greatest psychologists of all time, knew all that Paul told in that passage and would use his knowledge to help men become what they are meant to be by giving them, in the Second Week of his Exercise, a Model on which they can mould their lives and their real selves. He gave men a Leader whom they can follow. But the ex-soldier from Loyola put it all in a parable. It is an Exercise known as "The Kingdom" or "The Call of Christ."

He had Stepinac imagine that there was a leader, a man elected by God, endowed with every quality that makes a man captivating, and then blessed him beyond this personal magnetism with abilities for waging war far superior to any and all military geniuses known to man. This superb being issues an invitation to all men to follow him in a campaign "to reduce to subjection all the lands of the infidel." Then he goes on to say that whoever does follow him must be content with the food he eats, with the drink and clothing he has, to labor during the day and watch during the night as he does. It is a call to intimate companionship with a Magnetic Leader who, moreover, is sure of success. Finally, he promises his followers a share in the spoils of victory commensurate with the part they have played in the campaign.

It is a call that no man with blood in his veins would refuse to answer. More, it is a call that stirs genuine enthusiasm even in the phlegmatic. Stepinac was anything but that. So the soldier in him responded to this imaginary call. Then Ignatius turns this fiction into fact by having men hear the actual "call of Christ." If men would follow the imaginary leader with enthusiasm—and every real man would certainly do that—then what should the response be of a genuine Christian to the actual call of Christ, the most magnetic leader who ever lived? His Person and personality had drawn crowds in Judea, Samaria, and the lands beyond the Jordan; and He is, as St. Paul says, "the same yesterday, today, and forever." His "Cause"— the establishment of His Kingdom—is the very purpose of human life. And Christ cannot fail! Ignatius puts Christ's actual call in perfect parallel to that of the imaginary leader, and has Jesus saying: "My will is to conquer the whole world, and all enemies, and thus to enter into the glory of my Father. Whoever desires to come with Me must labor with Me, in order that afterwards he may share in the victory with Me."

Who would not follow the Son of God—and share in intimate companionship with Him? But Ignatius had Stepinac go further than mere following or accompanying. He told him there were two kinds of response open to thinking men: that of the good man and that of the better. The good man recognizes Christ as the Leader necessary for him to attain that end seen in the Fundamental Exercise: the salvation of his soul. He gives himself willingly to Christ and follows Him faithfully. But there is another kind of man who gives another kind of response. They see in Jesus more than a necessary Leader; they see a Model for generous, noble, lion-hearted manhood; they see in Him a Lover even more than a Leader—and their reply to His call corresponds to their vision. They, as Ignatius puts it, "wish to show *greater* affection, and to *signalize* themselves in their every service of this King of kings." *Insignis* is the Latin word used by Loyola, and it is a word that has summed up life for a multitude of real men since the Saint first wrote it. It made him what he was, and every other Saint of the Society of Jesus. It has made countless other saints, too. Stepinac, being who he was and what he was, took it to his heart, made it complementary to, and a necessary instrument for, his *unice*. He would not simply follow Christ; he would overtake Him. He would not merely serve his King; he would serve Him outstandingly. He would be *insignis* among the soldiers of Christ.

Ignatius follows this "Call of Christ" with a meditation on "The Two Standards." Again what seems like fiction is soon seen to be fact. Stepinac, the realist, saw that the Founder of the Jesuits had given him an exact picture of his own day: there were, in Croatia of the middle forties, in all Europe, and in all the world only two standards: that of Christ, and that of the anti-Christ. What chilled the Primate was the realization that in his own Diocese of Zagreb only one of those standards was really flying high—and it was not the standard of Christ. But to all in Croatia it was piercingly evident under whose standard the Primate was fighting. His *unice* and *insignis* had been manifest from the day of his arrival as priest, but never more manifest than since he had succeeded to the See once occupied by Ante Bauer.

But you may still ask: Why the statue of Judas for a man so single-minded, single-hearted, and totally committed to Christ? Ignatius, with his next Exercise, is the answer; for after the meditation on the "Two Standards" the sharp psychologist and shaper of souls places his meditation on "Three Classes of men." Herein he had Stepinac

223

look on those who would like to be full-fledged Christians, completely dedicated followers of Christ, but . . . it is a wishing on their part, not a willing. And this is painfully evident from the fact that they never make themselves really "indifferent," nor do they consistently use creatures *tantum quantum*—just insofar as—these will help them to their end. The second class are the compromisers. They have more than a wish; they have a real will to be what they were created to be. But that will is wavering and weak. It is a half-hearted thing. They will use some of the means, but not all of them. They will follow Christ—but never stay close to His side. The third class, however, are the whole-hearted, the utterly sincere, the chivalrous, selfless, generous. They use every means available. They use them *unice*, so that they may be *insignis*. The statue of Judas kept the Archbishop keenly conscious of the three possibilities and, in a certain sense, spoke to the Primate every day, saying: "*Unice, Insignis, Third Class.*"

Ignatius has laid his groundwork now. He has men knowing what manhood is and the way to achieve it. But the man from Loyola knew that just as no artist can reproduce unless he looks at his model, as no architect can build unless he studies his blue-prints, so no follower can succeed in following unless he looks at his leader. So in the "Second, Third, and Fourth Weeks" of his Exercises, this moulder of men has his maker of the Exercises follow Christ from the Annunciation to Bethlehem through every phase of Christ's life on to the Ascension from Mt. Olivet and His Enthronment in Heaven at the Father's right hand. It is pedagogy at its best. For how can anyone "put on Christ" (Rm 13:14) unless he knows Christ? How can anyone heed the injunction of St. Paul: "Let this mind be in you which was also in

Christ Jesus" (Phil 2:5) unless he knows the mind of Christ? Or how can any man heed that other injunction of this Apostle to the Gentiles: "Become imitators of me as I am of Christ" (1 Cor 11:1) unless he knows both Paul and Christ? Ignatius knew how to teach, and in Aloysius Stepinac he had a pupil who was anything but dull. Long before his Ordination to the priesthood of Christ, Aloysius Stepinac came to know and love the Incarnate Son of God better than he knew himself and love Him much more than he would ever love himself. That explains not only the fearlessness and fortitude of Croatia's Primate, but also that spirit of calm and obvious possession of quiet joy which puzzled even his intimates. Stepinac knew he was not only on the way, since he was a pilgrim on earth, but also "in the Way"—Christ. He had seen the Incarnate Son of God find life on earth not only rough and rugged, but even agonizing. When things grew more than rugged and rough for the Archbishop of Zagreb, when they became actually agonizing, he could smile calmly and tell himself that he now was truly "in Christ Jesus"—the one Way to the Father.

That phrase "in Christ Jesus" spells out the whole secret of Aloysius Cardinal Stepinac. But to understand what "in Christ Jesus" means one has to weigh well two words used by St. Paul when writing to his Philippians from his prison in Rome. He was pleading for union of minds and hearts among all Christians, and he gave the formula: "Be of the same mind as Christ Jesus, who, though he is God by nature, did not consider his equality with God a condition to be clung to, but *emptied* himself by taking the nature of a slave, fashioned as he was to the likeness of men and recognized by outward appearance as man. He humbled himself and became obedient to death; yes, to death on a cross. That is why God has *exalted* him and given him the name above all names, so that at the name of Jesus everyone in heaven, on earth, and beneath the earth should bend the knee and should publicly acknowledge to the glory of God the Father that Jesus Christ is Lord" (Phil 2:5-11).

Kenosis is the Greek word meaning to empty oneself. *Pleroma* is the other Greek word meaning to fill. They were dear to Stepinac; for he saw the way to fulfillment of self lay in emptying oneself. Christ had done it, and "that is why God exalted him." Any man who would be an *insignis;* any man who would use everything *unice;* any man who would belong to the *Third Class* as he answered the call of Christ to fight under His Standard must empty himself of self before he can be filled to capacity with Christ.

That was Aloysius Stepinac's plan for life and living, deliberately chosen even before his Ordination. Once he was ordained his *unice* became even more penetrating; for if as a man he was convinced that he had to live for God alone and use all things simply, surely, and exclusively for his Father's glory, as a priest he knew he would have to do the same even more intensively. For now he knew he had been made more than a man. Now he had a dignity that St. Ephrem had called "infinite," and St. Denis had named "divine." He weighed the words St. Charles Borromeo had used at the Council of Milan as he pointed to priests and said: "*Dei personam in terris gerentes,*" a repetition, as it were, of what St. Clement of Alexandria had said years before: "A priest is, as it were, God on earth." That this was no pious exaggeration Stepinac realized when he, bending over Host and Chalice while offering Mass, said not "This is Your Body—

This is Your Blood" but "This is My Body—This is My Blood." What could that mean but that Aloysius Stepinac was acting "*in persona Christi*"—in the very place of, and in the very Person of, Christ?

It was thrilling. But it was also something to set him trembling. He needed his statue of Judas more than ever after Ordination; for while he recalled what Christ had said to the first Ordination Class of the New Law—his own Apostles: "You have not chosen, but I have chosen you" (Jn 15:16), Stepinac never failed to add those other words of Christ: "Many are called, but few are chosen" (Mt 22:14), and paraphrased them for his own soul's good into: "Many are chosen, but few become choice." He would be one of the few. He knew that Ordination had stamped him eternally as priest according to the order of Melchizedek, but he also knew it did not, by the very power of the Sacrament, make him what he had to become if he would belong to that "Third Class." He had to use his *unice* with something like vehemence if he would become what he was: Christ's vicegerent on earth. He well knew that not all priests lived up to their dignity. That is why he kept that statue of Judas ever before him.

There can be no doubt but that Stepinac's life took on not only new meaning, but new depths once he was ordained. Long before it was practically defined by Pius XII, Aloysius Stepinac realized that between the priesthood given him by Baptism and Confirmation and the priesthood conferred on him at Ordination, there was an essential difference. Being a Christian he had to be like Christ. But being a Catholic priest he had to be Christ. It is one thing to act like Christ, quite another to act as Christ—and only the man who has received Holy Orders can act *in persona Christi*. It is a depth of being that is well-nigh unfathomable. Little wonder that St. Ephrem exclaimed: "The gift of sacerdotal dignity surpasses understanding!" and that St. Thomas Aquinas taught that "the dignity of the priest surpasses that of the angels"; that St. Alphonsus Liguouri would insist that "by a single Mass a priest gives greater honor and glory to God than all the Angels and saints, along with Holy Mary, have given, or shall yet give to Him." It is a startling statement until one realizes that the worship of the above can never be of infinite value, while that of a priest in offering Mass is. These truths made young Father Stepinac gasp, but they also made him glory in his priesthood, and had him making Mass the center of his life and all his living.

Like all true Croatians Stepinac had a special devotion to Mary, the Mother of God. He had early realized she was his own Mother because she had mothered Jesus. In some ways he was shocked as he read what some of the Fathers and Doctors of the Church had said about her when they were writing on the priesthood. But this shock soon led him into deeper depths and greater reality concerning himself as priest of God. Hence he came to love the gentleness and courtesy of St. Bernardine of Sienna for saying: "Holy Virgin, excuse me; for I speak not against you when I say it is the Lord who has raised the priesthood above you." Then he gave his reason: Mary had conceived the Christ but once, whereas the priest conceives Him, as it were, every time he offers Mass. But it was his favorite, St. Augustine of Hippo, who climaxed it all for him when this great Doctor of the Church wrote his exclamation: "O priest, thou art worthy of all veneration; for it is in your hands, as in the womb of Mary, that the Son of God becomes incarnate!"

The Jesuits at the Pontifical German-Hungarian

College had taught him well, and thanks to the Spiritual Exercises of St. Ignatius had centered his whole life on becoming what he was—first as a man, then as an ordained man—a priest. They focused his attention on the essence of the priesthood and brought him to a realization of its wonder, its dignity, and its responsibility. Thus they set a slow, sure boring process going on within him as he prepared, in 1931, for his ordination. Like an auger under the steady, expert pressure and turning of a strong man, bores into wood, so the truth God Almighty *needs* ordained men on earth to carry on and complete the work begun by His Only Son on Calvary bored into the being of this young man from Krasic. It was a slow, steady process and all based on truths divinely revealed.

During the year preparatory to Ordination, Stepinac read and reread Christ's Address to the first Ordination Class of the New Law—the Apostles. He reflected on its every line from "My little children . . ." which was spoken with affection by Christ to the fishermen from Galilee and the Taxgatherer just after Judas Iscariot had gone out into the night, down to the final words which Christ addressed to His Father: ". . . so that the love with which you have loved me may be in them, and so that I may be in them." The tenderness of the Heart of Christ had never been more manifest, nor the tremendousness of the priesthood so evident. But the passage that held Stepinac longest was the mind-stunning revelation Christ makes in the fifteenth chapter of St. John's Gospel.

"I am the true vine," said Jesus, "and my Father is the vinedresser. Every branch in me that bears no fruit he cuts away, and every branch that does bear fruit he prunes to make it bear even more. You are pruned already by means of the word that I have spoken to you. Make your

229

home in me, as I make mine in you. As the branch cannot bear fruit all by itself, but must remain part of the vine, neither can you unless you remain in me. I am the vine, you are the branches. Whoever remains in me, with me in him, bears fruit in plenty; for cut off from me you can do nothing. Anyone who does not remain in me is like a branch that has been thrown away—he withers; these branches are collected and thrown on the fire, and they are burnt. If you remain in me and my words remain in you, you may ask what you will and you shall get it. It is to the glory of my Father that you should bear much fruit" (Jn 15:1-7).

Stepinac would stop there and ask that he might ever "remain in Christ and Christ in him so that he might glorify the Father by bearing much fruit"; for he saw in these words the truths of the Spiritual Exercises of Ignatius put in other words—and these words were from the lips of Incarnate Truth. Being the man of one all-absorbing idea and one all-permeating will-action, Stepinac translated Christ's injunctions into his *unice, insignis,* and *Third Class;* for if Ignatius had led him on to the election and resolution to be as perfect a man as he could possibly be, St. John was now leading him on to the determination to be as perfect a priest as he could possibly be—and was showing him the way: remaining in Christ with Christ remaining in him.

The very next sentence from the lips of Jesus told him how to do this, for the Christ had said: "As the Father has loved me, so I have loved you. Remain in my love. If you keep my commandments you will remain in my love, just as I have kept my Father's commandments and remain in his love. I have told you this so that my own joy may be in you and your joy be complete. This is my commandment: love one another as I have loved you. A man can have no greater love than to lay down his life for his friends. You are my friends, if you do what I command you. I shall not call you servants any more, because a servant does not know his master's business; I call you friends because I have made known to you everything that I have learnt from my Father. You did not choose me, no, I chose you; and I commissioned you to go out and bear fruit, fruit that will last; and then the Father will give you anything you ask him in my name. What I command you is to love one another" (Jn 15:9-17).

Stepinac saw that it was a closely reasoned passage, dense with truths for life and living. He pondered it often, and after each pondering asked the Father in the name of Jesus for only one thing: not that he might know the joy Christ spoke of, which is the fruit of love; not that he might bear much fruit, fruit that would last; but simply and solely (his *unice* again) that he might love—that he might be transformed into Christ whom John had so succinctly defined by saying *Deus caritas est*—"God is love." And Stepinac knew what love is and what love does: it gives; it sacrifices; it suffers.

That insight came from the very next passage in Christ's Discourse. It was a passage that prepared Stepinac for his life in Croatia as nothing else could. In 1931 it was far from evident that a spurious axis for the world, running from Berlin through Rome to Tokyo, would be invented by men who had no love for Christ or His priesthood. But the young man from Krasic was ever a realist. He had seen what had happened in Russia after 1918. He knew that Priesthood in the New Law meant concommitant Victimhood—and he had seen it lived in fierce truth in Russia under the Communists. He saw that

231

Blaise Pascal had written no literary fiction when this French Philosopher penned the line: "Jesus Christ will be in agony until the end of time. . . ." After seeing what had happened in Russia, Stepinac did not hesitate to add: "especially in his priests." But he was not surprised, for Christ had prepared him for this brutal fact by this passage in His Farewell Discourse delivered at the first Ordination ever to take place in the New Law.

"If the world hates you," were Christ's words to His priests, "remember that it hated me before you. If you belonged to the world, the world would love you as its own; but because you do not belong to the world, because my choice withdrew you from the world, therefore the world hates you. Remember the words I said to you: A servant is not greater than his master. If they persecuted me, they will persecute you, too. . . . But it will be on my account that they will do all this, because they do not know the one who sent me" (Jn 15:18-21).

Christ had given His commandment. It was that they love. He had told them what He meant by love when He said: "A man can have no greater love than to lay down his life for his friends." Christ had shown that "greater love." Every true priest must love in the same way. Stepinac would be a true priest.

But, while he was ready to lay down his life, the time had not yet come, so he must live as Christ lived. He must "be about his Father's business." He must "go about doing good." What almost stunned the young Stepinac was the realization that Christ had actual *need* for him. This realization came out of this very Discourse of Christ, and most precisely from Christ's insistence that He was the Vine and that they were the branches. The Master had urged his priests to remain in Him so that as a branch joined to the vine produces fruit, so would they. But Aloysius was the son of a farmer. It was obvious to him that no branch could live without a vine. But the obverse of that proposition was what showed Stepinac the *need* Christ had for priests. For he well knew that no vine can produce fruit without branches. The vine gives the branches their life, but they in turn stretch out their "hands" to the sun, and through their tender "nostrils" breathe in the air, and thus sustain the vine in living. All that he had learned in the College of Agriculture after World War I helped him to understand the plumbless depths of Theology about the Mystical Body. Since he was a branch and Christ the Vine, Christ actually *needed* Aloysius Stepinac. It was a mind-stunning thought, even as it was simultaneously heart-stimulating; and Stepinac was as much heart as he was mind, if not more so.

This was the Damascus Road for Aloysius Stepinac; for here he learned what Saul of Tarsus had learned the day Christ knocked this zealot from his horse, and let him know that Christ and Christians are one. Stepinac took the passage in St. John's Gospel wherein the Beloved Disciple tells how Christ, when struck on the face in the house of Annas the very night He had been betrayed, asked: "Why strikest thou me?" (Jn 18:24). While lying in the dust of the Damascus Road Saul of Tarsus heard the identical question from the identical lips: "Saul, Saul, why persecutest (strikest) thou me?" (Acts 9:4). The guard had hit Jesus in His Physical Body. Saul was hitting Him in His Mystical Body so long as he was striking Christians. For the Person who owned both Bodies was the Second Person of the Trinity.

Stepinac saw clearly, then, that whenever he ministered to any Christian he would be ministering to Christ

233

Jesus Himself; and he better understood that saying of Christ concerning the Last Judgment: "... inasmuch as you did this to one of these the least of my brethren, you did it to me" (Mt 25:40). He also came to understand ever so much more clearly that statement of St. Paul: "I live, now not I, but Christ lives in me" (Gal 2:20).

This Theology about the Mystical Body gave the young Stepinac a deeper insight into Christ's need for him. For he saw that Jesus Christ could not "go about doing good" in the twentieth century as He had done in the first unless Aloysius Stepinac loaned Christ his feet, his hands, his heart, and his whole being. If Christ was to be heard in Croatia speaking "as one having authority" (Mt 7:29), Stepinac, and others like him, must lend Christ their tongues, their lips, their every ability to articulate. If Christ were to lay His hand on little children in the Europe of the 1930's as He had in the Judea of the 30's of the first century, then He had need of the hands of the men of the 1930's. Stepinac knew there were Magdalenes in his day who wanted to weep at the feet of Christ, women like the one at Jacob's Well who wanted the "water welling up into eternal life" (Jn 4:14), women like the one taken in adultery who longed to hear: "Neither do I condemn you. Go, and from now on, sin no more" (Jn 8:11), women like the sisters, Martha and Mary who yearned to send word to Jesus that "the man you love is ill" (Jn 11:2), men like Nicodemus who needed to hear the authoritative statement: "I must be frank with you: if one is not born anew, he cannot see the Kingdom of God" (Jn 3:3). But how could any of these needs of the men and women, and the children in his own day be satisfied save by men like himself who would give themselves entirely to God to act as Christ's vicegerents on earth? The need was real. He would make the answer to that need just as real. *He would be Christ on earth!*

His daring determination, phrased as it was, sent him to St. Paul's Epistle to the Hebrews; for he knew that in this letter Paul had revealed the depths of Christ's priesthood. "We have the supreme high priest—in Jesus, the Son of God. . . ." Paul had said, then a few lines later added: "Here we have an anchor for our soul, as sure as it is firm, and reaching right through beyond the veil, where Jesus has entered before us and on our behalf, to become a high priest of the order of Melchizedek, forever" (Heb 5:6). In the New Law, strictly speaking, there is only one priest—Jesus. Stepinac found Paul's letter corroboratory and complementary to what he had deduced from his ponderings on the Theology of the Mystical Body especially under the analogy of Vine and branches. Hence, he came to see that once he was ordained even the traditional title of "another Christ"—an *alter Christus—* did not tell the truth with fullness or precision. He would not be "another Christ"—he would be Christ!

He hesitated to state his conclusion until one day, while reading his favorite St. Augustine of Hippo, he found this Doctor of the Church exclaiming: "Let us rejoice and give thanks! Not only are we become Christians, but we have become Christ. My brothers, do you understand the grace of God that has been given us? Wonder! Rejoice! for we are made Christ! If He is the Head, and we the members, then He and we are the whole man. . . . This would be foolish pride on our part, were it not a gift of His bounty" (Jn 21). Since this was true of all baptized Christians, concluded Stepinac, how much more true of all ordained Christians. The priest had to "put on Christ" much more completely than mere

235

Christians. Hence, he had to be more thoroughly Christ. Stepinac was reassured now and went on to Ordination, shrinking back from neither the dignity nor the responsibility. But it was this latter that had him looking often at his statue of Judas; for it was the same St. Paul who had revealed his dignity to him, who also warned him: "whoever believes that he is standing firm, should beware lest he fall" (1 Cor 10:12).

Not long after his Ordination Stepinac was delighted to find in Emile Mersch, S.J. a kindred soul. For the Jesuit Professor of Theology at Notre Dame de la Paix brought out his monumental work *Le Corps Mystique Du Christ* in 1933 and in it substantiated with text after text from the early Fathers the insights Aloysius Stepinac had gained from his meditation prior to being made a priest. Then, ten years later, when he was in the midst of his difficulties with Pavelic and the *Ustashi*, an even more authoritative voice spoke out, and solidly reassured him that his convictions that Christ, Almighty God though He is, actually needed Aloysius Stepinac in His effort to save the mankind He had already redeemed, and in that other conviction that a priest was Christ. Imagine, if you can, the joy the then Archbishop Stepinac knew as he read in Pius XII's epochal Encyclical *Mystici Corporis*: "Because Christ the Head holds such an eminent position, one must not think that He does not require the Body's help. What Paul said of the human organism is to be applied likewise to the Mystical Body: 'The head cannot say to the feet: I have no need of you.' It is manifestly clear that the Faithful need the help of the Divine Redeemer, for He has said: 'Without me you can do nothing'.... Yet, this, too, must be held, marvelous though it appear: Christ requires His members" (M.C. no. 54).

Then, when speaking of the union that exists between Christ and His members, the Pontiff had said: "In Sacred Scripture it is likened to the pure union of man and wife, and is compared to the vital union of branch and vine, and with the cohesion found in our body. Even more, it is represented as being so close that the Apostle says: 'He (Christ) is the Head of the Church,' and the unbroken tradition of the Fathers from the earliest times teaches that the Divine Redeemer and the society which is His Body form but one Mystical Person; that is to say, to quote St. Augustine, the whole Christ. Our Savior Himself, in His high-priestly prayer, has gone so far as to liken this union with that marvelous oneness by which the Son is in the Father and the Father in the Son" (M.C. no. 82).

Now you can understand his *Caritas*. That work was not humanitarianism. It was sacramentalism. He was being what he was ordained to be: Christ ministering to Christ. As a human being Stepinac had a warm love for all other humans, but it was not the humanity in them so much as the divinity that won his love. He knew that by creation every human was an image of God, but by Baptism each baptized human was made divinely human. He was ministering to the divinity in them—and that was the Divinity of Christ. Father Aloysius Stepinac was a thoroughly Christ-conscious priest; conscious of his own Christness, and conscious of the Christness, actual or potential, in every other human being. That is why he would and could minister to Serb and Croat alike, to Orthodox and Roman Catholic, to Jew and Gypsy. He was ministering to human beings, but within each was Christ—living, or awaiting resurrection. He, Christ, was ministering to Christ.

When he was consecrated Archbishop he recalled all

these truths—and with reason. He had seen that the Communists in Russia had lunged at the very jugular vein of Christianity when they began their persecution of the Church in 1918. They were very like Longinus; for they aimed their lance at the very heart of the Mystical Body by lunging at priests and bishops. In that first year of the persecution twenty-eight bishops and four hundred and fourteen priests had been martyred.

It was not only his special devotion to John the Baptist that had this young priest, not yet in his forties, selecting the Feast of the Precursor, June 24, as the day for his consecration as Archbishop. It was insight and foresight. He had learned how the Archbishop of Perm had had his eyes gouged out, his face slashed, and then was buried alive; how the Bishop of Belgarod had been brutally beaten, and then buried in quicklime; how the Bishop of Youriev had had his nose cut off, then his ears, then after being stabbed again and again by a bayonet, had been finally cut to pieces. He, Aloysius Stepinac was about to be made an Archbishop. He might very probably be made a martyr. He was ready. He would be like the Baptist, and for those in high places who were not honoring God, he would say: "*Non licet tibi*" just as the Baptist had told Herod.

He had to credit the Communists with being sharper Theologians than many of his own Church's Theologians; for he saw that they well knew just where the heart of the Mystical Body was: in the priesthood of Christ. He knew how St. Thomas Aquinas had taught that the Eucharist is the greatest, noblest, most central sacrament of all; for from it all the others come, and toward it all others flow. It is rightly called the "sun" of the Christian's world, the source and center of the Church's life. Without a priest, there could be no Eucharistic Sacrifice or Eucharistic Sacrament. He had to admire the accuracy of the aim of the persecuting Communists. They would quench the very light of the "sun" for the Christian, darken his world completely, and stop the "heart" of the Mystical Body by exterminating priests—and as he enjoyed the plenitude of Christ's priesthood as Archbishop, he would be prime target for the Communists if they should ever take over Croatia. Indeed his Consecration could very readily spell martyrdom. But he was unafraid; for the only one he feared was "he who could kill body and soul"— and no Communist could ever do that.

But that he had to prepare for the eventuality of martyrdom came home to him day after day as he watched the happenings of his Europe. He was not in the Archiepiscopal See but a few years when he learned that the Bolshevik Persecution of Christianity, far from fading, had but waxed more furiously. In May of 1938 no fewer than two hundred and fifty priests had been shot in Russia. In 1939, as soon as the Communists occupied Poland, he saw a swarm of expert propagandists pour in, take over radio, press, and all other means of communication, and begin their campaign to put Christ to death. Their focus, of course was on bishops and priests. He saw the identical thing in Spain during the Civil War there. It is estimated that over six hundred thousand Catholics were martyred there before the advent of Franco; the first among these were bishops and priests.

One of the Archbishop's secretaries tells us that Aloysius Stepinac brought to the centuries-old Archiepiscopal Palace, the *Kaptol,* "an air of simplicity, seriousness, spontaneity, and asceticism." He could have well added: "a new Christ-consciousness" and thus have explained much that seemed inexplicable to many.

It was this, I believe, that manifested itself most clearly as soon as he took office after Ante Bauer had gone to God, and continued until Stepinac had joined him there. For, as with his priesthood, so with his Episcopacy, he based it all on Revelation, especially as he found it in St. John's Gospel. There he found Christ revealing Himself as the Good Shepherd. It is all contained in chapter ten which tells not only of the fold, the flock, and the shepherd, but also of the wolves who attack the flock, and the hired men who desert the flock and leave the fold.

He was not yet in office but only Auxiliary "with right of succession" when he saw more than one wolf coming toward the fold and for the flock. He studied Christ's own description of such a happening so as to reassure himself as to his own proper stance. Christ had said: "The hired man, since he is not the shepherd and the sheep do not belong to him, abandons the sheep and runs away as soon as he sees the wolf coming, and the wolf attacks and scatters the sheep; this is because he is only a hired man and has no concern for the sheep." Stepinac was not a hired man. He would never run away no matter how many wolves attacked his sheep.

Then the Christ had gone on: "I am the good shepherd; I know my own, and my own know me, just as the Father knows me and I know the Father; and I lay down my life for my sheep." Stepinac knew many in his fold even before he had been consecrated, but once he had been made their chief shepherd, he made superhuman efforts to know more and more of them. *Unice* was still his motto. At first he was "laying down his life for his sheep" by devotion to duty. All his energies were given to his flock. But as time went on he clearly saw that he might well be asked to lay down his life literally. He did not shrink back, far less run away. He went out to meet the wolves. It was not a pleasant prospect. But then, neither had Calvary been for the true Good Shepherd.

But Christ had not stopped there. He had gone on to say: "And there are other sheep I have that are not of this fold, and these I have to lead as well." That is why the young Archbishop of Croatia gave so much of his time, his talents, and his very being to those who "were not of his fold." Jew, Serb, Gypsy, Nazi, *Partisan*, *Ustashi*—everyone in Croatia—was somehow "of his fold." These he had "to lead." He felt some consolation when so many of these "others" listened to him. Christ had promised that in this same revelation when He said: "They, too, will listen to my voice."

With characteristic fearlessness and fidelity Stepinac applied the rest of the account to himself. Christ had said: "The Father loves me because I lay down my life in order to take it up again. No one takes it from me; I lay it down of my own free will" (Jn 10:17, 18).

The whole "secret" can be summed up in the words Aloysius Stepinac chose for his coat-of-arms. Many might be led to think his motto would be *"Fides et Fortitudo";* for his Faith and his Fortitude are so strikingly evident in his Letters, Sermons, Proclamations, and actions. But actually he took what can be interpreted as the same. His motto reads: *In Te, Domine, Speravi*—In You, O Lord, I have placed my trust.

Those words set other passages of Scripture running

through one's mind. They are so reminiscent of: "With God on our side, who can be against us?" (Rm 8:31) which will give any real man indomitable courage. And again of: "May the God of hope bring you such joy and peace in your faith that the power of the Holy Spirit will remove all bounds to your hope" (Rm 15:13) which can give one an imperturbable calm and a confidence that nothing and no one on earth can ruffle.

But it is the unwritten remainder of the sentence which begins with the Archbishop's motto that gives the entire secret of the man, the patriot, the priest and the prelate who was Aloysius Stepinac. The Psalmist had sung: *"In Te, Domine, speravi, non confundar in aeternum"* (Ps 30:1 & Ps 70:1) which Ecclesiasticus took up and rendered: ". . . know ye that no one hath hoped in the Lord, and hath been confounded." Stepinac's motto tells us that he knew though he might be beleagured and even beaten, he could never be conquered; knew with absolute certainty that, despite every lack of evidence of success, he could never fail; for while working in time, he was not working for time; that though fighting with men for other men, he was ever waging battle for God and for eternity. He hoped in the Lord always—and he knew his hope would always be fulfilled.

Whenever he looked at his coat-of-arms or at the statue of Judas he was reminded that there is only one failure in life for man: not to be on God's side. The Primate of Croatia would never be on any other side. His life was *unice.* His life was *insignis.* His life was "*Third Class.*" For he lived his motto: *In Te, Domine, speravi*—never more so than in the twentieth century's middle forties.

8 Masters of Deceit

WE LAST SAW THE TWO "Primates" in June 1945 and heard Josip Broz Tito claim that he knew how important it was to have the relations between Church and State clarified, regularized, and conflict avoided; that he realized how religious the Croatian people were, and what a role Religion played in their lives; and that he himself would do all in his power to spare human lives. He did add that it would be difficult, because "justice must be satisfied for the violations of humanitarian sentiments."

In July of the same year, just a few weeks after this meeting and all those promises, we find Archbishop Stepinac addressing a long letter to Vladimir Bakaric, President of the People's Republic of Croatia, regarding nothing less than the *"Persecution of the Church in the New Yugoslavia."* It is dated July 21, 1945. It is Stepinac at his most honest, direct, irrefutable best. He began:

Mr. President:

I have had occasion several times of late to write you regarding certain questions which are important to the proper regulation of the relations between Church and State. Although I have received no answers to these letters, I consider it most urgent that I write you again concerning these matters. There is first the question of the death sentence given to my priests who are momentarily awaiting execution. In connection with this circumstance I consider it necessary to explain to you, who are the responsible holders of governmental authority in Croatia, a number of things which are obstacles to the pacification of our present situation, and to that contentment which the people have awaited as following the war's end. I feel it my duty to explain these things to you frankly, so that you may avert in time the causes of the discontent which I see every day in association with great numbers of my faithful who, literally, besiege my palace asking for aid. In doing this I hope to find on your part a sincere and complete understanding; for all I am explaining is in the interest of the people in general and of the national community.

As first point the Archbishop took the promise made by Tito in Bakaric's presence to question all priests in concentration camps and free those who had "no blood on their hands." "It is true," admitted the Primate, "that a certain number of seminarians and some priests have been released. . . . But the seminarians from Zagreb were immediately called to the colors. It is also true that a number of my priests were taken before a military court and sentenced to death." Then came the spirited protest:

Mr. President! I cannot refrain from making some observations on the subject of the procedure of these courts martial. Every man with a sane mind and an honest heart knows that an accused person has the inalienable right of defending himself and of demanding in his defense the questioning of witnesses before any court that merits its name and which intends to exercise its function in the name of justice. Without the questioning of witnesses, who personally participate in the most important part of the proceedings, namely the trial, there cannot be a just sentence. I affirm that the military courts do not admit witnesses in their trials. . . .

Further, the courts martial function to the complete exclusion of the public, and the names of the military judges are not known, at least publicly. Now all that is possible and understandable in a regime that does not call itself popular and democratic, but which is universally known to be authoritarian. But it is utterly impossible to understand that such a trial system exists in a regime which emphasizes its democratic character, and the fact that it is the people who rule. . . .

The example of the death sentence given to Professor Kerubin Segvic may be advanced as proof of what I have just written. Although the Marshal clearly stated that priests who had not bloodied their hands, but who had only been indiscreet, would be pardoned, an old man of seventy-nine, K. Segvic, was condemned to death, although no proof of criminal conduct was adduced. He was accused of supporting the Gothic Theory of the Origin of the Croatian People. That is a somewhat preposterous theory which can hardly be proved. But the holding of a mere scientific theory does not justify, according to right reason, the sentence of death. It was not proved that Professor Segvic incited men to murder on account of his theory. The capital sentence given to old Professor Segvic has caused dismay in legal circles because of its lack of juridical sense, and has provoked among the people a great sympathy for the cruel fate of a powerless old man. These, Mr. President, are most natural human sentiments, and no theory or propaganda can accuse them of being 'false humanitarianism.'

The Archbishop was missing no opportunity in his effort to prod Bakaric, and the new State into sensibility. He was calling things by their right names, and was showing the President that the moves and methods of the new regime were known and recognized to be what they actually were. He ended his attack on the way Professor Segvic had been tried and condemned with: ". . . Segvic should rather have been taken before a court of national honor than before a court martial which condemned him to death for a reason no judge in his right mind could accept."

His attack on the next case was even more severe. He began with:

Can the natural good sense of the Croatian people accept the explanation of the death sentence given to Sister Blanda Stipetic? For the first time in Croatian history a nun has been sentenced to the supreme penalty by which the most hardened criminals are punished. And how had Sister Blanda bloodied her hands?—By hiding a *Ustashi*, the murderer Stjepan Hripka, under the name of Baric. She was assisted in this by Anka Zbornik and by Sister Beata Nemec. Let us assume that Stjepan Hripka was a proved murderer. The question was open whether Sister Blanda knew that he was. This fact was not brought out in passing sentence. On the contrary, Sister Blanda Stipetic asserted that she did not know what he was, nor whether he was a *Ustashi* or not. Hence, so long as subjective guilt for an objective act was not proved, no sentence could be pronounced according to any human law or to any reason; and least of all could the accused be sentenced to death.

The facts were that Sister Blanda and Anka Zbornik had been helped by a man, who claimed his name was Baric, in bringing food to Zagreb for the hospital there and the welfare kitchen for the poor. The man had hidden in a hospital for a time. The nun and her friend were accused of sheltering him from the law. They had never seen the man before, nor had they any knowledge of his crime. Further, Sister Blanda had frequently seen *Partisans* and their families hidden in the same hospital during the days of the *Ustashi* regime. None of these facts had been considered during her so-called trial. The Archbishop called Bakaric's attention to the fact that, though Hripka had already been arrested, he had, as yet, not been tried. Therefore, his crime had not been proved. So Stepinac asked: "By what law, by what logic can death sentences be pronounced because of aid given to a man whose guilt has not yet been legally proved? That, Mr. President, is indeed an example of 'justice' and law unique in the annals of our courts."

The next case cited by the Archbishop was that of Father Peter Kovacic, Pastor of the Holy Family Parish in the Kanal District of Zagreb. This good priest, against his will, had been decorated by the *Ustashi* regime. That was a "crime" in the eyes of the present government. Further, they accused him of the "crime" of telling parents to keep their children off the streets after dark in mixed company. For this "transgression" a sentence of eighteen months of hard labor had been imposed. Then, after passing that sentence, the judge accused him of having forced one of his relatives, long years before, to convert from the Orthodox to the Roman Catholic Church. For this the same judge sentenced him to six years of forced labor. Stepinac exclaimed: " 'The judge accuses, the judge condemns' was said of the Turkish courts three centuries ago. Here in the progressive People's Court in Zagreb, in the year 1945, is a practice of the sixteenth and seventeenth century. But the misfortunes of Pastor Kovacic did not end here. He was taken to the court martial of the City Commandant of Zagreb and condemned to death. The mind nor the heart are no longer capable of understanding Justice in this sense."

The aroused Archbishop went on with case after case that cried to heaven—and, in a certain sense, to earth—for vengeance. Then he began itemizing other acts of the Government which cried in like manner. He summarized forcefully: "Mr. President! when all that I have stated concerning the actions of the military courts against priests is taken into consideration; when the list of priests condemned to death is reread; when the great number of priests in prison is taken into account; when day after day the attacks against the clergy are repeated, and they are denounced as 'reactionaries'— which in the vocabulary of the times means placing them outside the law and defaming them; when the position of the Church in today's schools is realistically appreciated; when it is recalled that nearly all ecclesiastical buildings, such as schools and seminaries, are used for secular purposes; when, moreover, it is shown that the Catholic press in Croatia has been practically destroyed; when to Catholic institutions teachers are sent who in their classes directly attack the Catholic principles of education; is it not legitimate to conclude that the Church in Croatia is being persecuted?"

He had not finished even with that summary. He went on: "I have purposely not mentioned the kind of treatment to which Catholic priests are subjected in concentration camps and prisons, for that is too tragic a story. But the facts speak for themselves in a very loud voice— and their words are clear. The Catholic Church in Croatia is in a state of confusion. It is not persecuted openly, for today that is not as yet opportune, but under the pretext of the regulation of its activities in the political sphere and, in reality, by the evident tendency toward the destruction of all that forms the basis of the life of the Church, namely the freedom of the clergy and their activity in administering to the souls of the faithful, it is most certainly being persecuted. For, as statistics show, the clergy is fast disappearing from the surface of free life, either in the prisons or under the bullets of firing squads."

That was how he ended the first half of the letter. In the second half the Archbishop addressed himself to the task of explaining to the President the nature of the requests that were presented to him in the Archiepiscopal Palace day after day. First was that the condemned be allowed a priest before execution. He scored sharply when he told Bakaric that similar requests, presented by him to the *Ustashi*, had been honored. He scored again when he pointed to the fact that under the new regime there were no courts of higher appeal, no possibility of pardon for those sentenced to death, and no remotest possibility of commutation of sentence. "Such an institution exists in every juridical system in the twentieth century." Then the Archbishop added: "I must not pass over in silence the fact that such an authority, during the *Ustashi* regime, saved the lives of several persons who, today, are in high office. Why go backward in this respect, when it is being emphasized that we are a progressive people?"

Now thoroughly aroused the prelate went on to charge the regime with crying out against the *Ustashi* when the latter buried the condemned unknown or at the site of execution, but were now doing worse: denying relatives— mothers, brothers, sisters, wives and children—of all knowledge as to the place of execution as well as of burial. "It is well known," stated Stepinac, "that Roman Law permitted the burial of the executed; for after execution 'justice is satisfied.' Therefore, there is no reason why the body of a Christian should not be decently buried." He insisted that relatives should be allowed to take the bodies of the executed "to family graves, in Christian cemeteries, as pious Christians have done with their dead since time immemorial."

He went on to tell of other requests that came to him

day in and day out, each pointing to another specific injustice committed by the regime. It was a long letter. It was a strong letter. For it was written by a man in the strictest sense of that term; by one who loved his country far more than those who were now tyrannizing over it. It was a letter written by a priest of God who had been moved to "righteous indignation" and who was as "angry," if that be the proper word, as was the Christ when He found His Father's House turned into a "den of thieves." It was a letter which could have been written only by a man who could bring issues to as clear and as hot a point as that of a skilled electric welder's arc; by a man whose heart ached with every aching human heart, and yet could swell with resentment for any and every injustice until it was veritably a lion's heart.

For this courageous representation all he received was:

Archbishop:

Through Monsignor Rittig I received your letter containing complaints against our authorities' methods of procedure.

I am grateful to you for having sent me your sincere opinions.

I find that on certain subjects you are badly informed, on other subjects that I do not share your point of view, on still others I am of the opinion that you are absolutely correct.

I hope in a few days, as soon as my health permits, to discuss these matters with you and find a solution that will satisfy both parties.

Please accept the expression of my respect.

Dr. V. Bakaric

His Excellency could not be but sorry that the President was unwell and, at the same time, grateful to him for the seemingly frank and honest reply, even as he could not be other than hopeful concerning the promised meeting and discussion. But we can well imagine how he felt when, a few days later, he read in the papers how the "unwell" President had addressed the Sabor (Senate) almost immediately on receipt of the letter and had touched upon many of the points the Prelate had posited in that bit of correspondence.

In typically Communistic fashion Bakaric had twisted some of the Archbishop's statements and presented them to the Sabor as admissions of complicity and guilt. The President had said that he was in possession of "authentic statements from the highest ranking ecclesiastic that most of the pilgrims (in the Procession from Marija Bistrica) were members of *Ustashi* families, many of whom had fled, were in hiding, or in concentration camps."

That sat Stepinac into his desk again, penning a reply to the President. "If these words refer to my letter, I reiterate that I made no such statement, and that the conclusion does not follow from what I did write. My words were as follows: 'Responsibility for this falls upon those who have filled the concentration camps and prisons with the relatives of the Marija Bistrica pilgrims.' It does not follow that the relatives of the Marija Bistrica pilgrims were *Ustashi*. There were a great many who were not *Ustashi*, but who have relatives in the concentration camps and prisons. This is universally known. . . . I cannot accept your statement that at the time of the procession a fundamentally *Ustashi* campaign was organized.' The reason is that I am convinced that the great majority of the pilgrims had nothing in common with the *Ustashi*

Movement, and, consequently, were not pro-*Ustashi*. . . .
I take vigorous exception to the charge that the Church
is political and, especially, that the organization of the
procession from Marija Bistrica was pro-*Ustashi* in character."

Then the Primate took up another charge the "unwell"
President had made in his speech to the Sabor. "At one
point you speak of an office that draws up lists for the
'English,' and at another you say 'among these who are
drawing up these lists are priests. . . . In fact a political
party is in the process of formation. All this is the work
of enemies.' Mr. President! As I pointed out in my recent
letter, every day I receive requests for aid and many
petitions for information. I stated this sincerely and
openly. Hence, I must energetically reject the accusation
that anyone in my secretariat is 'making up lists for the
English.' I do this because the whole city knows that
hundreds of persons have come to my office with the
addresses of their relatives from whom they have had
no news up to the present. This is not the result of my
own initiative or that of my priests. If you have been
otherwise informed, I assure you that the information is
inaccurate. In concluding this reference to the gathering
of information, you stated further in your speech: 'We
affirm that we know whence comes the inspiration for
these actions, and we are following the development of
these matters attentively.' In regard to these words I say
sincerely that I am unaware whence comes the inspiration
in gathering the information on the subject of missing
persons."

As the Archbishop affixed his signature to the letter
he knew that he had made an honest reply to the charges,
and had shown that each was a distortion of truth. How

Bakaric would receive the letter he did not know, but he did know for certain that the newspaper reports of the President's speech to the Sabor had done irreparable harm to the Church. He was tempted to sigh in helplessness and to shake his weary head in discouragement and disgust. But then, as he was replacing the pen in its holder, his eye fell on the little statue of Judas that stood always on the front-center of his over-laden desk. The Archbishop's shoulders straightened; his lips firmed; his chin jutted. With strong hands he folded the letter and as he sealed it a new energy coursed through his whole frame. "No," he said quietly, then with incisiveness added, "not for thirty, not for thirty thousand, not for thirty million, not for all the wealth in the world. Help me, O Lord, to be what I am."

The summer of 1945 was a hot summer for Archbishop Stepinac. He used it to write to just about everyone of any importance in the Provisional Government telling them openly what they were doing to the people and what they were obliged to do. The people, for the Primate, meant everyone in Croatia and even in Yugoslavia. The people, for those in power—and only the Communists were in power!—meant stooges. The final battle was on months before the plebiscite. It was Armageddon. And the forces of evil in this Armageddon were driving toward triumph. For Stepinac it was Calvary that loomed ahead. But for a Christ-conscious man Calvary, while spelling physical death, also spells true victory. Death itself is not a pleasant prospect for any man, but for the genuine human it is not death that matters, but what death leads to. So the Archbishop fought on.

In early August he was telling the President of the Croatian Government, the Religion Commission of the same Government, and the Federal Ministry of Public Instruction of the Yugoslav Federation just what was going on in education and precisely what the Catholic Church has always demanded should go on. The two, of course, were antithetical. By the middle of August he was writing Marshal Tito, President Bakaric, and the Presidency of the Council, the Commission for Religious Affairs in the Federation just what was going on under the title of "Agrarian Reform"—and what the Catholic Church had always held should be going on. Again the two were antithetical. By the end of August the Primate was sending telegrams to Tito and the Presidency of the Provisional Popular Assembly vigorously protesting the methods being used to carry out what they were calling "agrarian reform" but which he, and every man with eyes, saw to be nothing other than "confiscation, without reimbursement of any sort, of ecclesiastical properties."

It was wearying work, this of protestation, but it had to be done. It was also quite frustrating. For few were the acknowledgments, let alone replies, that he ever received. Yet one came from Tito on September the first. It was both an acknowledgment and reply. But it was not couched in terms that would lift the heart. Tito had said "On the subject of agrarian reform many discussions had been held . . . in which there was always unanimity on one point: that the reform must include the Church lands. This unanimous point of view is, of course, the result of the state of mind of the peasant masses, not the will of the deputies themselves." Of course the Archbishop could have asked the Marshal if there had been any ecclesiastics present for those discussions. However the Marshal did close with: "I reiterate the possibility of reaching an agreement on questions pending between the Church and the

255

State, for I think that that is in the interests of an easier domestic readjustment." The plebescite had not yet been held. Hence, the Marshal had to state that he believed "in the possibility." But the Archbishop knew how to read letters from Communists. He also knew how to write letters to them. And yet the Letter which set the two parties on the inevitable collision course was not addressed to the Communists but to his own people. Still Stepinac was never one for indirection. He was no compromiser, no pussy-footer. He addressed the Marshal first and gave him the contents of the Pastoral Letter he would send out in the name of and after meeting with the entire Yugoslav hierarchy. It read:

Marshal:

The Catholic hierarchy, meeting in plenary session in Zagreb from September 17 to 22, 1945, considers it its duty in these critical times to address you, as the highest authority in Yugoslavia, in the interests of both Church and State and for the general welfare of the people.

The Catholic hierarchy had on its agenda a discussion of the general situation of the Catholic Church in Yugoslavia. In the course of its meeting the Catholic hierarchy was compelled to take cognizance of certain distressing facts, which compel us to present to you, Marshal, our attitude regarding the future relations between Church and State.

Out of one hundred Catholic magazines and newspapers not one exists today; almost all our publishing plants have been confiscated, as well as our paper supplies. This means that the existence of a Catholic press has become impossible.

The Seminaries have been, with few exceptions, liquidated; as have been, to a greater or lesser degree, all Catholic educational and welfare institutions.

By the abolition of compulsory catechism in the schools, the education of youth has been placed, to our greatest regret, in gravest danger, and through action contrary to the freedom of religion which is guaranteed to all citizens by law and by Government declaration.

The abolition of all Catholic private schools has been announced in contradiction to the elementary rights of parents and the Church, these two essential elements in education.

By the constant organization of all sorts of celebrations which last late into the night, the youth of our cities and villages are exposed to great moral danger.

The performance of religious duties on Sundays has been made difficult because different classes of persons, such as youths and office workers, are called upon on that day to perform compulsory work or engage in sports contests.

In the delicate question of marriage the Church has had the following *faits accompli* placed before it: the introduction of civil marriage and the practices of certain local officials of making marriage decisions which are not lawful, and which are even opposed to the civil code in effect up to the present.

As a result of the agrarian reform and the suspension of the salaries of the clergy and other officials of the ecclesiastical institutions, the reduction of the Church to a state of pauperism has been brought about.

The graves of soldiers in Catholic cemeteries have not been spared although contrary to international law, the cultural traditions of Europe, and the practices of Christianity.

Marshal, the Catholic hierarchy has reached the conclusion that the present situation of the Church in Yugoslavia is tantamount to open persecution, however much the Government may deny it.

Marshal! We consider it necessary and our duty to communicate these facts to you as the President of the Federal Government.

The Church wants no conflict with any government, especially with that of Yugoslavia, our Fatherland. For that reason we address you directly, Marshal, hoping by personal contact to avoid possible misunderstanding between Church and State.

That was the Archbishop at his usual astuteness. He was acquainting the Marshal with what was actually going on, and telling him that he and the rest of the hierarchy had read aright the activities of the Government. But the Primate of Croatia did not stop there. He would now openly present the demands of the Church. He did it this way:

We demand most urgently the reparation of the injustices listed above. We await from you the unconditional release of Bishop Simrak so that the Holy See will not be called upon for a decision in that case. We await from you the release of all our priests who are innocent of crimes.

We demand complete freedom for the Catholic press, for Catholic private schools, other educational and welfare institutions, seminaries, and the restitution of all confiscated properties.

We demand absolute respect for Christian marriage, a complete course of religious instruction in all primary and secondary schools, the possibility for the performance of Sunday religious duties, a revision of the agrarian reform in agreement with the Church, and respect for Catholic cemeteries.

We await, through your intervention, the solution of the question of the admission of priests to military and civilian hospitals, as well as to prisons. In our opinion this constitutes one of the most essential features of religious freedom.

These are our demands and our requests. We set them before you forcefully as our Faith and our conscience as pastors dictate.

Then as if adding a postscript that might take the note of intransigence from the list of demands the Primate began with: "Marshal! We are profoundly convinced that a peaceful solution to these misunderstandings can be found, for the benefit of both parties, Church and State. We hope for peace and harmony with the State. If on the State's part there is equal good will, we can arrive at a peaceful solution by means of an agreement with the Holy See, such as the President of the Bishop's Conference proposed in his first conversation with you." But then the Archbishop seems to have stopped and thought back on that first meeting and the subsequent happenings so his quasi-postscript went on with:

If, on the contrary, this good will does not exist, the State will suffer as much as the Church. You may be certain, Marshal, that the Church cannot, at the price of all its sacrifices, recede from its fundamental principles, for that would be a denial of itself.

Marshal! We confidently express our hopes to you, a son of our country, who knows the soul of its people, its religious sentiments and needs. On the basis of your statements to the Zagreb Clergy, we are convinced that you will understand us; for we ask this in the name of the religious freedom that is guaranteed by all modern states.

In spite of the difficulties we have just set forth, we declare ourselves to be loyal citizens of the State in which we live; that we will respect its authorities; and are ready to collaborate for its reconstruction.

Before any acknowledgment or reply could be given that letter, the Primate had read at all Masses in his Cathedral, and had ordered read at every Mass in every church in the Federation, a Pastoral Letter that was longer, but which was substantially the same as the one he had sent the Marshal. It was longer because it detailed the excesses, giving names, numbers, times, and places. It was a clear statement of Catholic Doctrine concerning the proper relations between Church and State, based on that dictum of Christ: "Render, therefore to Caesar the things that are Caesar's, and to God, the things that are God's" (Mt 22:21). It was also a very clear statement of Catholic Doctrine concerning the relations existing between those who serve in the Church and those who are served. The hierarchy had a duty to fulfill in order to help their respective flocks on to God. "Aware of the jeopardy in which the Catholic Church, and the priceless spiritual good of its millions of faithful have been placed," they wrote, "we consider it our duty to bring out into the open all the calamities and vicissitudes which confront and plague the Catholic Church. All of us make up one spiritual society, the Mystical Body of Christ. 'So we, the many, are one Body of Christ, and severally members one of another' (Rm 12:5). And to us in these days is directed the fiery call of the Apostle to the Nations, St. Paul: 'But doing the truth in charity, we may in all things grow up in Him who is the Head, even Christ: From whom the whole Body, being compacted and fitly joined together, by what every joint supplieth, according to the operation in the measure of every part, maketh increase in the Body, unto the edifying of itself in charity'" (Eph 4:15-16).

Having set forth the purpose of the Letter, the Hierarchy then went on to place before the people the precise state of affairs. First came the fact that two hundred and forty priests had already been killed, one hundred and sixty-nine were still in prison and concentration camps, while eighty-nine were listed as missing. A total of five hundred and one priests from the one Archdiocese. "Balkan history for many a century has not witnessed such a slaughter of God's chosen ones. But what has most grievously offended us is that they, like hundreds of thousands of other Catholic faithful, are denied the Sacraments in their last moments—which all civilized nations allow to the most depraved criminal."

The Primate used clear, forceful language throughout the entire Letter. There was nothing of the timid, the cautious, the hedging, the hesitant in the Letter. Stepinac would never be any of those. He was even so forthright as to say: "There is something else that especially pains us. It is the materialistic and godless spirit which today is being openly and secretly, officially and unofficially, propagated throughout our country. We, Catholic Bishops of Yugoslavia, as teachers of truth and representatives of our Faith, condemn unreservedly this materialistic spirit from which mankind can hope for no good. Likewise we condemn all ideologies and social systems not based on the eternal principles of Christian Revelation, but on the shallow material foundations of philosophical atheism."

Then came the explanation: "All that we have laid before you, dearly beloved, has been said with no intention of provoking a conflict with the new authorities. We do not seek it. We have never sought it. Our thoughts are directed toward peaceful, orderly civil and public life. That peace today is necessary to all, but if there is to be peace, and if the wounds of war are to be healed, it can only be done by respecting our Christian religion and its moral laws. We anticipate that there will be unjust attacks and accusations ... but we are not concerned, nor are we fearful. We are one with our people. We guard its most precious heritage: its Faith and its honor, its desire to be free and united in love with all citizens of this State regardless of creed and nationality."

From all we have seen of this man that passage is typically Stepinac, but the summation at the end of the Letter is even more typical. He had written:

"Therefore, we seek—and under no circumstances shall we desist—full and complete freedom for the Catholic press; full and complete freedom for Catholic schools; full and complete freedom for Religious Instruction in all grades of elementary and secondary schools; full and complete freedom for Catholic Societies and Organizations; full and complete freedom for man's dignity, and personality, and inalienable rights; full and complete freedom for Christian marriage; return of all confiscated properties and institutions. Only under these conditions can the situation in our country be solved and lasting internal peace be realized."

He realized that such a summary was as explosive as a bomb and possessed a clarity that was blinding, yet his conscience and his character would not allow him to posit it in any other terms.

He did append a paragraph that was calculated to lift the hopes and the hearts of his people—and again he wrote it clearly, with courage, and with confidence.

"Most dearly beloved flock," he said, "we wish to bring these facts to your attention so that you may understand clearly the present position in which the Church finds itself. Come what may, we look with confidence to the future. We take courage from the awakening religious spirit in the great masses of our faithful in all parts of our country. Especially are we consoled and made joyful by the lively and overflowing devotion to the Mother of God, who is so near and dear to our Catholic people. This is proven by the overwhelming number of pilgrimages, such as never before visited our national shrines. Cherish and nourish in your hearts and that of your families that deep and abiding devotion to the Mother of God. Pray her rosary together in common, imitate her virtues, and it is certain that the Mother of God will be our special Protectress. Under her powerful protection our flock in all circumstances and vicissitudes shall remain faithful to their forefathers' religion. The Mother of God will not abandon us, but will, through her intercession, provide God's guidance in all our needs."

The reaction of the government was instantaneous and volcanic. Even as the Bishop of Dubrovnik read it to his own people there were those in the congregation,

263

unquestionably "planted," who shouted "Down with Christ!" Then came the morning papers with column after column of denunciation and attack. The Monday after it had been read, countless hastily arranged Political Meetings were held throughout the land in which speakers attacked the Hierarchy viciously. Next day graffiti appeared wherever it could be scratched or painted, telling in no delicate terms, just what should be done to all who signed that Letter, to all priests, nuns, and Catholics. In the month that followed this kind of thing waxed instead of waning. And yet, not a word from the Government officially. Stepinac knew the reason: the plebiscite had not yet been held.

Early on All Saints Day, November 1, some members of the OZNA, Croatia's Secret Police, came to the Archiepiscopal Palace to tell the Primate that were he to speak out in the Cathedral that day in such a way as to lead the people to think he was attacking the Government, "the people would rise up against him."

"What people?" asked the Primate.

"That's our business," was all he got in way of reply.

He could have told them that they had spoken truth; for he knew just what "people" would rise up against him: those who had been planted in his congregation with instructions as to when to cry out and what to say. Of course he spoke out and proclaimed God's truth in such a way that no one could miss the contrast between what he was saying and what the Government was doing. Yet there was no "rising of the people against him."

On November 4, Father Salic, secretary to the Archbishop, stood waiting for His Excellency to come to the car which was parked at the curb before the *Kaptol*, ready to take both the Primate and his secretary to

Zapresic where His Excellency would open a new parish and dedicate its church. The secretary was uneasy, for he had just heard how the day before a stranger had arrived in town by train, had been met at the station by a boy from Childrens' House, a known Communistic Center for youth, who took the stranger to what they called a commune. Once there the stranger had stated apodictically: "Stepinac will not have time to open the new parish at Zapresic." What could that mean, wondered Father Salic? Whatever it meant it was a remark that did not put the secretary in any holiday mood. But before he could sink any further into his gloom he saw the slender figure of the Archbishop emerge, hurry down the steps, and head for the car.

"Praised be Jesus Christ! Good morning, Father. Hope you are feeling up to this trip and the dedication," was the cheery greeting from the prelate. The secretary returned it as pleasantly as he could but he was marvelling all the time at the Archbishop's energy and cheerful calm. Little did he know that his Primate had reflected long that very morning on what he had seen and heard about the activities of the Communists in the city of Zagreb and in the entire Federation of Yugoslavia. What he saw in them was exactly what Christ had seen after His prayer in Gethsemani: a mob coming "with swords and clubs" as for a "brigand" (cf. Lk 22:52). He was also wondering who it would be who would give him (Stepinac) "the kiss."

The car started but it had not gone far when the Archbishop was noting the large paintings of the hammer and the sickle on houses he knew to be the homes of priests. He shook his head a bit sadly. Then his eye was caught by slogans painted on walls, windows, and even on the

265

sidewalks. They all said the same thing, though in different words: "Down With Clerical Power"—"Down With The Blackrobes"—"Death to the Remains of Fascism"—"Death to the signers of the Pastoral Letter." Suddenly in the road ahead he espied a huge drawing. He asked his driver to slow down so that he could view it more thoroughly. No one could fail to recognize, crude as the drawing was, the Cathedral of Zagreb. But as they drew closer the Archbishop was heard to draw in his breath sharply. Father Salic looked and saw that the "artist" had placed figures of priests on the roof and the towers and had them shooting down on the people in the street. The Secretary groaned aloud. The Archbishop turned to him and said: "Cruel. Diabolically cruel and clever. They want to turn the people against us. They will never succeed. Not with the real people of Croatia." Then as he waved to the driver to resume speed, the Archbishop said as if to himself: "No persecution of the Church. No. None whatsoever." When the driver asked: "What is that, Your Excellency?" all he got in reply was: "The hour is come when the Son of God is to be glorified." The driver thought he was referring to the dedication of the Church about to take place in Zapresic. The Archbishop was thinking of Christ's words at the Last Supper "on the night He was betrayed."

As they sped on they could not miss the *graffiti*, the caricatures of the Archbishop himself, and the cartoon of priests obviously drawn to stir up contempt for the clergy. Just as they reached the outskirts of Zapresic two motorcycles came toward them, circled their car, and then drove off toward the town. The Archbishop could not miss the way the two motorcycle riders had looked at the car and at him. He turned to his secretary and quietly

266

asked: "Should we name that a Reconnaissance Patrol?" Father Salic did not smile. The chauffeur was too busy with his driving to catch the query. But all three grew more alert as they came in sight of the church that was to be dedicated, for on the left side of their car as it approached they saw a fairly huge throng of people standing—the parishioners, obviously, but on the opposite side of the street a group of about twenty men and women were posted. There came a strange light of questioning into the Primate's eyes as he noted that the men on the right side of the street were in uniform and armed, while all the women were wearing *Partisans'* hats. Father Salic paled noticeably.

The driver slowed the car as it approached the front of the church. But before he had brought it to a full stop a rifle shot rang out, then more, then on the right side of the car and on its roof fell a rain of stones, eggs, and mud. Father Salic was hit by one of the rocks. The Archbishop and the driver escaped all injury. At that moment Father Pasicek, pastor of the church, came out the church's front door and hurried toward the crowd that was gathered near the church. He, obviously, wanted to reach the Archbishop's car, but just then, from the opposite side of the street came a group of men and women shouting obscenities about priests and prelates. The pastor stopped in unbelief and bewilderment. But the group came on with knives opened. They closed in on the pastor, banged him with their fists, slashed at him with their knives, threw stones, and finally knocked him down. The parishioners, stunned by the onslaught, now moved. They circled their fallen pastor. Above their murmurs of indignation and consternation, the voice of one

267

of the attackers was heard to shout toward the few who had remained on the opposite side of the street: "He has no revolver."

The Archbishop, as soon as he had seen the group move in on the pastor, had bolted from his car. Now, as the parishioners parted to allow the Primate closer, one of the approaching *Partisans* tossed a revolver to the side of the prostrate priest. Whether the attackers realized they were outnumbered or were frightened by the sight of the Primate on the ground helping the assaulted pastor it is difficult to say, but the riot they intended to provoke never came off. The pastor was helped to his rectory. The parish was opened and the church dedicated. Fr. Salic had his slight head wound as a memorial of the affair.

But two days later the papers were carrying lurid accounts of the event and the Minister of the Interior had the brazenness to put forth an official statement in which he claimed that "the assembled group (meaning, of course, the parishioners) began to make a demonstration to hail the agrarian reform; they threw eggs, mud, and small stones at the Archbishop's car. The attack was begun by the people who opposed the growth of the Church. It reached its climax when an armed priest fired into the people in order to put down the opposition. . . ."

That was too much for the Primate. He began to do some investigating on his own. He soon had the whole thing in focus. It all began shortly after the publication of his Pastoral. On October 7 there was a public meeting at Zagreb at which one of the speakers had said: "If someone needs to be shown our power, we will know how to choose the time to show him, since he has asked for it. We force no one to be our enemy, make no one provoke us into showing our fangs, but if anyone has not sufficient wit to see for himself what is going on about him, then it is our duty to show him what is happening." Then there was the stranger who visited the commune on November 4 who stated that the Archbishop would not have time to open the parish, far less to dedicate the church. Added to this was the fact that there had been a meeting of the Communist Youth Union of Yugoslavia the very morning the dedication was to take place. During the meeting it was decided that that was the day and Zapresic the place for them to "show their fangs" by attacking the Archbishop. One hour before his arrival it had been asserted here and there in the town that the Primate was to be attacked at the church's door. Once he had his evidence, the Archbishop protested in the only way left him. He wrote President Bakaric.

"The events to which we have lately been witness compel me to send you this letter. The campaign directed against the Pastoral Letter of the Catholic Episcopate waged in the newspapers, in political meetings, by posters plastered on walls, by the jeering words painted upon the houses of priests and religious, reached its culmination on the fourth of this month in a physical attack made on me and my attendants at Zapresic. . . ."

Then he took the Minister of the Interior's communiqué and showed the President that the Minister was either grossly misinformed, or was deliberately trying to place the blame on the innocent party. The Minister had said that the attack had come from the left side of the car—the side on which the parishioners were standing. The Archbishop told the President: "it came exclusively from the right, as the damage to my car is witness." Next he asked the President if the eggs, mud, and stones that had been hurled at him "had suddenly fallen from heaven into the hands of the so-called demonstrators. Then he exclaimed: "In what a superficial way—to speak of it with the greatest moderation—in what a deliberately misleading manner was the Minister's communique composed! He says 'small stones'.... The fact remains that two stones were found in my car, one weighing about 70 decagrams (7½ lbs) and another weighing 20 decagrams (2¼ lbs). I am keeping these stones as an historical document, and I can show them to you, Mr. President, so that you may be convinced of the character of the Minister of the Interior's communique and his conception of what constitutes a 'small stone.' To be struck on the head by such a stone would, in the opinion of trustworthy physicians, cause either a serious wound or death."

The Archbishop ended his letter in characteristic style: "Mr. President! I must hold you personally responsible for all future excesses, now that you are in possession of the above facts. I hold you all the more responsible for you are also the highest official of the Communist Party in Croatia which, as every one knows, controls all public political activity. In this double capacity, then, you carry before the court of history full responsibility for events which follow from the above enumerated facts."

The plebescite had been held November 11, and Tito along with his Communist-dominated "National Front" had, as is to be expected in such plebescites, won a substantial majority.

The Archbishop had watched Communist tactics in Russia, Poland, and in every country they had "liberated." He was not surprised when the only reply he received to his honest representation was constant villification in the Press. He knew the ultimate purpose of this campaign —himself.

On November 29, 1945 the "Federal People's Republic of Yugoslavia" was proclaimed. Backaric was maintained as President of Croatia. That fact alone tells what he was all along. Tito wouldn't keep any but close collaborators in power. Now the President showed his true colors openly. Instead of answering the Archbishop's letter directly, he published, on December 16, what he brazenly called a statement on "*Ustashi* Activity in Ecclesiastical Institutions." It was the usual Communistic concoction: a cascade of lies and distortions of facts.

The Archbishop read it and saw its ultimate objective. He prepared for arrest and trial. Not, however, by sitting back and waiting for the OZNA to come to the *Kaptol*. Instead he prepared his clergy and, through them, his people for what he was sure would eventuate: his arrest and trial.

On December 17, 1945, the day for beginning the Novena in preparation for Christmas, he sat into his desk and penned a letter to his clergy, telling them that "out of respect for truth and justice," he proposed to examine the charges made in the President's statement which had appeared in every paper in the land. But he began with what reads like a "final testament." The Archbishop attested: "To all the complaints directly or indirectly lodged against us, we can reply that we have nothing with which to reproach ourselves. Our conscience is clear and tranquil before God, who is the most faithful Witness and the Just Judge of all our actions. Our conscience is clear and tranquil as well before all the Catholics of this country who judge events calmly and soberly. Our conscience is clear and tranquil, too, before the Croatian people to whom we belong, according to the Will of God, by ties of blood, and whom we serve wholeheartedly in

271

our position, without regard to their different points of view or political parties."

Then he addressed himself to each charge in particular. The first was about clerics in politics. His defense was air-tight before any jury of thinking men; for he cited his Circular Letters of 1935, 1938, and 1943, each of which forbade all active priests to become candidates on any ticket whatsoever. "I am of the same opinion today," he wrote, "and see no reason for changing it. Each priest is alone and personally responsible for what he does in the political sphere. Consequently, if a priest does something contrary to the regulations of the law in force, he must personally answer the consequences of his actions."

Next, the Archbishop had been accused of conspiring with the ousted *Ustashi* on the basis of a visit by Eric Lisak, a *Ustashi* Colonel and former Director of Public Order in the now defunct Independent State of Croatia. He was also accused of having received Lela Sofijanec, a woman who was then held by the Tito regime to have been a spy. The President was making the Archbishop out to be a conspirator for the restoration of the *Ustashi* State.

His Excellency calmly replied: "Numerous persons have sought entrance into the Archiepiscopal Palace at all times. Innumerable persons came there during the later years of the war. Their opinions, religions, nationalities, and political affiliations were the most diverse. We welcomed all people paternally as is befitting our ecclesiastical position. If someone came to our Palace under an assumed name, we are not omniscient and cannot penetrate all manner of disguises, nor are we responsible for those who abuse our Christian charity."

272

To state it that way was true Christian charity; for the facts of the case were these: Colonel Lisak had come to the Palace, but had posed as a "Mr. Petrovic" who needed, for personal reasons, a private audience with the Archbishop. Father Ivan Salic had received the man and had announced him to the Primate as "Mr. Petrovic." In the kindness of his heart the Archbishop consented to see him. But as soon as His Excellency opened the door to the reception room where "Petrovic" was waiting, the latter put on his glasses and the Archbishop immediately recognized him as Colonel Lisak. After an involuntary gasp and a quick questioning look at Fr. Salic the Archbishop bowed to the Colonel who began talking, saying that he had not come for any political or terroristic action, adding that there had been enough of that already. His Excellency interrupted Lisak's flow of talk to ask first what had become of the children of the refugees abroad, and then what had become of Father Tiso, former President of Slovakia. The visit lasted little over a quarter of an hour. The Primate then expressed his displeasure that the Colonel had come to the Palace, regret that he had allowed himself to be deceived, then ordered Father Salic never to receive the Colonel again. That was the "conspiracy" the Archbishop engaged in!

Father Salic was not on hand now to type this letter for the Archbishop since, shortly after the experience at Zapresic, the secretary and two other members of the Archbishop's household had been arrested and imprisoned for "association with the *Ustashi-Krizari*, opposition group to the government." The President had charged the Archbishop with keeping the *Krizari* in his Palace; that he had fed, clothed and helped arm them from his Palace even while they were in the forests. He had added that His Excellency had hid the Archives of the *Ustashi* in his Palace, and had correspondence with politicoes.

As the Archbishop looked at the word *Krizari* he shook his head in sadness as he muttered sadly: "What masters at deceit!" He had reason for the exclamation; for *Krizari* means Crusaders, and he well knew that a non-political body of Croatian youth had been organized twenty years earlier as part of Catholic Action and had called themselves *Krizari* or Crusaders with the approval and under the patronage of the Yugoslav Hierarchy of which he was president. But how different was the group which formed in the last year of the Pavelic regime—strongly nationalistic and violently anti-Communistic—which had taken the same name, *Krizari* but were known as "hot heads" rather than Crusaders! With swift, firm hand he wrote his denial of all knowledge of anyone hiding in his Palace under the flag of the *Krizari*, admitted that he had received the Archives of the *Ustashi* Foreign Minister, but immediately added that he had transferred the same to the present Government as soon as it had come into power, and had a receipt of the transfer from them. The charge of having had "political correspondence" he repudiated with the simple phrase: "a lie." Then with characteristic forthrightness he wrote: "We have defended, do defend now, and will defend until the last breath of our life the right of the Catholic Church to complete freedom in fulfilling her mission."

More deceit was unmasked when His Excellency referred to some photographs that had recently been published by the newspapers. One picture showed high officials of the Pavelic government, military as well as civil,

with the Archbishop among them. The paper had cap-
tioned it as a photo of a "political meeting." Actually this
picture was of a New Year's gathering, a purely social-
civic event, to which the Archbishop, as representative
of the Church, had been invited, and which courtesy and
his position as Primate demanded he attend. The Communistic press made it appear as "cooperation with the
enemy." Of course everyone who was not a Communist
was an "enemy." And any association with them led to
"condemnation by association."

Another picture showed the Archbishop amidst a very
similar group of officials. This time the caption tried to
make him out a supporter of the Nazis! They did it by
deceitful arrangement of the picture. The Archbishop
looked to be giving the Nazi salute, but a closer look
proved that the arm up in that salute belonged to the
Ustashi official who was standing behind the Primate and
had his arm just over the Archbishop's right shoulder.
The fact was that the Archbishop was the only one in the
picture who was not giving the salute!

Yet another picture showed the Archbishop outside
historic St. Mark's church surrounded by the *Ustashi*
officials. The caption read "Friend and Helper of the
Ustashi and Nazi governments." The fact was that His
Excellency was celebrating a Pontifical Mass for the
opening of the Croat Parliament, which was traditional
in its own way. The further fact was that the Archbishop
had used that very occasion to preach a fiery sermon
demanding that the new government respect the rights
of the Church, have reverence for each man's conscience,
and abhor anything like violence and persecution. But
"one picture is better than a thousand words"—and there

was the picture of the Archbishop with the *Ustashi* who were supported by the Nazis. Was this not "collaborating with the enemy"?

Here is how the Primate handled the pictures: "The daily press carried some photographs of a reception on the occasion of New Year's Day in 1945. Civic courtesy demands that one perform certain conventional acts on such an occasion. But they do not, in any way, signify the approval of a particular political attitude. Therefore, these photographs do not disturb us. The same applies to the flood of caricatures by which we have been ridiculed in the different newspapers, magazines, and posters. You, brother priests, are able to judge clearly on the basis of published documents what my relations were with the former authorities. It is characteristic that we were then, as today, attacked and humiliated when we defended the principles of justice and Christian charity."

After admitting that certain people would welcome the President's "statement" and use it to "crib, cabin, and confine" the Church in its work, he added: "However, neither material measures, mockeries, threats, nor physical attacks, such as that at Zapresic, will shake us in our defense of the Church, and its right to fulfill its mission."

The Archbishop knew precisely what the Communists were doing. These masters of deceit, well aware of the shortness of memory span for ordinary people, cognizant of the power in emotion-packed words, conscious of their ability to make assertions without ever offering proof, and recognizing the effect of allegations backed by specious evidence, especially that of a few photos they could caption with misleading titles, they were conditioning the reading public for an all-out attack on the Church—and their first victims, of course, would be the Hierarchy.

"Collaboration with the enemy" was *the* catch-phrase of the moment. They would use it in every conceivable context and thus "prove" that the Church had "collaborated." The people, unknown to themselves, were being "brainwashed." The Archbishop realized exactly what was being done. But he saw no way to offset the process since the State had monopolized all means of communication. All he could do was what he was now doing: write his clergy and have them enlighten the people. He ended his present letter with: "Whatever may happen in the future we have nothing to add to our defense. Our defense is in God, our conscience is clear, and our witness, besides all you Reverend Brother Priests, is the mass of our faithful people and the representatives of the Holy see in Zagreb."

It was a calm, logical, complete refutation. It was also a revelation of character. Stepinac was still using his *unice,* following the voice of his conscience, discharging his duty as he fought under "the standard of Christ" in such a way as to be *insignis,* and a man of the *"Third Class."*

To men distant in time and space from the actualities of Zagreb in 1945 it all appears incredible that anyone would make such groundless charges with hope of having them stick. But that is to forget the effect of a constant barrage from a controlled press and radio. The Communists know that "a lie repeated often enough comes to be accepted as truth." And they are skilled in the use of the press.

Just before Christmas in 1945, one of the leading dailies, *Vjesnik,* "proved" that the Archbishop had "collaborated with the enemy"—this time the Italians—by printing a letter, alleged to have been written by the Primate, asking Pope Pius XII to give a "special blessing to the Independent State of Croatia and the Pavelic regime." The paper carried no facsimile of the letter, nor the signature of the Archbishop. Hence, in the mind of any one acquainted with Communistic techniques, a question as to the genuinity of the letter arises. It is true that His Excellency wrote to the Vatican often, especially during the war years, and that he, practically always, asked for a "special blessing," but from the extant letters of the Primate it is evident that his request was always for "the Croat people" or "the Croat nation," and never for any particular party or any form of government. But there it was in print in *Vjesnik;* and who is he who is not influenced by what he sees in print?

This particular paper seemed to have a real obsession on the matter of "proving" that His Excellency was a "collaborator with the enemy." One day it would be a letter, like the above, "proving" that he had "collaborated" with the Italians. The next day it would be a picture to "prove" that he had "collaborated" with the Nazis. One such "proof" came from a "spokesman for the people" —always "the people"—who claimed to have been "an eyewitness to the daily visits of SS-General von Kasche, the German Minister to Croatia, to the Archiepiscopal Palace," and that he "knew the purpose of such visits was to plot against the people." The truth of the matter is that General von Kasche never once visited the Archbishop, never entered the Archiepiscopal Palace, and, hence, could never have "plotted against the people with His Excellency." But, there it was in print.

On January 26, 1946, *Vjesnik,* accused the Archbishop of neglecting Catholic priests who had been thrown into the concentration camp at Jasenovatz. His "proof" came from a priest who, after his release, came to the Palace to protest to the Archbishop about His Excellency's inaction. The fact is that the Primate all but deluged Pavelic himself with protests and pleas for these very priests; and the one who had come to the Palace had come not to protest, but to thank His Excellency for his heart-deep concern and his effective protestations. He himself was living proof of the effectiveness; for it was due to the Primate's protest that he had been released. But, there it was in print in *Vjesnik*.

On January 28 of the same year, *Vjesnik* carried an anonymous letter in which Stepinac was accused, not only of neglecting his duty of protecting the persecuted, but of actually approving and encouraging it!

It may have been a little consolation to the Primate to learn that Randolph Churchill, son of the famous Winston, after a visit to Tito's "Democray" in this same month of January, 1946, had written to the *Daily Telegraph* in London: "The Yugoslav propaganda against the Archbishop of Zagreb has only one purpose: to prepare the trial of the Archbishop." Stepinac himself did not question the purpose of the attack. He knew he would one day be arrested and then tried. Just what day only the masters of deceit knew. But that it was nearing he realized when a new tactic was employed: that of "mass demonstrations."

Of course all such "demonstrations" were "spontaneous"; and they showed "the invincible will of the people." But the truth is that "street secretaries," that is, Communists in charge of individual streets, lined up the inhabitants of their various streets, and marched them to fuse with the "marchers" from other streets. In these "spontaneous demonstrations" the "marchers" were commanded to shout what the leaders told them to shout, and to do it when and where they were commanded. Workers from factories and the men and women pouring out of office buildings at the end of their day's work, were similarly pressed into line and commanded to march and shout. Anyone who refused to line up, or anyone who dropped out of the "march" lost his or her job. Still the papers announced them as "spontaneous demonstrations" which clearly showed "the invincible will of the people."

This kind of thing escalated during the spring, especially among the youth who would be called to meetings, whipped to frenzy by clever "orators" who knew much about "mob psychology." The youths would then be placed in trucks, driven through the streets, shouting when commanded, and then hurling rocks at convents, monasteries, and rectories.

A warm spring really fevered into a blasting, hot summer when the third step in the process was made: Trials in People's Courts. On August 30, 1946 His Excellency, Gregory Rozman, Bishop of Ljubljana, Capitol of Slovenia, and Dr. Miha Krek, former Vice-Premier, Minister and Chairman of the Slovene's People's Party, both of whom were living in exile, were tried *in absentia* for "Collaboration with the enemy." The tactic so often used by Communists of trying an entire group, some of whom were actually guilty of the charges proffered against them, was employed. Thus bringing about "condemnation by association." The Prince Bishop and Dr. Krek, the two most prominent Catholic leaders in the land, were tried because the Slovene's People's Party while fighting against the Axis invaders had also strongly resisted Tito's *Partisans*. Of course both were found guilty by "the people" and sentenced to eighteen and fifteen years of forced labor respectively, loss of all civil rights, the confiscation of their properties, and an added ten years' loss of both civil and political rights.

Similar "trials" were held in various parts of the country, but the one that held the Archbishop's attention most grippingly was opened in Zagreb on September 9. Eighteen men were charged with "collaborating with the *Ustashi-Krizari.*" Twelve of them were priests, one of whom was Fr. Salic, the Primate's secretary who had been arrested shortly after he was hurt at Zapresic when the Archbishop went there to open the parish. For nine months Fr. Salic had been held in prison before being arraigned with the seventeen others for this "show-trial." The main charge against Fr. Salic, as against two other priests from the Archbishop's household, was that he had provided medical aid to the *Ustashi* underground. Among the eighteen being tried was a group of Franciscans, one of whom was the Provincial of the Franciscans in Croatia, a certain Father Modesto Matincic.

On September 17 the radio and press of Croatia had a field day; for Fr. Martincic had said that "the center of all terroristic action and intervention from abroad was Archbishop Stepinac," and then Fr. Salic claimed that "the Archbishop's Palace in Zagreb was the center of *Ustashi-Krizari* and terrorist action." That was bad enough, but when the Public Prosecutor introduced the Circular Letter the Archbishop had sent his clergy after the "statement" by President Backaric, and asked Fr. Salic whether he thought that the Archbishop's statement that his conscience was clear was true or not, and Fr. Salic replied: "I think the Archbishop's conscience was not clear," the "Court" was visibly stirred. Then came the climax: The Prosecutor asked Fr. Salic: "What did the

Archbishop want?" Fr. Salic answered: "He wanted the Independent State of Croatia which the *Ustashi*, Germans, and Italians established." Near pandemonium broke out in "Court."

The Public Prosecutor waited for some semblance of order before he said that "evidence is piling up that Stepinac is the immediate accomplice, promotor, and collaborator in the crimes of the eighteen men then on trial." After that statement "Court" was adjourned. On the 18th of the month the case was resumed, but the Public Prosecutor announced that because the evidence continued piling up, he had "ordered that Stepinac be put in prison and that investigations be initiated against him. When the investigations are complete, I shall indict him for offenses against the people and the State."

A ten-day adjournment was agreed upon so that the Archbishop could be charged jointly with the eighteen already on "trial." That very same night the radio announced that Archbishop Stepinac had been arrested at six o'clock that morning!

Why the State wanted ten days was evidenced when from press and radio day after day, and almost hour after hour came denunciations of the Archbishop. That it was "spontaneous" is clear from the fact that every paper and every radio announcer used the identical words and repeated the identical charges. Then came the "petitions" demanding the death of the Primate because of his crimes against "the people." Every government office, the factories and shops received these "petitions," and woe to the employee who did not sign it "spontaneously." Next came the "marches" and the "popular spontaneous demonstrations." The chant was: "Death to all priests! Death to Stepinac!"

When some protest against the "demonstrations" was made, the answer came back that "the people" had a "right" to demonstrate against "anti-nationalists." All this, note, before the indictment, let alone the trial!

On Sunday morning, September 22, at five o'clock OZNA agents were knocking on the doors of all the rectories in the Archdiocese to forbid all pastors and priests to read the Circular Letter which had been sent out from the Zagreb Chancery expressing the conviction that the Archbishop was innocent, and asking the prayers of the faithful for their Primate.

The faithful needed no urging. As soon as the news broke about the Archbishop's arrest they had poured into the Cathedral and into every other church in the city as well as into those all over the Archdiocese. To counteract this mass movement and genuinely spontaneous demonstration, OZNA agents informed all priests in Zagreb that they would be prosecuted for "disturbance of the peace and public order" if they permitted any more than five people to gather in front of their churches at any time. More OZNA agents were seen standing in front of churches taking down the names of all who entered. Fathers of families, if their names appeared on such lists, lost their jobs immediately. Mothers, widows, and orphans of fallen *Partisans* lost their State pensions if they assisted at Mass. When they protested, they were told: "The priests are your friends. Go to them for help."

The Most Reverend Joseph P. Hurley, Bishop of St. Augustine, Florida, U.S.A., was Regent of the Apostolic Nunciature in Belgrade at the time of Stepinac's arrest. Being an American, he went into action immediately. He went to see Tito. It is the Marshal himself who tells us that he "informed the Pope's representative, Mr. Hurley, that in the new Yugoslavia everyone is equal before the law, and priests who break the law will be punished." Then the Yugoslav Embassy in Washington, D.C. tells the story this way:

When Archbishop Stepinac was arrested and brought to trial in September, 1946, one argument of the critics ran along these lines: Why did the Yugoslav Government not arrest Archbishop Stepinac immediately after the liberation if his offenses were so grave? If they really had the evidence, why did they wait so long?

The answer is that the Yugoslav Government, far from being motivated by vengeful feelings, made a serious effort to avoid the necessity of taking court action against Archbishop Stepinac. It endeavored earnestly and patiently to reach a *modus vivendi* making possible a settlement of the Stepinac case.

When the War Crimes investigation produced evidence of the Archbishop's complicity in the barbarous regime of Ante Pavelic in puppet Croatia, the Yugoslav Government informed the Vatican of the nature and the volume of this evidence and asked that Stepinac be withdrawn. What happened was described by Marshal Tito in an address at Zagreb on October 31, 1946:

"When the Pope's representative to our Government, Bishop Hurley, paid me his first visit I raised the question of Stepinac. 'Have him transferred from Yugoslavia,' I said, 'for otherwise we shall be obliged to place him under arrest.' I warned Bishop Hurley of the course we had to follow. I discussed the matter with him in detail. I acquainted him with Stepinac's many hostile acts toward our country. I gave him a file of documentary evidence of the Archbishop's crimes" (p. 8 of brochure published by Yugoslav Embassy, Washington, D.C.).

That testimony merits scrutiny. It shows how to use words so that you can lie truthfully. To the undying credit of Archbishop Stepinac be it said that when he heard of the Marshal's magnanimous offer to allow him to leave the country, he replied: "My place is with my people."

The Archbishop had been arrested at 6 A.M. September 18. On the 24th of that month an indictment, dated the 23rd, reached him. It charged him:

1) As a member and instigator of the *Ustashi-Krizari* terrorist group of the defendants Lisak, Salic, and their accomplices, he helped to organize the crimes of the *Ustashi-Krizari* groups;

2) He collaborated with the occupying forces, and most closely with the so-called Independent State of Croatia of Ante Pavelic, and helped the *Ustashi;*

3) He organized the rebaptism of the Serbs in Croatia, Bosnia, and Hercegovina to the Catholic Faith;

4) As Military Vicar to the *Ustashi* and other military bands he was responsible for the hundreds of Chaplains who incited the *Ustashi* and others to strife, hatred, and crimes against the Croat people and other peoples of Yugoslavia, and against their struggle for liberation;

5) He made the Catholic Press, especially `Katholici List*, the semi-official organ of the Archdiocese of Zagreb, a channel for propaganda for the occupying forces, for Pavelic and the *Ustashi*, for justifying terrorism against the people and forcible conversions to the Catholic Faith, for a filthy campaign against the national liberation struggle, and for the instigation of national and religious hatred;

6) In agreement with Pavelic, he hid the Archives of the *Ustashi* Ministry of Foreign Affairs, and other

criminal *Ustashi* documents, in the Archbishop's Palace. Do not be appaled at the brazenness of such groundless charges. But gasp when you learn that His Excellency was indicted under the "Laws on Crimes against the People and the State," a statute which was approved only in August 15, 1945, and amended July 9, 1946. Practically every charge in the indictment refers to acts allegedly performed by the Primate before the statute was adopted.

How those members of the Pavelic regime who had escaped the country must have gasped at the charge that His Excellency had supported the *Ustashi* Government, and how members of the Vatican Diplomatic Corps would have been forced to join them. For both knew that when Archbishop Stepinac made his *ad limina* visit to the Pope in 1942, Pavelic had made a special request of the Holy See, asking that "the archbishop of Zagreb be persuaded to desist from his severe attitude toward us." Six months later the Minister of the Interior was complaining to Rt. Rev. Abbot Giuseppe Ramiro Marcone, O.S.B., Apostolic Visitor to the Yugoslav Hierarchy, that "Archbishop Stepinac has never uttered a single word to show his adherence to the present Government."

Sitting in his prison cell the Archbishop could not avoid meditating on what it cost to be a man, then on the higher cost one has to pay to be a Catholic man, then on the still higher price one has to pay to be a genuine priest, but, finally, on the supreme price exacted from one who will be a Good Shepherd. But then the lines from the Bible about the "pearl of great price" echoed in his mind even as his heart told of the "pebble" to be given to those who "overcome" mentioned in the Book of Revelation (Cf. Rev 2:17). Any price was worth paying for the purchase of that "pebble." He was arrested. For a full week he did not know the charges, but from the moment of arrest he was quite sure of the verdict. True, he had not yet been tried, but he well knew he had already been condemned. He was calm even though he expected the sentence to be what the "spontaneous demonstrations" had been demanding: Death. That brought on a new series of thoughts. He had never felt himself worthy to be a priest. As for being a prelate he had always felt himself distinctly unworthy. Now it looked as if he were being selected to become a martyr. That was what this imprisonment meant. The Tito regime would exterminate the Church. The first step would be to besmirch the name, the character, and all the acts of him who was the Church's chief representative in the land—the Primate. "*Domine, non sum dignus*" was his final word to such a series of thoughts.

Life is a Passion Play. In it individuals, not by assuming any character, but by actually repeating the acts of the first characters, are alternately Judas, Peter, John, Pilate, Caiphas, Annas, judge and condemned man, executioner and victim. The Primate knew he was taking on that last role now. But, after all, was it so surprising? What is a baptized person but a sharer in the Priesthood of Christ; and what is a share in His Priesthood but a share in His Victimhood? After all, God seemingly was simply asking him to be what he had been made by God. If he thought of his statue of Judas at all in these prison hours, it would only be to set him praying that since he was now in his "Grotto," he be strengthened to carry on: go to Annas' house, then to Caiphas,' on to Pilate and the Praetorium, and always as Christ—never as Christ's betrayer.

As he thought of the testimony that had brought him to

his prison cell—that of Fathers Salic and Martincic—he had to shake his head in wonder at the similarity between his own experience and that of Christ. He hoped that the similarity, as far as the two priests were concerned, was only a surface similarity. He knew they had been in prison for months—a Communist prison. Father Salic had been there for nine full months. The Archbishop told himself that anything can happen to the mind of a man under pressure for that length of time. "Forgive them," was ever on his lips, even though memory would suggest that other phrase: "one of the twelve."

Life is a mystery, he admitted. Life as a Christian, even more mysterious. As for life as a priest—what is it but an abyss of shadows, not of light; and abysses are never easily explored. He was calm; even happy. But he did have to tell himself that "intimacy with Christ" can be both simultaneously exhilarating and frightening. Who will question about his use of Christ's words: "Father, if it be possible, let this chalice pass from me. Yet, not my will but Thine be done"?

He had met God daily. But this meeting at this hour, in this place, with this prospect was different, very different—and yet, as he went back over the years, he saw it was not essentially different. He told himself that St. Paul had been exact when he said: "Jesus Christ, yesterday, today, and the same forever." By Baptism, Confirmation, Ordination and Consecration he had been made Christ. How could he be surprised, then, to find himself where he was? The morrow could only bring something very similar to the "trials" of Christ—and at their end, Christ's condemnation. He simply said: *"Fiat voluntas Tua"*—"Thy will be done ... *by me!*"

9 The Light Still Shines In the Darkness

THE TEMPTATION HAS BEEN STRONG, almost over-whelming. Yes, the temptation to say right here: "The case rests." You have looked upon a *man.* You have seen him prove his manhood many times and in many ways. He is one who based his whole life and all his living on principle. You have looked upon a patriot: a man who loves his country without ever hating any other land; a man who is ever working for the good of his country, and ready, if necessary, to lay down his life for her. You have seen a priest: a man sanctified by the Sacrament of Holy Orders who is naught but sacrifice for God and others. You have gazed long at a prelate who was in every breath and heart-beat a Good Shepherd. If you know anything at all about the present day, you know how nearly desperate is our need for men, patriots, priests and prelates. So you know now why Aloysius Cardinal Stepinac has been called THE MAN FOR THIS MOMENT. So you see how justifiable it would be to say: "The case rests."

But the temptation must be resisted; for the whole story has not yet been told. Further, it may yet be said that "in his end was his beginning." Not only because his compatriots are appreciating him more day after day; not only because the world of thinking men outside his country are seeing him for what he was; but because in his end we see him at his best.

And still the temptation to rest the case here still nags and gnaws; for it seems almost inhuman to take you into what they called a "Court Room" where was held, for some twelve days, what they named a "Trial," and thus submit you to the torture of watching truth twisted out of all recognizability, seeing justice jaundiced over as the "Blind Goddess" was rendered deaf and the scales in her hands so heavily weighted on one side that all she could dispense was vengeance. It seems more than unkind; it appears cuttingly cruel to seat you in this "Court Room"—which was actually a school gymnasium in Zagreb— from September 30, 1946 until October 11 of the same year, and have you enveloped in an atmosphere saturated with hate.

I have been into this "Court Room" often. It has always impressed me as dark, very dark, despite the way it is lighted up. And that kind of darkness is spreading over our world at THIS MOMENT. So the cruelty may be genuine kindness at that. For while you have had opportunity to gaze on THE MAN, it is possible that many of us have not stared long enough, nor often enough at THIS MOMENT. It is possible that too few have actually seen it for what it is. Hence, the taking you into this "Court Room" may be something of a necessity, not to hurt you, but to help you. It can enable many who call themselves "Realists" to see Reality in all its nakedness; bring those who deem themselves "Existentialists" into intimate, personal contact with existential actuality; and show those who are clamoring for "co-existence" just what and with whom they will have to "co-exist" if they ever get their way. But I will spare you as much as I can of the horror. . . .

It is horror; for the darkness mentioned above is chilling darkness, and the chill seeps deeper and ever deeper until it gets into the blood, then into the bone, and finally into one's very being. It is a darkness and a chill that moves. It is never still. It writhes. It whirls. It eddies. One feels it pressuring from all sides. On the senses first; then on the psyche; finally into the very soul. It is the pressure of evil. It is the fierce pressure of hate.

I do not exaggerate. The whole affair is especially repulsive to Americans brought up under the 14th Amendment. It was Acting Secretary of State, Dean Acheson, who remarked when asked for comment on the trial. . . . "It is the civil liberties aspect of the thing which causes us concern: aspects which raise the questions as to whether the trial has any implications looking toward the impairment of freedom of religion and of worship; the aspects of it which indicate, at least to reporters who reported it from the spot, that the actual conduct of the trial left a great deal to be desired. You will recall that under the Constitution and law of the United States

291

fairness of trial is guaranteed under the 14th Amendment, and the Supreme Court of the United States has set aside as not being legal procedure at all trials in which the courtroom has been dominated by feelings adverse to the defendant by demonstrations of prejudice. That is deeply inherent in the American system, that the very essence of due process of law is that in trials we shall lean over backwards in being fair to the defendant, in the atmosphere of the courtroom, in forbidding demonstrations of spectators, in opportunity of facing and cross-examining witnesses—all these matters seem to us to be absolutely inherent in the matter of a fair trial. It is that aspect of the thing . . . which causes us concern and deep worry."

That comment was made on October 20, 1946, nine days after the verdict had been given. To see why the Dean was worried read this article from the *New York Times* of September 23, 1946, seven days before the trial opened: "The Zagreb newspaper *Vjestnik* today denounced Catholic Archbishop Stepinac as the 'Supreme Head of all the dark and bloody crimes committed by pro-Fascist bands since Allied forces drove the Germans out of Yugoslavia. . . . Stepinac will answer for the heavy crimes he has committed during the occupation and since Yugoslavia's liberation. He is responsible for four years of collaboration with the enemy. He is responsible for a protection of *Ustashi* slaughterers, for diplomatic activity before the collapse of the Croat Independent State, for the Episcopal Letter directed against the National Liberation struggle and for the anti-national spirit that he propagated as supreme head of the Church among his subordinates.'

"Zagreb papers and the provincial Croat press opened a concerted editorial attack against Archbishop Stepinac himself. . . . The general Croat press theme today was: 'The entire population, with great interest, is awaiting the continuation of the trial of *Ustashi* criminals before the Supreme Court of Croatia at which time Dr. Stepinac will appear on the defendant's bench.' "

There you have it a week before the trial opened: the Press is not saying that the Archbishop should be *tried* for these alleged offenses, but that he is *guilty* of them. Note again that while the *New York Times* names only one paper, it adds that "Zagreb papers and the provincial Croat press opened a concerted editorial attack"; further it gives "the *general* Croat press theme." You know what has happened to a case thus prejudiced by the press in our United States.

As for the conduct of the "Court"—its impartiality and decorum can be judged from this one sentence from the *London Times* of October 2, 1946: "Frequently both the president of the court and the prosecution were directing so many questions at him (Stepinac) that he was cut off in the middle of a sentence."

As for witnesses—on October 7, the judges announced that the defense witnesses would be heard, but before a single one of them took the stand "The Court" made this statement: "These witnesses cannot contribute anything to modify the substance of the indictment. They can only testify regarding details. They might be able to show that Stepinac protected a few isolated Serbs and Jews. But to pretend to base a defense on this would be an intolerable affrontery in a Peoples' Court. The defense witnesses are notorious Fascists, and Fascists cannot testify on behalf of Fascists in our country. This would be placing the Court and democracy on the level of a country where Fascism and not the people had been victorious. Stepinac supported terrorism . . . his conduct was identical with that of Pavelic. If there were differences it was on the personal level and does not affect the general situation."

After that impartial and completely unprejudiced statement, the same "Court" proceeded to disqualify fourteen of the twenty it allowed the defense to summon—and on the grounds of some of them being "Fascists." All that despite the fact that the Prosecution had called and had been allowed as witnesses three men who were awaiting trial as "Fascists: the former Minister of Defense, the former Minister of Finance, and the former Minister of Foreign Affairs for the Pavelic regime. On top of that, most of the Documentary evidence submitted by the Defense was arbitrarily ruled out. That the "Judges" had already judged is evident from an incident that would never be so much as allowed in our Courts. A woman witness at the trial of Colonel Lisak, with whom the Archbishop was being tried, showed the Court a piece of rope by which she said her daughter had been hanged and demanded that Colonel Lisak be hanged by the same rope. Then the Court President asked the Archbishop whether he still considered it his civic duty to attend dinners and banquets "with Lisak and other criminals." Lisak had, as yet, not been proved a criminal! Yet here was the judge already branding the Colonel as a criminal. The Archbishop calmy replied: "My conscience is clear." Then this impartial President of the Court snapped: "You must have a very loose conscience if you could be in the company of such people."

As for "the jury"—they were "the people"—And just precisely what people? Only those who had tickets for admission. These tickets had been given out by members of the OZNA—the Secret Police of Tito's Yugoslavia.

No one received a ticket unless he or she was rabidly attached to the Communist State and feverishly antagonistic to the defendant. No one was allowed into that "Court" who was not ready to hiss, jeer, scoff and sneer at every word that favored the accused and to applaud, cheer, and shout approval at every phrase that seemed to serve the State.

It was a very fair trial. The judges: Zarko Vinpulsek, Ante Cireneo, and Ivan Poldrugac were "good sons of the people." The "jury" was made up of the same—after having been conditioned, actually brainwashed, by a full year of planned propaganda which poured from press and radio with ever increasing malice until hate had reached hysteria. The Public Prosecutor for the Popular Croat Republic was one Jakov Blazevic who closed his case with the calm, reasoned, legally temperate, and thoroughly humane statement:

"In conclusion, there can be no question of the persecution of the Catholic Church, her priests, or her faithful. It is a question of the prosecution in criminal law of the defendant Stepinac who, as a simple traitor to our people, supported the occupier and with Pavelic and the *Ustashi* collaborated against the National Resistance Movement. He incited the people to civil war and a fratricidal struggle, and after the liberation, continued to incite, aid, encourage, and support the former *Ustashi* regime who, under the guise of crusaders, continued to commit crimes.

"Therefore, our whole people, eager for peace, work, progress, and freedom, demands that the defendant Stepinac, with the other defendants be punished as they deserve.

"Death to Fascism! Freedom to the People!"

You now have some idea why the Acting Secretary

of the United States was concerned and deeply worried. You also should see why I feel darkness and chill, venom, hate and evil in the very atmosphere of this "Court." But those are only some of the realities and existential facts that marked the twelve days in Zagreb in the fall of 1946. When you learn that the Archbishop was allowed but one hour with his counsel, Dr. Ivo Politeo, on September 27th; that every obstacle was placed in His Excellency's way as he prepared his defense; that not even the privilege of consulting with Archbishop Hurley, the acting Papal Nuncio in Yugoslavia was granted him; when you learn that the "Court" rejected one of the two lawyers the Archbishop's friends proposed to defend him—"for reasons not given out"—when you learn that at one point in the trial when the "Court" accused Dr. Politeo of "unduly prolonging the trial," this good man was so moved by the prejudice of the "Court" that he retorted: "By actual count the prosecution talked for forty-eight hours, the defense for exactly twenty minutes"; you have a clearer idea why I have saved you as much as I can of the actual horror, and why I have insisted on giving those who would "co-exist" some inkling of what and with whom they would have to co-exist.

If you will go deeper into reality, plumb the depths, theologically, of the existential facts; you will see that, thanks to the dignity in the person of Aloysius Stepinac we actually co-exist with none other than Jesus Christ. As we watch this prelate stand before his accusers and listen to him as he gives his last words and recall Blaise Pascal's words about "Jesus Christ being in agony until the end of time," we will see in the Primate of Yugoslavia during his agony the agonizing Christ.

There were two men in that crowded "Court Room"

who recognized "the defendant Stepinac" for whom he was: Archbishop Hurley and the Public Prosecutor, Jakov Blazevic. The Papal Representative, because of his position, was allowed into the "trial." After all, there are some limitations even the brazen Communists dare not pass. Every time Archbishop Stepinac was taken to or from the dock, Archbishop Hurley rose and bowed to the one he saw in "the defendant Stepinac"—Jesus Christ. Jakov Blazevic showed his mind, and actually exposed the purpose of the State in this prosecution, when he turned, at the conclusion of his case, to the silent and truly majestic Archbishop and angrily exclaimed: "You are trying to assume the role of a martyr like Jesus Christ before Pilate."

How apt a simile. How exact a similitude. The "judges," like Pilate, were representatives of a foreign power; for what Rome was to Judea, Communist Yugoslavia was— and is—to Croatia, and what Pontius Pilate was to Annas, Caiphas and the rest of the ruling class in the first century, Zacho Vimpulseck, Ante Cireneo, and Ivan Poldrugac were to Tito, Stalin, and the Kremlin in the twentieth. The Prosecutor's angry words set echoes of what the demoniac in the country of the Geresenes testified to the moment Jesus stepped from the boat in which His disciples had carried Him across from Galilee the time He calmed the wind and the waves by a word. To all within earshot that day the demoniac testified that Jesus was "son of the Most High God" (Cf. Lk 8:28). One can go further and say that Jakov Blazevic by his outburst tells the thinking man what the Voice from Heaven told Saul of Tarsus the day he was knocked from his horse on the Damascus Road: Christians and Christ are one. Hence, it is obvious to these that Aloysius Stepinac was not the lone man who was being badgered and bullied in the "Court Room" at Zagreb during that travesty of a trial in the fall of 1946; it was the Vatican as well, and with the Vatican the Catholic religion, and ultimately, yet most really, that Religion's Founder—Jesus Christ. Tito, Yugoslavia, and atheistic Communism were persecuting God.

Small wonder I find that "Court Room" black, cold, and writhing with hate. Small wonder I have been tempted to spare you the horror of contact with incarnate evil.

But there was one light in that blackness—really "the Light of the world"; for Christ did say: "You are the light of the world" (Mt 5:18). That light was the thin, tall prelate, clothed in a loose-fitting black soutane who always talked with calm composure, ever walked with real majesty, and comported himself with genuine dignity. That light was Archbishop Aloysius Stepinac, Primate of the Catholic Church in Croatia.

History was repeating itself. In the house of Annas, in the house of Caiphas, and before Pilate, Jesus Christ had shone in the first century. He was shining again in the person of Croatia's Primate in the mid-twentieth. But history repeats itself with some variations. The People's Court in Zagreb on October 3, 1946 heard more from the pre-judged but as yet not condemned "criminal" than did the other "courts" in Jerusalem on the 14th day of the month Nisan before the mid-first century. Jesus Christ answered Annas—only to be struck on the face by a guard. Jesus Christ answered Caiphas—only to have the high priest rend his garments, name God a "blasphemer," and declare the Author of Life worthy of death. Jesus Christ answered Pilate—only to have that petty potentate, after learning whence he got his authority, learning that Jesus Christ was indeed King, learning that He had declared Himself Son of God, after learning truth from Truth

298

Incarnate, sneeringly ask: "What is truth?" And then, though he had told the people time and time again that he "found no cause in Him," in other words, that he found Jesus innocent, this weak-kneed representative of all-powerful Rome, handed Christ over to be crucified. Yes, Jesus spoke to His three so-called judges; spoke forthrightly, fearlessly, and with faultless truth. But He always spoke briefly. In the mid-twentieth century He would speak again to His three so-called judges, speak faultless truth, speak with utter fearlessness and stout-hearted forthrightness but, through the lips of Aloysius Stepinac. He would speak more at length. Yet the substance of His reply in 1946 sets echoes ringing in one's memory of what Christ had said with His own lips and in His physical body, when He spoke to Pilate: "For this purpose was I born, for this purpose I came into the world—to give testimony to the truth. Only he who is open to the truth gives ear to my voice" (Jn 18:37). No one in Pilate's court gave ear then—though Incarnate Truth was speaking. No one in the so-called People's Court gave ear now—though it was the same Truth speaking through the prolongation of His Incarnation in Aloysius Stepinac.

That reads like mysticism, doesn't it? Some will ask: How can a man, born twenty centuries after Christ lived and died, be called Christ? Give us reality. Others will insist that Aloysius Stepinac was but a man, born of a human father named Joseph and a human mother named Barbara; that the same Aloysius Stepinac lived and died a mere man. Why, then, name him God-man? Others will simply say: Have done with romanticism and sheer rhetoric. Give us existential fact. Call him Christian if you like, but not Christ.

That is precisely why this chapter had to be written.

299

For we would give reality to Realists, incontestable fact to anti-romanticists, and mere prose, but prose that pierces to and probes the heart, to opponents of rhetoric. Sophisticates of the twentieth century need to learn that Christians and Christ are one; that humans, by Baptism, are divinized; that when a body is struck, it is the person who owns that body who suffers. And the unsophisticated, who are usually the much more wise, need to know that Communism, no matter what its type: Chinese, Russian, Polish, East German, or Yugoslavian, actually persecutes but one Person—the Second Person of the Blessed Trinity—when it persecutes individual Christians.

We all need to recall again and again the Damascus Road and hear that Voice from heaven asking Saul: "Why persecutest thou Me?" and grasp the truth of the reply that came to Saul's query: "I am Jesus whom you are persecuting" (Acts 22:6).

What has been said of Christ can be said of anti-Christ: "the same yesterday, today, and forever." And that is said with full cognizance of the "dialogue" which the leading theoretician of the French Communist Party, Roger Garaudy, would institute between Communists and Christians; with full cognizance of all the key leaders of the U.S. Communist Party, including party boss, Gus Hall, and the leading theoretician, Herbert Aptheker, had to say in the July, 1966 issue of *Political Affairs,* the official monthly organ of the Communist Party U.S.A. There they stated that Communism and Religion are no longer incompatible; that Christians and Communists not only can, but that they should, work together. They even went so far as to say that in a Communist United States "full freedom of conscience and worship will be guaranteed." When did they ever say anything different? When did they ever allow either?

In 1905 Lenin wrote: "Religion is the opium of the people. Religion is a kind of spiritual vodka in which the slaves of capital drown their human shape and their claims to any decent human life." In 1927 Stalin wrote: "The Party cannot be neutral toward Religion.... Antireligious propaganda is a means by which the complete liquidation of the reactionary clergy must be brought about." In 1946 *Young Bolshevik*, an official organ of the Party stated: "Dialectical materialism, the philosophy of Marxism-Leninism and the theoretical foundation of the Communist Party, is incompatible with Religion ... the Party is bound to oppose Religion." Earl Browder, for years the leader of the Communist Party U.S.A., stated that "the Communist Party is the enemy of Religion."

Has there been a "thaw"? Do Garaudy and Aptheker represent the truth? Have present-day Communists repudiated Marx, Lenin, and Earl Browder? Read *Pravda* for the 12th of January, 1967: "In true accord with Leninist tradition our Party is continuously giving great attention to the problems of atheism. The fight against religious remnants is not in the nature of a campaign of an isolated or self-sufficient event. Rather, it is an inseparable part of the entire ideological activity of the Party organization. The Party orients all its organization and its ideological institutions towards aggressive, atheistic activity." Read *Communist of the Armed Forces* for February, 1967: "Religion and scientific Communism can have nothing in common nor be related to each other, as was proved by scholars of Marxism-Leninism. In the future all the forms of Religion will be thrown in the rubbish heap of History."

301

There has been no "thaw." There never will be. But "the masters of deceit" will propagandize. *Pravda* is ever so much more reliable than Roger Garaudy. Herbert Aptheker or Gus Hall. Like Christ, the anti-Christ is "the same yesterday, today, and forever."

The cry today is for tangible reality, naked truth, existential fact. That is why the temptation to "rest the case" has been rejected. Whittaker Chambers, a man who knew Communism from the inside, gave some naked truth, existential fact, and tangible reality when he wrote in the mid-twentieth century: "I am baffled by the way people still speak of the West as if it were a cultural unity against Communism though it is divided not only by a political, but by an invisible cleavage. On the one side are the voiceless masses with their own subdivisions and fractures. On the other side is the enlightened, articulate elite which, to one degree or another, has rejected the religious roots of the civilization—the roots without which it is no longer Western civilization, but a new order of beliefs, attitudes, and mandates. In short, this is the order of which Communism is one logical expression, originating not in Russia, but in culture capitals of the West. . . . It is a Western body of belief that now threatens the West from Russia. As a body of Western beliefs, secular and rationalistic, the intelligentsia of the West share it. . . . If they could have Communism without the brutalities of ruling that the Russian experience bred, they have only marginal objections. Why should they object? What else is socialism but Communism with the claws retracted? . . . What is more, every garage mechanic in the West, insofar as he believes in nuts and bolts but asks: 'The Holy Ghost, what's that?' shares the substance of those same beliefs. Of course the mechanic does not know, when he asks:

302

'The Holy Ghost, what's that?' that he is simply echoing Stalin at Teheran: 'The Pope—how many divisions has the Pope?' That is the real confrontation of forces. The enemy—he is ourselves. That is why it is idle to talk about preventing the wreck of Western civilization. It is already a wreck from within. That is why we can hope to do little more now than snatch a fingernail of a saint from the rack, or a handful of ashes from the faggots, and bury them secretly in a flowerpot against the day, ages hence, when a few men begin again to dare to believe that there was once something else, that something else is thinkable, and need some evidence of what it was, and the fortifying knowledge that there were those who, at the great nightfall, took loving thought to preserve the tokens of hope and truth."

In the blackness of the "nightfall" I am showing you a Light to give some "fortifying knowledge" to all, along with some "hope and truth." That is why I say that Josip Broz Tito put Jesus Christ on trial when he had Archbishop Aloysius Stepinac brought before the so-called tribunal of the People's Court September 30, 1946. He, and all his henchmen, knew more clearly than Pilate that an innocent man was on trial and would be condemned. On that last day of September, 1946, Jesus Christ stood before judges and people in that Zagreb gymnasium just as really as He stood before people and judges when Pilate brought Him out from the Praetorium back in Jerusalem and cried: "Behold the man!" Further, Jesus Christ heard in the mid-twentieth century as He stood before the people in Zagreb, just what He had heard in the early first century when He stood before His own people in Jerusalem; for group dynamics, or, if you will, "mob psychology" worked as successfully in the Croatian

303

capital as it had that first Good Friday in the capital city for all Abraham's sons. Jesus Christ is "the same yesterday, today, and forever."

It is no cause for surprise then, that, when He stood before modern pharisees, He said again what He said then: "I speak the truth, and therefore you do not believe me. . . . Which of you can prove me guilty of sin? . . . As it is, you want to kill me—a man who has told you the truth. . . . Suppose I do testify in my own case: my testimony is valid even then, for I know where I came from and where I am going. . ." (Cf. Jn, ch. 8). In 1946 He, through the lips of Aloysius Stepinac, said: "My conscience is clear. . . . You can bring a thousand proofs, but you will never be able to prove a single crime." That was the Archbishop's reply to the indictment the first day of the trial. It was as clear a challenge as Christ's: "Which of you can convict me of sin?" It was as well founded, as the world learned on October 3, 1946, when the same "criminal"—and the same Christ in, through, and with him,—spoke out fully and fearlessly, and accused the accusers as he said:

"To all the charges brought against me here in Court, I answer that my conscience is clear in every way. (Even though the public here present ridicule this statement.) I seek neither to defend myself, nor to appeal against the verdict. For my convictions I am able to bear not only ridicule, hatred, humiliation, but, because my conscience *is* clear, I am ready at any moment to die.

"Hundreds of times here in this Court I have been called 'the defendant Stepinac.' There is no one so naive as not to know that with 'the defendant Stepinac' here on the bench there sits the Archbishop of Zagreb, the Metropolitan of Croatia, and the head of the Catholic

304

Church in Yugoslavia. You yourselves have many times appealed to the accused priests here in this Court to acknowledge that only Stepinac is guilty for their, the people's and the clergy's, stand. Stepinac, the man, could never have had such an influence; only Stepinac, the Archbishop, could.

"For seventeen months there has been waged a campaign against me in public and in the Press; and for twelve months I have been in actual internment in the Archbishop's Palace.

"You accuse me of having re-baptized Serbs into the Catholic Church. But you use the wrong word; for he who has once been baptized, need never be re-baptized. What you actually accuse me of is not re-baptism of Serbs, but of having caused conversions of Serbs to the Catholic Church. I shall waste no words on this matter, but only repeat that my conscience is at peace, and that the time will come when history will establish the truth. As an illustration, however, of what actually happened, I may reveal today that I had to transfer parish priests to other parishes because they feared reprisals from the Orthodox. Some Serbs wanted to kill these priests because they had refused them admission into the Catholic Church. It is a fact that during the late War the Church had to find her way through many terrible situations, but we can calmly say that we have done all that was possible to help the Serbian people.

"The honorable judge has produced evidence that I sought an abandoned Monastery in Grahovitza for the Trappists who had been driven from their own Monastery at Rajhenburg by the Germans. That is true. But let me say first of all that this Monastery at Grahovitza was once a Catholic Monastery belonging to our own Pauline

Fathers. Secondly, this monastery was empty. Thirdly, the Trappists had been thrown out of their own home by the Hitlerites. I considered it my sacred duty to aid my brother Slovenes in such circumstances.

"I am accused of having instituted the office of the Military Vicariate. The President of the Court here asked me if I did not consider myself a traitor to Yugoslavia because in this matter I sought an understanding with the Independent State of Croatia. I was Military Vicar in old Yugoslavia. I labored through eight to nine years to bring about a definite solution of this religious problem between Church and State. The question was finally solved through the Yugoslav Concordat. But that Concordat, after having been signed and ratified, collapsed in the streets of Belgrade. At a time when the Yugoslav Army had already capitulated and the war between Yugoslavia and Germany was at an end, I had to look after the spiritual welfare of the Catholic soldiers in what remained of the old Yugoslav Army and in the Army of the Independent State of Croatia. The State had collapsed, but the soldiers of the Army remained, and we had to do our duty toward them.

"I was far from being a *persona grata* either to the Germans or the *Ustashi*. Much less was I a *Ustashi* myself. I did not take the oath of allegiance as did some of the officials of this Court whom I see sitting here today. The Croatian nation unanimously declared itself for the Croatian State, and I should have been a despicable man had I not heard and understood the beating of the heart of the Croatian people who were slaves in the former Yugoslavia. A Croat could not get promotion in the Army or in the Diplomatic Service unless he changed his religion or married one of the other faith. That is the fact which

306

served as basis and background for my sermons and my Pastoral Letters.

"Whatever I have said about the right of the Croat people to their national freedom and independence is in complete accord with moral law, and no one can reproach the Croats for wanting that freedom and independence. Such a desire is in perfect accord with the basic principles laid down by the Allies in the Atlantic Charter. If, according to these principles, every nation has a right to independence, why should it be denied the Croatians? The Holy See has many times solemnly emphasized the fact that the small nations have the same right to be free as the big nations. Do you really think that a Catholic Bishop and a Metropolitan should never so much as mention the matter? If we have to perish for that, we will; but it will be for having done our duty.

"If you think that the Croat people are satisfied with their present fate, I challenge you to give them once more the opportunity of expressing freely their own will. Let there be no doubt about my attitude. No difficulties will come from my side. I have always respected, and still do respect, the will of my own people, so long as that will does not contradict the principles of the Catholic Church.

"You accuse me of being an enemy of the State and of the people's authority. Do tell me, please, which was the lawful authority for me in 1941? Was it the Shimovitch Government which, as you say, put in a King illegally, against the Constitution? Or was it the 'traitorous,' as you call it, government in exile in London? Or was it the government set up in Palestine? Or was it Mihailovic, who was not known at the time? Or was it your government, functioning 'in the woods'—which did not even exist then? Is it possible to serve two masters at the same time? Of course not. That is impossible according to Catholic morals, the law of nations, and common sense. We could not ignore the Government in Zagreb, even though it was the *Ustashi* Government. It was here. You have a right to question me and make me answer for my deeds since May 8, 1945, and only since then.

"As for my so-called 'acts of terrorism,' you have no proof, nor will anyone believe you. If Lisak, Lela Sofijanec, and others came to me under assumed names, if I received a letter which I never read, and if it be a crime for men to come to me, I shall accept the verdict with equanimity. It does not trouble my conscience to have issued a certificate of free movement to Rev. Maric, for I did not do so for the purpose of creating disorder. If this be a crime, then I shall go to the other world with my soul at peace. Whether you believe me or not does not matter. The accused Archbishop of Zagreb knows not only how to suffer but also how to die for his convictions.

"Premier Backaric of Croatia himself made this statement to Father Milanovic: 'We are convinced that the Archbishop stands behind these acts, but we have no proof.' That, for me, is sufficient acknowledgment of my innocence.

"But now let us come to the core of our controversy and ask just why these vicissitudes, and why no peaceful solution. The Public Prosecutor has again and again asserted that nowhere else in the world is there such 'freedom of conscience' as there is here in this State. Let me give you a few facts to prove the contrary:

"First of all, I again affirm that between 260 and 270 priests have been killed by the National Liberation Front. There exists no civilized country in the world where so many priests would have been put to death for such so-called crimes as you have brought up against them. For example, Father Buerger, Pastor of Podravska Slatina, a member of the *Kulturbund*, should have been sentenced, at the very most, to, let us say, eight years in prison. But no. You killed him—because, as was his sacred duty as Dean, he had saved the sacred vessels of a National Shrine. Then take the case of Father Povolnjak—without any trial whatsoever, he was killed in the street like a dog. And the same must be said about the fate of the accused Sisters. In no civilized country in the world would death have been meted out to them; but only, at most, a prison sentence.

"You have made a grave error, a fatal mistake, when you began murdering priests. For the people will never forget; nor will they ever forgive you for that. Such is your 'freedom.'

"Now look at our Catholic Schools. We built them in difficult times, and with great personal and national sacrifice. You have thrown us out of them, and taken many away from us. Had not American friends sent us this year seventy tons of various materials, we should not have been able to carry on even in our provisional Seminary, since the original Seminary had been taken from us. And who are the seminarians—Capitalists? No! They are the children of our poorest peasant population. You looted the Seminary and forcefully took over all its property. In doing this you did nothing less than the Gestapo did when it robbed the Seminary at Mokritza of all its farm lands. Why have you done such things? We are not against agrarian reform. The Holy See has issued many Encyclicals on the Social question. But we do insist that such reforms concerning Church property should have been made in agreement with the Holy See.

309

"Our Catholic Press has been destroyed. Our Catholic printing presses have been silenced. Our plants taken away. We no longer have a Press of our own—that Press which has been so savagely attacked in this very Court. The Dominican Fathers were unable to publish a spiritual book which I had translated from the French, and was to have been printed at a cost of 75,000 dinars. Is that your 'Freedom of the Press'? Is it not manifestly scandalous to maintain that nowhere in the world does the Church enjoy such 'freedom' as here?

"The St. Jerome Society has ceased to exist. To treat thus this their greatest and oldest cultural institution is a grave offense against the whole people.

"Look at our Catholic Orphanages and institutions for the poor. You have liquidated them! Not the buildings, but those who gave help and consolation there. Our nursing Sisters in the Catholic Hospitals must bear untold miseries and hardships. And yet you have the audacity to claim that the Church is nowhere so 'free' as in Yugoslavia.

"You have reproached me for the work of my *Caritas.* But I tell you in this Court: *Caritas* has performed untold services for our people and for your very own children.

"Then there is the question of religious instruction in the schools. You have laid down the rule: In the higher grades religious instruction is forbidden; in the lower grades it is according to choice. How can you give to children who have not yet grown up the right to choose for themselves, while to those in higher grades, who are actually capable of choosing for themselves, you deny all freedom of choice in the matter?

"Against the overwhelming opposition of the people you have introduced civil marriage. Why do you not interpret this freedom in accordance with the mentality of the people? In America—where rules a wise republic—one is free to choose either civil or religious marriage; and that is wiser! We do not deny you some control over marriage. But it grievously pains our people when they first must enter a civil marriage before they can enter a religious one. If you had turned to us, we would have given you suggestions on this matter.

"The buildings of the Religious in Bachka have been confiscated. Some Churches in Split—I do not know whether it is still the case—have been converted into storehouses. Without agreement with the Holy See, Church lands have been seized. It is because of this sort of agrarian reform that the people refuse to take such lands from you.

"But the material question is the least of our concerns. The tragic thing is this: not a single Bishop, not a single priest in this country knows in the morning if he will be alive that evening, or knows at night if he will ever see the dawn. Bishop Shrebnic was attacked at Susak by youngsters at the instigation of responsible elders. For three hours these youngsters tormented him and even invaded his quarters, while your police and militia stolidly looked on. I myself suffered a similar experience at Zapresic when I was attacked with rocks and revolvers. Bishop Lach, when on a Confirmation tour—and this fact was known—was turned back from the Drave and held a whole night in prison at Korivnica. In fact your own men who were 'in the woods' came to me and stated: 'This conduct is unbecoming. We shall protest to the authorities.' While Bishop Buric was on a Confirmation tour rocks were hurled through the windows of the house in which he was staying. Bishop Pusic, as I heard, was the target recently of rotten apples and eggs. Such 'freedom' we hold to be an illusion. We do not wish to exist like outlawed bandits. We shall fight for our rights with all just means—and do so right here in the State.

"Just that you may know why we fight, I will add three or four more examples of your 'freedom.' In the class-rooms, in defiance of all historical proofs, it is officially taught that Jesus Christ never existed. Know you, then, that Jesus Christ is God! And for Him we are ready to die. Yet today you teach that He never actually lived. If any teacher dared to teach the contrary, he would most cer-tainly be expelled. I tell you, Mr. Public Prosecutor, the Church is not 'free'; but slowly will be annihilated. Christ is the foundation of Christianity. You claim to have con-cern for the Orthodox Serbs. But I ask you: How can you conceive of Orthodoxy without Christ? How can you conceive of the Catholic Church without Christ? It is an utter absurdity.

"Another thing: In the school-books it is stated that the Mother of God is an adulteress. Do you not know that in the minds and the hearts of Catholic and Orthodox the Mother of God is enshrined as holy?

"As official doctrine you have proclaimed that man originated from the apes. Perhaps some people may have that high ambition, but why decree as an official theory what no scholar of any repute holds to be valid? Accord-ing to your understanding materialism is the only accept-able system, and that implies the elimination of God— and of Christianity. If there be nothing but matter—then thank you for your 'freedom.'

"One of your most influential men has boasted that there is no one in this State whom you cannot bring to Court—and sentence. So to these outrageous charges whereby you place us among murderers and associates of terrorists, I say to you that not all the evil committed in the former Independent State of Croatia was the work of *Domobrani* or the *Ustashi*.

"Let no one think I want conflict. Let the present authorities come to an understanding with the Holy See. The Church does not recognize dictatorships, but she is not against honest understandings. If that could be achieved, then the Bishops would know what is their duty, and there will be no further need to seek out priests, as was done here, to point out their Bishop's guilt.

"Finally I want to say a few words to the Communist Party, which, in reality, is my accuser. If you think we have taken the present stand because of material things, you are wrong; for we have stood firm even after you have made us poor. We are not against workers obtaining greater rights in the factories; for this is in line with Papal Encyclicals. But let us make it plain to the leaders of Communism: if there shall be freedom to spread materialism, then let us also have the right to confess and propagate our principles. For that right Catholics have died—and will die.

"I conclude: With good will, an understanding can be reached. The initiative lies with the present authorities. Neither I nor the Episcopate are the ones to enter this basic agreement. That is a matter between the State and the Holy See.

"As for myself and the verdict: I seek no mercy. My conscience is clear!"

The tall, slim figure, silhouetted above the antagonistic crowd which sat in that Court Room, stood a moment after his last words, and looked at his three judges—not with anger, not with defiance, but with a look that can only be described as filled with pity and love. No pectoral cross sparkled on his breast. No Episcopal ring shone on his finger. But the simple soutane which hung loosely on his somewhat emaciated body told of his priesthood, while the calm of his strikingly beautiful face and the light which shone from his deep-set, dark eyes, bespoke guiltlessness, as well as nobility, tranquillity, pity and love. That light said more than had his words. I cannot but think of the eyes of Christ as He looked out over the crowd that would not enter Pilate's Praetorium "lest they be defiled" yet would cry out "Crucify him! Crucify Him!"—the Man in Whom Pilate "could find no cause." The eyes of Christ had been wet with tears one eventide as He looked down upon Jerusalem—and He had heartbrokenly lamented: "How often have I longed to gather your children, as a hen gathers her chicks under her wings, and you refused" (Mt 23:37). There must have been heart-break in His eyes as He looked on them that first Good Friday morning—and listened to their shout: "Away with Him! Not this man, but Barabbas" (Lk 22:18). There was heart-break in the eyes of Archbishop Stepinac as he looked on his judges—and for the same reason: They were rejecting Christ!

Reading the October 3 speech at any hour in any day of any year will show any thinking man that despite the inhumanity of the Communists there was a man of integrity in their midst who could not be cowed; that omnipotent though their State was at that moment, it was utterly powerless before the will of an innocent Archbishop; and that militant atheism, which could—and did—kill the body, could never so much as touch the soul of one committed to Christ and dedicated to Croatia. That speech, rightly interpreted, tells you why Aloysius Stepinac is THE MAN FOR THIS MOMENT.

We have snatched more than "a fingernail of a saint," more than "a handful of ashes from the faggots." We have saved the words of a man who shows all men that they can have "hope and truth" if they will believe that there is "something else"—than materialism and Communism; "something else worth living for and even grasping death for"—than this world; Someone else worth living for—and, if necessary, dying for. He is and ever will be—Christ.

How the men of this moment need to know that! How they need to watch a man "draw that thin, straight line" and "*rule* that little . . . little . . . area . . . within himself" and say: "I can go no further, but put all in the hands of Him, for fear of whose displeasure, for the safeguard of my soul, stirred by mine own conscience (without reproach to any other man's) I suffer and endure this trouble." At this moment we all need to see that Whittaker Chambers out of the depths of his own bitter experience gave us the master idea which has actually mastered the Communists. He said: "The tie that binds Communists across the frontiers of nations, across the barriers of language . . . in defiance of religion, morality, truth, law, honor, even unto death is a simple conviction: *it is necessary to change the world. . . .* It is man's oldest faith. Its promise was whispered in the first days of creation under the tree of the knowledge of good and evil: Ye shall be as Gods. The Communist has chosen between irreconcilable opposites. He has chosen man instead of God; mind instead of soul; Communism instead of freedom." He does add: "there has never been a society or nation without God, while history is cluttered with the wreckage

315

of nations that became indifferent to God—and died" (*Witness*—pp. 16, 17). And we of the West? Has not David Raphael Klein given us the true picture when he says: "It is hard to say where it started. With Gutenberg? Galileo? The industrial revolution? Darwin? Somewhere along the way Western man began to lose his belief in God as a personal force, as decider of his fate, as ultimate judge of his actions.... Just as some primitive people have accepted Christianity by transposing their old gods onto the new religion, so have many moderns transposed their ethic onto another structure: the needs of society." He goes on to show the terrifying consequences of such a transposition. But all I ask is: Is this not chosing man instead of God? If so, how can any man of this society ever draw that "thin straight line" and then put himself as did More and Stepinac "in the hands of Him, for fear of whose displeasure, for the safeguard of my soul.... I suffer and endure..."? Without such a possibility, is life worth living? Has it not been well said that "for the thinking man there are only two choices: worship or suicide"? The Western world darkens. We need the "Light of the World." We need men like Stepinac.

But that brilliant speech did not end the "trial"; it but intensified it. From September 30th to October 3rd the sessions had run from eight in the morning until three or four in the afternoon. After October 3rd, they ran from eight in the morning until eight and nine in the night. But finally on October 11th a verdict was handed out: three Franciscans were found "Not Guilty." The other fifteen on "trial" received varying sentences. Colonel Lisak and Pavle Gulin heard: "Death by hanging." Father Matincic, Provincial of the Friars, received: "Five years of forced labor." Father Ivan Salic: "Twelve years of forced labor" and finally it came: Archbishop Aloysius Stepinac: "Sixteen years of forced labor." The crowds in the "Court Room" cheered. The Primate looked straight ahead, not a sign of emotion on his noble features.

He had forty-eight hours in which to appeal to the National Assembly of Croatia. He made no appeal. Had he not said: "I seek neither to defend myself nor appeal against the verdict" long before that verdict was given? Had he not told that "Court": "My conscience is clear— I am ready at any moment to die"?

On the very day the Archbishop was speaking in Zagreb, the *New York Times* ran this Editorial:

"Archbishop Stepinac has been tried and convicted in Tito's slave Press. No one outside Yugoslavia doubts that the verdict of the four-man Court, at once Judge and Prosecutor, is already signed and sealed. But the churchman, dragged to the bar, is proving more formidable than when he was free. He is unafraid, unbroken, and seems careless of the fate reserved for him. He refuses to defend himself as an individual, but defends his right to exercise his ecclesiastical functions among his flock and bestow the blessing of the Church on all his faithful. Not since Cardinal Mercier, Roman Prelate in the First World War, and Pastor Niemoeller in Hitler's Protestant Germany, has any churchman so boldly faced entrenched tyranny, shielded only in the armor of his conscience.

"The Communist dictatorship will not tolerate among the masses any influence it cannot digest and use for its own nutriment. It will acknowledge no control over men's minds other than its own. The Catholic Church, especially powerful among the

Croats, is the strongest bulwark against Communism in Yugoslavia today. Therefore it must be crushed. Murders of priests by the secret police have failed to crush it. The trial of Archbishop Stepinac is the heaviest weapon against the Church Tito has yet rolled out. If the lessons of history mean anything, he is merely making a martyr, whose spirit and influence he cannot kill."

We add that the West must thank Tito for having lit a light in our darkness. And, because we have used the truth of Christ and Christians being one so often, we dare use the Gospel text and say: "... and the darkness never put it out..." and never will!

From a Serb, Bishop Dionisije Milivojevic, Head of the Serb Orthodox Church in the United States and Canada, we have this testimony: "This trial was prepared in the political sphere. It was for the purpose of dividing the Catholic Church in Croatia from its leadership at the Vatican. Tito has openly expressed this purpose. The strategy, which comes definitely from the Kremlin in Russia, is to break the leadership of religion. It is to be noted that opposition to atheism is stronger when there is an outside leadership. I refer to the Pope. The trial was not based on justice, but was an outrage on justice. Tito's regime has no interest in justice. It seeks only to stifle opposition. . . . I see only martyrdom for Archbishop Stepinac if the sentence of the Tito Court is carried out—sixteen years of forced labor. May God keep his spirit high and to endure, that through his courage Christianity may win!"

But perhaps the best testimony comes from one of Tito's own. Basil S. Rusovitch, Yugoslav Consul in New

Orleans, wrote on October 12, 1946, the day after the sentence:

"I no longer feel that I can belong to such a mockery of Government. . . .

"My decision was prompted by the unjust trial and execution of General Draza Mihailovic, the killing of American pilots over Yugoslavia, and finally the infamous trial of Archbishop Stepinac, an innocent man, beloved in Yugoslavia. I am an Orthodox Serb, but I think the accusation and sentencing of Archbishop Stepinac is very unjust, as was the trial and execution of General Mihailovic, and I sincerely hope that proper steps will be taken to liberate Archbishop Stepinac."

The thinking man needs no such testimonies, but since we so seldom really think, they are good to have. Better still is it to have the Light that shone in Zagreb as the world, especially the Western world, grows darker and darker. God forbid that the German poet turn out to be prophet. He wrote:

> "The dark of night drew on still nearer
> In dumb rest lay Babylon."

We are Babylon. We are Confusion.

Has Gilbert K. Chesterton given us reality when he wrote?:

> "I tell you naught for your comfort,
> Yea, naught for your desire,
> Save that the sky grows darker yet
> And the sea rises higher."

Aloysius Stepinac can put on our lips, if we but do as he did, the words Chesterton put on the lips of King Alfred when he had him speak at Ethandune:

"The high tide!" King Alfred cried.
"The high tide and the turn!"

10   Candles... Always Candles

OLIVER WENDELL HOLMES once said: "A word is not a crystal, transparent and unchanged; it is a skin of a living thought, and may vary greatly in color and content according to circumstances and the time in which it is used." Almost universally true as that statement is, it could be never more true than when the word "Lepoglava" is used. Literally it means "beautiful head," but let any Croat hear it and he will think of anything but beauty; he will think of horror.

Geographically, it is the name of a tiny town, some fifty miles from Zagreb, situated below the mass of the

Ivanscica mountain. For the tourist the name seems natural; for there is rare beauty day in and day out as shadows run across the mountain and the sun darting through different cloud-patterns dapples and dances over the meadows and fields of the hamlet. But dominating that village are the white walls of the prison which turns the word Lepoglava from the name of a quiet, and truly beautifully set little town into the name of a place that, historically, tells of horror.

Those white walls with their regular breaks for high, square observation towers were built while Croatia was part of the Austro-Hungarian Empire. The horrors began then; they continue, to some extent, even now. At least that is the connotation the word carries for any and all Croatians. How could it be otherwise when, from the very beginning, right up to today, patriots and opponents to the ruling power have always been lodged there? Under the Hapsburgs how many Croat patriots suffered in Lepoglava? How many Croatian nationalists gave their lives within this prison for their undying ideals?

I have only seen two large prisons in our own United States. But with the beauty that surrounded them, and the magnificence in nature that surrounds Lepoglava, I have asked myself: Was it Tantalus or the Marquis de Sade who selected the spots for prisons? My first glimpse of Sing Sing caught my breath in my throat. To look across the vast sweep of the gently flowing Hudson, on up the sides of those green covered slopes of what must be the foothills of the Catskills, to watch cloud shadows run across those slopes playing tag with one another, then to rest one's eyes on what in the blazing sunlight looks like white walls of a dominating castle is to see beauty at its best. But then to learn that what looks like a castle is but a prison, to think that behind those walls are men who have forfeited their freedom because of an abuse of that freedom is to know the "tears in things" the Latin poet spoke of in the long, long ago.

To enter the narrows that lead one to San Francisco Bay, pass under the majestic sweep of the Golden Gate Bridge and then be met with the rocky, yet green-splotched island of Alcatraz and look at those buildings blazing in the sun while the waters of the Bay lap at the base of the rock is to gaze on splendor. But then to learn that on that bold thrust of enchanting beauty, standing there in solid defiance of the ever-moving waters, there are humans to whom "each day is like a year, a year whose days are long" clouds over the gorgeous sight no matter how golden be the sun.

And Lepoglava—does the quiet and charm of the surrounding country and the calm solidity of the beetle-browed mountain in the background taunt the inmates? Are their eyes wistful as those Oscar Wilde told about in his Ballad of Reading Gaol?:

> I never saw a man who looked
> With such a wistful eye
> Upon that little tent of blue
> Which prisoners call the sky,
> And at every wandering cloud that trailed
> Its ravelled fleeces by.

It was to Lepoglava that the "condemned" Archbishop of Zagreb was sent to serve out his "sentence" of "sixteen years at forced labor." Was it malice—Victor Hugo did say that "the malicious have a dark happiness"—that had

323

Tito's men sending the Catholic Primate to the same prison wherein Josip Broz spent five years—learning more about Communism? Whatever be behind this assignment we can say with certainty that in this one "prisoner" Wilde's description was invalidated. He had said:

> The vilest deeds like poison-weeds
> Bloom well in prison air:
> It is only what is good in Man
> That wastes and withers there:
> Pale Anguish keeps the heavy gate
> And the Warder is Despair.

Archbishop Stepinac knew neither Pale Anguish nor Despair. His way of living was changed but not his way of life. He still had his *unice,* his *insignis,* his *"Third Class";* for he still had his Christ. It is the author of the *Imitation of Christ* who has said: "Never less alone than when alone." If that be true for any man it was especially true for Aloysius Stepinac when he found himself in "solitary confinement."

That last phrase is not to conjure up some dark dungeon in which the Primate dwelt with never a human voice to break the stillness or human companion to break the aloneness. No, from what meager information we have of the five years in which the Primate was incarcerated at Lepoglava, we have to say that his "solitary confinement" was only relatively solitary and comparatively confinement. He was assigned to a room about nine by twelve feet. Its window was barred, but not in such a way as to exclude the light of the sun. It held a simple cot which boasted of sheets, a pillowcase, and blankets. A single chair enabled one to sit into the lone table;

close to the wall was a bureau on which stood a wash-basin, a pitcher, and a tin vacuum bottle. Hooks on the wall served to hold up a few clothes and a towel. Different, indeed, from his quarters at the *Kaptol,* but far from anything like a "dungeon" for the solitarily confined. Further, there was a wooden door in one of the walls which led into a somewhat smaller room which held a single table covered with a white cloth. It was the Archbishop's "chapel"; the table served as "altar." Again, quite different from Zagreb's magnificent Cathedral, and yet sufficient for the heart of any priest; for on that table and in that "chapel" he could re-present the greatest Act of Love ever performed by Man under the sun. Did the authorities realize what they were allowing the Archbishop to offer to God, and what, through his daily Mass, he could obtain from God for all men? If so, they had more wisdom than many other acts of theirs bore witness to.

Nor did the Archbishop have to offer Mass alone. There were two other Catholic priests of the Roman Rite imprisoned at Lepoglava at the time, and these were allowed to assist the Archbishop, pray with him, and be in all truth what they were ordained to be. In the Old Law priest and victim were separate. In the New Law they are one. Jewish priests offered bullocks, sheep, goats—victims distinct and separate from themselves. But the Priesthood of Christ allows for no distinction or separation. Christ offered Himself in the New Law's one and only Sacrifice. Every priest must be one with Christ in the Sacrifice of the Mass. How could the Holy Sacrifice be more meaningful to Zagreb's Archbishop or to his assisting priests than in the mornings they met in that little room, gathered around that lone table, and consecrated wheat and wine? Could they not say then, as never before: "With Christ I hang upon the Cross" (Gal 2:20)? Each morning as they offered God to God and said: "*per Ipsum, et cum Ipso, et in Ipso*," how the words of St. Paul to the Romans must have pierced their beings: "When he died, he died once for all to sin, so his life now is life with God; and in that way, you too must consider yourselves to be dead to sin but alive for God in Christ Jesus" (Rm 6:11). The Communists had granted a boon to God and a blessing for all mankind by sentencing Zagreb's Archbishop to such a "solitary confinement"; for no greater act for God or man can be offered than the Holy Sacrifice of the Mass.

Nor was that the only boon this "confinement" brought to Heaven and to earth. Now the Archbishop had time to do what he had always been doing, but in a very different way. Now he had time to pray, to meditate, to contemplate. Ever since his ordination Aloysius Stepinac had been busy; busy with a schedule that crowded more into one day than most men can cover in a week. Thanks to his "God-consciousness" he was ever praying; for as Francois Mauriac once said: "Prayer is taking a direction; it is pointing things to God." Stepinac never pointed anything in any other direction from the day he had answered God's call to "Come, follow Me." But now that he was "confined" to his two small rooms; now that he was allowed but one visitor from the outside world only once a month; now that he was "solitary" as far as his far-flung Archdiocese was concerned, he could "enter into his room, and speak to his Father in secret."

Then there were books. Yes, the prison officials allowed

Stepinac's sister to bring him books once a month. Of course they were scrutinized, but they could hardly find any "political matter" in lives of the saints or in certain books on the history of the Church. But in them both, the "prisoner" found much not only to sustain him but to encourage and inspire him. He saw that now, as never before, he was living his priesthood and could do much for his flock by prayer and genuine sacrifice. He might be physically alone in his comparatively tiny room, but he lived with great minds, great men, great souls as he delved into the various volumes of the biographies of men who had given their all to Christ and for Christ, or relived the different crises through which the Mystical Body of Christ had passed—and triumphed.

To the guards and the prison officials it looked as if the Archbishop was leading a loveless, lonely, fruitless life. But the "solitary" prisoner knew that, crowded though his life had been up to this date, it had never been thronged with such delightful companions, such stimulating thoughts, such a deepening love. His earlier attraction to the Joannine theme of the Vine and the Branches stood him in good stead now that his world had shrunken to the length, breadth, and height of two small rooms. That promise of Christ about those who would "abide in Him and He in them" bringing forth "much fruit" assured him that no breath or heartbeat of his was without meaning for both God and man. His incarceration was naught but "the Father's pruning." The All-wise "Vine-dresser" knew how to bring forth "much fruit."

The sentence of "sixteen years of forced labor" and the consequent imprisonment of the Primate brought protests from all over the world: Catholics, Protestants, Jews, in every nation, save Russia; heads of many Governments; Councils of individual Church Bodies; voiced their indignation—and the United Nations itself received petitions from Catholic War Veterans, from the National Conference of Christians and Jews. The only one who seemed to accept the sentence and the imprisonment with equanimity was the "condemned" himself.

Tito took cognizance of the world-wide reaction and with customary Communistic brazenness, in a speech in Zagreb on October 31, 1946, boldly told the lie to the world that he and his regime were not persecuting the Church but only prosecuting war criminals. To add insult to injury the Marshal then predicted that "the world will soon forget all about Archbishop Stepinac."

The Marshal was speaking at a "People's Front Election Rally" that Halloween in 1946 and without mask or makeup, with seeming sincerity, said: "Accusations are levelled against us throughout the capitalistic world. A campaign is on foot in the United States and in Britain about something of which we are not guilty. It is alleged that we are against the Church. I declare from this place: It is not true that we persecute the Church. We simply do not tolerate that certain people serve with impunity foreign interests instead of the interests of their own people. . . .

"We are accused of wanting to deprive Stepinac of his freedom in order to get rid of him. When the Pope's representative, Mr. Hurley, came to see me, I approached the question of Stepinac, and I told him: 'Take him away and relieve him of his duties, for if you do not do this we shall arrest him; we have to arrest him. . . .' We waited for several months, but there was no reply, so we arrested and tried Stepinac, and we shall deal in the same way with whosoever acts against the people. . . .

"I think that the overwhelming majority of the people fully agree with our measures. But nobody could reproach us with being against the Church because of these measures. No. We firmly reiterate that we are not against the Church, and that we only demand that our priests be with our people. Let them carry out their religious functions, but let them not become estranged from the people or serve foreign interests. Let them serve instead the interests of their own people, and let them be the people's priests. That is what we demand and nothing else. . . .

"We need not fear any campaign. They will shout to their heart's content, and then the storm will abate, because they will weary of it. . . ."

Mr. Broz shows some knowledge of the shortness of the general public's memory in the brazen effrontery in that speech. But how often has he been surprised since that Halloween at the tenacity of some men's minds!

In 1946 Cy Sulzberger, Foreign Correspondent for the *New York Times*, was in Belgrade. He managed to obtain an interview with the Marshal and heard him swaggeringly state: "We arrested Stepinac and we will arrest anyone who resists the present state of affairs whether he like it or not. We prosecute anti-Nationalist Front elements, whether these elements are from the clerical ranks or any other profession."

Four years later the two were meeting again and the American correspondent had but one special request: Could he visit Archbishop Stepinac? Obviously the world had not forgotten. The request was granted.

As Sulzberger was being driven through the lovely countryside of Zagorije region of Croatia on an exceptionally beautiful autumn day he was juggling thoughts and impressions. He had seen Archbishop Hurley in Belgrade

.

that very spring and had asked him about the "prisoner" only to learn that he was well, allowed a visit from his sister once a month, and was being pressurized by the regime to resign his See. The Primate resolutely refused to do so, saying it was a matter for the Holy See to decide. Sulzberger had found the Papal Nuncio restrained in his expression of views about the regime, but could easily see that he was bitter about it. He told the journalist that there had been no change in the attitude of the Government toward the Catholic Church since Tito's split with Stalin in 1948. In 1949 alone some ninety-seven priests had been arrested, nuns expelled from convents, all ecclesiastical property confiscated except a very few churches which were kept open for "show purposes." Then there were the Orthodox Serbs who had sidled up to him growling: "Stepinac should have been hanged. He condoned the murder of thousands of Orthodox." But then there were the Croats who came once they learned he had permission to see the Archbishop, saying: "You should know before you see him that, no matter what they tell you, we adore him. He is the great hero of the people, and no slanders launched against him are believed. He is our martyr." Whom was he to believe?

A few hours later he was standing before Josip Speranic, Commandant of Lepoglava, a former Major in the *Partisan* Army of Marshal Tito. When the purpose of Sulzberger's presence was made clear, the Commandant frowned, but when he was told that Marshal Tito himself had granted the permission, Speranic brightened. He told the man from the *Times* that there were about a thousand prisoners in Lepoglava, but only one "special prisoner"—Archbishop Stepinac. The others live in dormitories and work eight hours a day, six days a week, in the fields or shops. The Archbishop had exceptional quarters and was given exceptional treatment.

The Commandant summoned the Assistant Prison Director and with Sulzberger and a companion set off for the prison proper. They passed idling militiamen and some UDBA (secret police) troops, then came to the gate itself. A young soldier with a tommy gun flung the gate open and saluted the Commandant. The four entered a courtyard. They passed many guards in blue uniforms as they crossed the yard and passed through a second gate. Once inside this they climbed a stairway to a brick building. Just inside the doorway they halted in a corridor on each side of which was a row of wooden doors, each having a tiny peephole in it covered by a wooden disc. Speranic said something to the Assistant Director who took a key from his pocket and opened the first door on the right. They entered.

Sulzberger tells us that he had been wearing sunglasses because of the glare in the prison courtyards, hence it took him some time to adjust to the relative darkness of the room, but soon he discerned a "slender man of medium height standing behind a table, looking first at Speranic and then at me. It was Archbishop Stepinac. The Archbishop is a man of pale but evidently healthy countenance, fine features, thin brown hair and a facial expression that clearly denotes a tremendous inner passion."

It soon became evident to Sulzberger that the Archbishop had not the faintest idea of who he was, nor why he was there. The journalist did what he could to ease the awkwardness of the situation by speaking for himself, telling the Archbishop who he was, how he happened to be there, and that "with due respect to the circumstances of the interview and to his own desires, I wished

331

to report to the world any messages he might care to send on how, in general, he felt about his physical treatment and psychological condition."

Sulzberger had spoken in French. The Archbishop, after apologizing for any mistakes he might make, and adding that he was more fluent in Italian and German, nevertheless went ahead in French and, as Sulzberger himself says, showed that he had mastered that language, too. When asked about his health, the Archbishop replied: "I feel well. I am in no way ill. I have lost no weight since I came here four years ago."

Then the journalist asked the Primate how he occupied his time only to hear that His Excellency devoted many hours to prayer and contemplation; then he added that at the moment he was translating some lives of saints. He showed Sulzberger the book he was then examining. It was a Latin tome on the Franciscan Order by an Irish prelate named Wadding.

Sulzberger had been watching the Commandant, the Assistant Director and their companion while he spoke with the Archbishop. He says he was convinced that they did not understand a word he or the Archbishop was saying. It was evident, he says, as the interview progressed that His Excellency could not have cared less whether they understood or not. When Sulzberger told the Primate what Tito had said about the possibility of release provided he went either to a Roman Catholic monastery within Yugoslavia or into exile without any possibility of return, he got a reply that sounded as if it had come out of the Fundamental Exercise of St. Ignatius' Spiritual Exercises: "Whether I go to a monastery, or whether I remain here, or whatever should happen to me, I am utterly indifferent." Then the Primate touched again the very center of the whole affair as he said: "Such things do not depend on Marshal Tito. They depend only on the Holy Father, the Pope, and upon no one else."

Finally Sulzberger asked the Archbishop if he had any kind of a message he would like to transmit to the world outside Lepoglava. His Excellency deliberated for a short while and then said: "I have nothing to say. I am content to suffer for the Catholic Church. Whether or not I shall ever again resume my office depends only on the Holy Father. I am completely indifferent as to the possibilities of my liberty. I know what is at the root of this matter. It is a question which only the Holy See can resolve. My freedom, or what I may do afterward, is not for the Government to decide. I am completely indifferent concerning any thoughts of my liberation. I know why I suffer. It is for the rights of the Catholic Church. I am ready to die each day for the Catholic Church. The Catholic Church cannot be, nor ever will be, the slave of any regime. If Marshal Tito wishes to free me he should speak with the Holy See. The Catholic Church cannot be the slave of any regime or of any country."

When Tito read that statement he must have been reminded of the first meeting between himself and Croatia's Catholic Primate. Stepinac had said the same thing in almost the same words.

Sulzberger and the Archbishop parted after that statement. As they, the Commandant and the others, came across the courtyard, Speranic, with evident curiosity, asked: "What did he say?" The American journalist repeated the conversation as exactly as he could. The Commandant thought for a moment, then said: "That is not entirely true. For instance, he has never asked for that paper, *L'Osservatore Romano* (which Stepinac had told

Sulzberger he missed). What he asks for he gets. Why he lives better than the guard here. In the morning he gets coffee, bread and butter. For lunch he has soup, meat, dessert, and a half liter of Dalmatian wine. In the evening he is given either a Schnitzel or eggs, or a half liter of coffee. Every day he has either slivovica or a liquer. . . . How can he complain? We can never forget the crimes he committed—we who fought the war. . . ."

On the way back to Zagreb the *Times'* correspondent had plenty to think about, but even as they drove along one companion expressed admiration for the courage of the Primate only to be counterbalanced by the growl from the Montenigran-Serb who was driving: "They should have killed the pig."

In Zagreb itself two men rushed up to Sulzberger in the street and asked: "Are you the American journalist? Did you see the Archbishop? Ah, he is a fine man, a saint. Tell the American people he is our hero."

Cy Sulzberger made his report to the American people and won a prize for it. But one wonders if it was not all a tactic on Tito's part. In 1948 he had broken with the Kremlin. In 1949 Stalin imposed his vengeful commercial boycott. Yugoslavia was hurting economically. The Marshal and his more intelligent economists saw that they would have to turn to the West for aid. In the same year and in the same month that Sulzberger was allowed to visit Lepoglava Ambassador Allen had been advised by our State Department that it was very much afraid that Congress might add a rider on the Yugoslav Aid Bill demanding the Archbishop's release as a precondition. On the 27th of November Allen suggested to Tito that he send the Primate out of the country. He made it clear to the Marshal that the United States, while asking the prelate's liberation, was not asking that he be restored to his See. Two days later Tito's reply came back: he claimed he could not release the Archbishop right then; for the man was "too stubborn." He did add, diplomatically! that he would be glad to release him three or four months *after* Congress had passed the Aid Bill. He explained to the Ambassador that if he released Stepinac then it would appear that he had yielded to pressure from the United States—and that is something he could not afford.

The Bill, of course, passed—as did the Aid pass to Tito. It has been estimated that between 1949 and 1955 the United States in grants, loans and food sales gave "Aid" to Tito to the tune of 600 million dollars in economic aid and another 588 million dollars in military aid. Tito's tactics pay off.

But more than "three or four months" passed after Allen's request and the passage of the Aid Bill without any release of the Archbishop. In the fall of 1951, almost a year after Sulzberger's visit to Lepoglava, Averill Harriman was "negotiating" with Tito. Our expert brought up the question of Archbishop Stepinac and explained to Tito "the political importance of Catholic opinion in the United States." All he got from the Marshal was "a bored reaction." How could he have hoped for anything else since the Marshal had much of our money and was going to get more?

Yet, in that "bored reaction" Harriman describes there may have been more of the Marshal's "tactics." Communist leaders are superb actors. At any rate, in December of 1951 the news came that the Archbishop of Zagreb had been released from the prison at Lepoglava and had returned to his native village of Krasic. Whatever was behind this move one can be sure it was not mercy, humanity, or justice. For the Archbishop was as much a prisoner of the State in Krasic as he had ever been in Lepoglava. He did have more than two rooms in that brick building which Cy Sulzberger had visited; for he now resided in the modest rectory of the Pastor of the Church in Krasic, but he had no more genuine freedom. There were guards at Krasic just as there had been guards at Lepoglava. True, these guards were not in the blue uniform of the others, nor did they march up and down with a tommy gun in their hands, but guards they were.

Still the Archbishop did have more consolations in a tangible priestly way than he had at Lepoglava; for now he was able to assist the Pastor in hearing confessions, giving instructions and sermons at Mass, and distributing Holy Communion. He was back as a priest with the poor of Christ. But there was a difference from those first days in Tresnjevka. There was a huge cloud in the sky over Catholic Croatia, and it was anything but luminous: Atheistic Communism with its Secret Police, its brutal persecution, and its purges.

Tito had "prophesied" that Stepinac would be forgotten. But in 1952, the observant individual was reminded of a song which said: "Forgotten you?—Yes, if forgetting means thinking the whole day through"; for in that year the world which had paid scant attention to the Archbishop's "release" from prison, was electrified by the news that Aloysius Victor Stepinac was to be created Cardinal of the Holy Roman Catholic Church.

He had been loyal to Rome—that was the core of the whole conflict between himself and Tito. Rome was, and ever would be, loyal to him. On October 14, 1946 the *L'Osservatore Romano*, the Vatican daily, had published on its front page the following declaration of the Sacred Congregation of the Council:

The judicial action by which the Most Excellent and Most Reverend Aloysius Stepinac, Archbishop of Zagreb, was arbitrarily thrown into prison and wrongfully condemned by a Yugoslav Civil Court has profoundly disturbed the whole Catholic world and the civil society of Yugoslavia.

The Church, especially by three provisions in the Code of Canon Law, protects the holy Pastors and their dignity and freedom, threatening *excommunicatio ipso facto* to:

1) Whosoever shall bring a bishop without due permission of the Church before a secular court, especially an Extraordinary Court (Canon 2341);

2) Whosoever shall lay violent hands on the person of an Archbishop or Bishop (Canon 2343, paragraph 3);

3) Whosoever shall directly or indirectly obstruct the exercise of ecclesiastical jurisdiction or authority both *pro foro interno et externo*, having recourse for this purpose to any secular authority whatsoever (Canon 2334, section 2).

All excommunications in these matters are reserved, according to the occasion, in a simple or special manner to the Holy See.

THEREFORE, the Sacred Congregation of the Council, which is entrusted with the discipline of Christian priests and people, the aforesaid offenses having been deemed in no way to have seriously mitigating circumstances (Canon 2205, paragraph 3; Canon 2229, paragraph 3) but rather having aggravating circumstances, particularly on account of the high dignity of the Most Excellent and Most Reverend person offended (Canon 2207, section 1) hereby declares all those who may have shared, either physically or morally, in committing the aforementioned crimes, or who have been essential co-operators in them (Canon 2209, paragraph 1-3) to have incurred the excommunications described above, and to remain subject to them until they have sought and obtained Absolution from the Holy See.

Given at Rome, on the fourteenth day of October, 1946.

Cardinal Marmaggi, Prefect

F. Roberti, Secretary

Tito might greet such a declaration with a Stalinesqe sneering: "What effect excommunications on the Party?" But in his heart he read this document aright: the Holy See supported Archbishop Stepinac in his every thought, word, and deed during the Pavelic regime, and was now supporting him in his opposition to the atrocities of the Communist regime.

The Marshal wanted Aloysius Stepinac removed from the Primacy of Croatia officially. All through the Lepoglava years the Archbishop maintained he was the Ordinary of Zagreb, and Primate of Yugoslavia. The Holy See corroborated his contention by appointing a "temporary administrator" to the Zagreb Archdiocese, one Dr. Salis Sevis. It was not until after Stepinac had been designated Cardinal that Dr. Francis Seper was consecrated Bishop of Zagreb—and then only as "Auxiliary." Obviously Rome still considered the imprisoned Cardinal-designate to be

Primate of Croatia. That was loyalty. That was intransigence. That was diplomacy at its highest and best.

The world admired the deftness of Vatican diplomacy and rejoiced that there was one power in the world that would not compromise in any way with Communism, no matter what its type or where its Politburo. Tito, of course, was outraged—because he saw he had been outmaneuvered. He severed all relations with the Vatican. The Vatican survived the cut. The Marshal came creeping back, and is still creeping back.

The Cardinal-designate thanked God for the consolation this recognition and elevation brought to his human heart, but, other than that, was unmoved by all the commotion Pius XII's subtle congratulations and indirect rebuff to Tito was causing. Aloysius Stepinac recognized the kind hand of his Father in this designation by the Pope. He himself was suffering mental agonies as he helped the pastor; for this was Krasic, his native village. How sharply he could recall his childhood and boyhood and early manhood days in that same village. Then the Church would be crowded. Today.... Oh he knew the people longed to come. He knew their hearts. But he also knew the ugly realities of the "freedom of worship" allowed by the Tito Government. Where the peasants should have been walking toward the Church there were agents of the secret police not only watching him, but watching everyone who entered to worship God. He admired the courage of all who came. He understood the difficulties of all who remained away. But it was agony.

He also thanked God for the encouragement Pius XII's act would give to all Catholics in various Republics of Yugoslavia. The Bishops who were being stalked in every diocese; the priests who found themselves shackled by

339

governmental regulations concerning not only what they could do, but even concerning what they could say; people, many of whom were wandering "like lost sheep"— all heard what the Vicar of Christ on earth was saying when he named Aloysius Victor Stepinac to be Cardinal of the Holy Roman Catholic Church. It was very like what Christ had said to the frightened disciples that night of the storm at sea when He came walking toward them over the raging waters: "Fear not. . . ."

As soon as he had heard of the Archbishop's elevation the Honorable Josip Broz Tito manifested his powerful intellect and showed what sharp insights into actuality he enjoys by speechifying at Smederevska Palanka on December 16, 1952:

> The Vatican is pursuing an Imperialist policy. The Vatican and Italian policies complement one another. The Italian government is contributing to Vatican domination by spreading reaction in the world, while the Vatican helps the Italian Imperialist aspirations toward Yugoslavia and others.
>
> The Vatican has insulted Yugoslavia by appointing the war criminal Stepinac as Cardinal and wishes to present him with the Cardinal's hat. The man is a political Bishop. He served in the arrangement between Alexander Karogeorgevic and the Vatican on the occasion of the Concordat—and became a Bishop over night. He did not become a Bishop because of his holiness or great services; it was a matter of politics at that time, as it is today. However, they will not see Stepinac installed at Zagreb.

After that exposition of "facts" the Marshal let it be

known that the Archbishop could go to Rome for the "red hat"—provided he never returned to Croatia. The "stubborn" Stepinac remained "stubborn"—which is properly translated as *unice, insignis* and *"Third Class"*; which means utterly uncompromising where objective principles are involved, a man of character, a true priest, and a fearless and loyal Good Shepherd. His reply was: "My place is with my people."

He did not go to Rome. He never received the "red hat." But he was created a Cardinal of the Holy Roman Catholic Church. Tito might imprison a body. He could never imprison a mind. He might dictate to his people— who are to a great extent "imprisoned" in his Yugoslavia, but he could never dictate to the Vatican.

The elevation changed the newly-made Cardinal's life not a whit. He arose at 3:15 every morning, spent long hours in prayer, meditation, and contemplation, then offered what had become his life—the Holy Sacrifice of the Mass. After that he did what he could to assist the pastor in ministering to the needs of the parishioners, read, prayed some more, and soon found that it was 9:00 P.M.— his time for retiring. Thus did his days as "prisoner" pass on to eternity, empty as the world evaluates a day, but filled to the overflowing with acts of love for God and man as the all-seeing eye of God and His People price human efforts made by one in the state of Grace.

But soon it became evident that the Cardinal was suffering physically as well as spiritually. Doctors had difficulties with the Government about going to see the Cardinal, but finally his disease was diagnosed as Policythemia—a rare blood disease, difficult to treat.

Archbishop Hurley had not forgotten the Christ he had bowed to in Stepinac during that showcase of a "trial."

He arranged for American specialists to go to Krasic to see what could be done for the suffering Cardinal. A Dr. Lawrence from California reached him, as did a Dr. Ruzic from Chicago. They brought medicines and gave their expert attention and services to the ailing "prisoner." But the Cardinal did not improve.

Now he knew he was "one with Christ." He not only had his share in the mental agony of the Head of the Mystical Body but was granted a share in His physical passion as well. He suffered, but he suffered with Christ, in Christ, and as Christ. His life now was truly a Mass. He was priest to the core of his being; for he was also a victim. He did not say: "Father, forgive them for they know not what they do"; for he felt that Tito and his Communists had far greater insights into reality than did the Jews and Romans at the time of the Crucifixion. But he did say his favorite prayer, the *Our Father,* with ever deeper and constantly deepening meaning; especially that clause about "Forgive us our trespasses as we forgive those who trespass against us."

As 1960 dawned the Cardinal's condition worsened. Yet he was up at 3:15 every morning and the Christ in the Eucharist saw him in the parish Church for long hours every day praying for his flock, many of whom he saw wandering as if they had no shepherd. Early February saw him confined to his bed. Now he was "on his Cross" for the pain reached saturation point.

On February 10 he knew he was dying. He had already been anointed so he called for a candle. His sister was present, and as is natural for a sister, she began to weep. The Cardinal asked her to recall an earlier day when he had stood by her bed which many thought would be her death-bed. He asked her to remember what he had said to her at that time; how he had told her what a glorious thing it is to die in the hands of the Lord. She dried her eyes. Then he asked her to say the *Our Father* with him. All that day they prayed. At 2:15 in the afternoon he once again began the prayer he loved so long and so ardently. When he reached *"Fiat Voluntas Tua*–Thy Will be done"* he stopped praying, fixed his eyes on the statue of Our Lady of Lourdes he had in his bedroom, gave three little gasps and was gone–into the hands of God.

He had no need for his little statue of Judas at that moment. He had been loyal and loving to the end. He had used his *unice,* been one of the *"Third Class,"* and thus been truly *insignis.*

Tito's press endeavored to hush up the fact that the Cardinal was dead. The Belgrade newspaper *Politika* reported the event in a few lines. But the news got out to the world–and the entire world reacted. Tributes were paid to the deceased by countless Governments. Cables, telegrams, letters came pouring into the Vatican–and into Yugoslavia. Tito and his Government had second thoughts. Originally they had decreed that the Cardinal should be buried in his native village, Krasic, but when Foreign Correspondents flooded into Zagreb, the Marshal and his cronies decided to allow His Eminence to be buried in his own Cathedral.

We all know that "evil news travels fast," but there are occasions when good news travels even faster. Word that His Eminence was to be buried in his own Cathedral swept through Croatia despite the silence of the official press and the radio. On the day of the burial eighteen bishops and over five hundred priests were in that Cathedral, while inside and outside its ancient walls more than one hundred thousand of the Faithful gathered to pay their tribute to the mortal remains and thus honor one they had looked up to as their Good Shepherd and now could look upon as their martyr—and, as many of them said, "their saint."

The free press of the world, both religious and secular, reported the death and burial widely. Most ran long articles and editorials honoring the deceased Primate and patriot, even as they told of the persecution the Catholics had suffered, and were still suffering under the Tito regime.

Ten years later Daniel M. Madden, who had held public information posts for the United States Government in Paris, Brussels, Copenhagen and Vienna, made a visit to Zagreb. Being what he is he went to the Cathedral and picked up the guidebook. Paging through it he came on the reference to the Bishops and Archbishops who were buried in the various crypts behind the main altar. They were identified rather off-handedly as "Alagovic, Vrhovac, Haulik, Mihalovic, Posilowic"—and others—no name registered in any impressive way on the young New Yorker. But then he saw "Bauer, Stepinac." His eyes widened. He remembered. He went to that crypt—and found there a young lady praying. He found there fresh flowers. He found there candles—many candles burning. He snapped a picture of the girl, the flowers, and the candles. Later he talked to the girl and learned that while neither the Church nor the Government encourages visitors to the crypt there are always visitors there—then she added: "Always flowers, and always candles—yes, candles always—and always burning."

He who was a "light to the world" had burned out—but because of what he was and what he did, he not only has lighted candles—always candles, but has kindled a flame that will never die in Croatia—and may never die in the world: the Flame of Faith—the Fire of Fortitude— the unquenchable flame of loyalty to Christ through loyalty to His Vicar in the Vatican.

A man died February 10, 1960 at 2:15 P.M. in Krasic. But the memory of that man will never die so long as men appreciate character. There will be candles—always candles in Zagreb's Cathedral—and if that should be rendered impossible, there will always be candles in the hearts of Croatians—and those candles will be burning.

A fellow Trappist brought this photo back to the author in May of 1971 with the information that among the many wreaths found today at the tomb is one from, among all people, Marshal Tito.